Dear Suzette,

Protect Our
Children for
Survival of
America!

Georgina Prohar
9/11/04

Dear Suzette,

...

9/11/04

Seeds of Deception

Planting Destruction of America's Children

by

Georgiana Preskar

authorHOUSE

1663 Liberty Drive, Suite 200
Bloomington, Indiana 47403
(800) 839-8640
www.authorhouse.com

First published by AuthorHouse 07/02/04

ISBN: 1-4184-0180-3 (sc)
ISBN: 1-4184-0181-1 (dj)

Library of Congress Control Number: 2004093163

Printed in the United States of America
Bloomington, Indiana .

This book is printed on acid-free paper.

DEDICATION

For my husband Michael and our children Michael Pierce and Michelle Lee

AND

AMERICA' s CHILDREN

GRATITUDE

I give thanks to my Mom, Dad and Brother for wonderful memories and the solid foundation of my life, to my Husband's family for sharing love and friendship through the years, and to Helen and Josilyn, and their families for caring. I acknowledge old friendships that have endured the test of time and new friendships that will endure the test of time.

My appreciation I give to Eagle Forum of Sacramento board members and to our local Chapter members who support our endeavors. I also thank speakers, authors and radio talk show hosts ready to give of their time and knowledge. I thank all organizations and citizens willing to share in our common cause, *Protection of Our Children for Survival of America.*

The editing of this book by Michael and Michelle Preskar and Teri Lawrence, along with the cover sketch by Amy, made possible its completion. I thank J.R. Harris of AuthorHouse and all who encouraged me through this adventure.

Thank you to Michael, my husband of 29 years, for realizing my dream and sharing with me another adventure in our lives. I am grateful for our children Michael and Michelle, whose daily lives are true examples of the American Spirit.

Above all, I thank God for the strength and courage to write this book.

Contents

APPENDIX

FOREWORD

Elk Grove, California, my home for the past 22 years, was once a sleepy town. It was quiet, reserved and solid in appearance. Then, in 2002, we gained National attention with the desperate attempt of a father to remove "under God" from the Pledge of Allegiance. Our voice is now heard loudly as many debate the content of the Pledge. Lurking in the corners, however, are issues unknown to the town folk. They remain behind "closed" doors, SEED and similar programs with philosophies unknown to the average parent and citizen. The secretive organizations are worldwide, planting seeds of deception.

My story began in January of 2002. Our country seemed foreign to me; it was different than the land I grew up in. The New Year began my quest to find the reasons behind this change. The Journey awakened quiet times of research, exhilarating times of education, threatening times of media criticism, and fearful times of harassment. The reassuring answers came in the silent moments, in recognition of God, Family, Country and the solid principles upon which we are founded. Bad seeds planted, through erroneous indoctrination, will destroy our land. We must protect our children to guarantee survival of America.

Transformation is taking charge of our minds and ultimately our World. If uncertain about change in your school, community and government, begin to find your answers by reading this book. I invite you to travel with me on my adventure of discovery. My book will take you through the past and present, giving you answers to discern fact from fiction. It gives you concrete ways to dig out seeds of deception to help stop our destruction. Activism is noticed, awaken your sleepy towns and be silent no more. Begin your journey of discovery today.

I welcome you!

1

DELUSIONAL DIALOGUE

I could feel its presence. It would not go away. Morning, noon and night intensity grew. The weight of its influence urged me to reexamine its structure. I sat in my comfortable blue chair, pretending to read but was unable to concentrate. I felt it listening as I debated aloud that perhaps we could be friends.

Year after year I returned home with diplomas following classes of instruction. I ran upstairs to our office filled with anticipation and hope of a new beginning. Each time I imagined it would be different, until I turned the corner seeing the enormous head with a tiny body holding it in place. There was no smile, no hello, just a cold glare. My fantasy turned into reality; it would not change. I wanted to reach out grabbing all it offered but did not know how. It kept its same position and never spoke; I felt its silent doubt of us ever becoming friends. As I sat in my comfortable blue chair I wondered how anyone could ever befriend this awful contraption more commonly known as a computer.

At the same time that I decided my relationship with the computer would never improve, I joined my first Bible Study. One of our members, Pauline, was sick with a medical condition that appeared to be life threatening. She would not, however, reveal information pertinent to the truth of her disease. I was eager to learn more so as to offer support in the future course of her illness.

I embarked upon this adventure with great enthusiasm. Unfortunately my medical books gave me no information and my husband's were no different. I could not find information on her condition anywhere. Devastation took hold. I was frozen with anticipation knowing this was placed in my life for a reason. The time had come. I pressed the master switch to the computer quickly. Though my hands were sweaty and my heart was racing, my decision to finally make peace with the computer did not falter. I saw the monitor light up and I was on my way. It took but a minute and pages of information became available. It seemed endless. I satisfied my curiosity as all of the facts concerning Pauline's illness became available to me.

Pauline did not have long to live. Her symptoms were true to the course of her disease as I saw her declining physical status. She became comfortable with our desire to be there for her in this time of need and within weeks she died peacefully in the presence of her family. We miss her.

I remember Pauline. She forever will be a part of my life. Her illness is what encouraged me to make a new friend with my computer. Our decisions in life enable us to move forward in new directions. The object I loathed became a symbol of stability that encouraged me to move in directions I never thought possible. In sadness we usually grow in ways that prove beneficial to others and ourselves. Human beings are amazing creatures, just as computers are amazing objects. I am grateful I grasped the opportunity when I did. My computer and I have a great relationship now! As I sat in my comfortable blue chair in winter of 2002, I smiled about the mini miracles in life.

2

MANIA

The rain had not stopped for days. I sat in my blue chair watching it fall. The sounds on the rooftop were distinct as it made its statement. The gloom of January was well under way and no one dared to say when it would end. If we took hope of it clearing we were almost certainly disappointed. Simply accepting the rain seemed to work best.

The pounding drops mesmerized me and my thoughts of days gone by were strong. How I enjoyed remembering our children and their "growing up" times. It passes quickly, as does life. I thought of my mother and how proud she was of her grandchildren. I recalled how I thought she would live forever; she was after all my mother! However, death avoids no one. This is perhaps the one package I did not like opening.

My mother's death ten years ago, though devastating, had a profound effect on me. I realized that mourning is a process that takes time and patience. It is a journey, different for each person. The length of the trip and how we travel it define its success. My trip was lengthy. I did, however, emerge with a renewal of life filled with newfound treasures of self-awareness that have now enabled me to follow a course I never dreamed possible.

Our daughter Michelle had left for college, at UC Davis, in September of 2000. Time stood still and so did our home. The town of Davis was close to Elk Grove, but that fact did not make up for the hurt I felt in the absence of her presence. However, our son Michael was still living at home. We clung to this comforting feeling. This worked as a band-aid for our sorrow and seemed to mend it. He kept the idea of children alive in our home, and we reached to him to fulfill

3

our desires of still being needed. Two years later Michael moved closer to CSU at Sacramento, where he was attending classes. He was only 20 minutes away, but it felt like 20 thousand miles. As I sat in my blue chair, the mourning process began again and I was no longer comfortable. It was January 2002 and I prayed for a miracle to get us through this time in our life.

My husband Michael and I were devastated. His days at work were fast paced, blurring some of the pain, while mine were slow, giving me much time to dwell on it. Supportive words from friends were deafening to my senses. I wandered around our home aimlessly, as if in a desert, looking constantly for some way to quench my thirst for what was draining out of my body. There was a gnawing in my stomach; I soon began to fill the empty pit with popcorn. A journey of food seemed different, perhaps even fun. Popcorn is my comfort food and I definitely gave myself permission to eat as much as I wanted, as frequently as I desired. My delight came in the fact that I felt no guilt for this act of gluttony. It was my only salvation on a daily basis. Anticipation of the moment began to rule my life. I now know how people become overweight. Through these times, I recalled how important feeling pain is for the mourning process. Feeling this pain though, did not seem bad for I would just grab my big bowl of popcorn and eat. The tiny white fluff balls became my friends and popping them was easy, within minutes they were done.

Around six weeks after our last child left home I was ready to move on. Lucky for me I made the decision when I did, for I could have gained weight not easily lost. My husband and I eventually worked through our pain replacing it with the joy of seeing our children grow into young adults with solid traditional values and mores.

I finished the popcorn-gobbling phase in my life, happy to be done with this episode. I learned years ago if people wait patiently, living each moment fully with awareness of daily miracles, they find the message of their next adventure. Mine was right around the corner; I didn't have long to wait for the unraveling of my roller coaster ride through the next two years. In the meantime I sat in my comfortable blue chair and watched the raindrops fall as they may.

3

LOBBY DAY

My friend Susan left a message that began what would be my journey for the next two years. In it she mentioned that Capitol Resource Institute (CRI) was sponsoring a lobby day at the State Capitol. Questions flooded my mind. What was a lobby day? I called immediately to find my answer. Lobbying fascinated me. It was an area unexplored in my life. I liked exploration!

The answers were many, enough to encourage participation in my first lobby day. The morning arrived and I put on my suit knowing my decision was the right one. The drive to the Capitol was a learning adventure unto itself. People everywhere struggling to get to their destination. The freeways were mobbed with humanity that had forgotten its true purpose in life. I have traveled extensively in my life, but the experience of travel never seems to ease the tension of beginning a new adventure. This adventure came along with an adrenaline rush that would last the whole day through.

The auditorium that CRI occupied drew me in; I felt like I belonged. I carefully sat myself in the back so as not to be noticed. Karen England, the program coordinator for CRI, is a spirited lady. Her enthusiasm as coordinator for the day encouraged me to soak up as much knowledge as I could. My ears were ringing with facts that were both welcome and unwelcome. Tim LeFever, lawyer and chairman of the CRI Board, spoke about public acquisition of legislative material and working to make changes. Senators spoke on legislative bills and Karen explained how a bill became law. I heard the atrocities of abortion and human cloning. A Pro-life youth leader, Sarah Dawson, spoke courageously on how to answer the opposition when debating abortion. Jesse Petersen, the President of Brotherhood Organization of a New Destiny (BOND) was our featured speaker. He spoke on his book *From Rage to Responsibility*, which brings a message of hope to black America. His words were inspirational and uplifting. John Stoos, a radio talk show host on KFIA radio in Sacramento spoke next on our constitutional government. After listening to all of these amazing individuals speak, I began to feel at home with my surroundings.

The afternoon was busy. Karen explained the lobby process asking for volunteers to lead different groups. I am an assertive person, but I retreated, this day, into a shell of protection. What would I say to the legislators? What if they asked me a question I could not answer? Visiting the Capitol Building was comfortable but approaching a Senator with our concerns was uncomfortable. I followed our leader, a young man eager to move forward for our task at hand.

We walked a few short blocks to the Capitol. I enjoyed the beautiful site of this majestic building, aware of the power that lay within. Due to September 11th, admittance took longer than usual. We waited patiently and soon we were on the elevators leading us to our first senator's office. My palms were sweating as we entered the first threatening door. If I didn't have to say a word, why was my heart beating so fast? I saw our representatives as a force foreign to me; they seemed to exist in a world apart from everyday people. I wondered if I could overcome my detachment and be able to communicate with them.

We stayed only a short time. It was easier than I thought. Our leader began with an introduction, stated our purpose, sought the senators stand on a bill, gave our position on the bill and in closing we asked for his vote. My apprehension lightened and I found myself looking forward to the next office. As time passed, each encounter had its own flavor. Debate seemed to add some spice to the outcome. If the Senator was not present, we requested to see his legislative assistant and spoke with him. If he was absent, we pursued conversation with the receptionist and shared our concerns. It proved to be a positive afternoon and on the return walk I saw things differently than I had prior to the lobby day. Our representatives are people like you and me. It is apparent, however, that many do not

6

represent us; but instead, special interest groups. The reality of how difficult change would be finally set in. What we really needed were new people in office.

After follow up discussions and evaluations, we said good-bye to our daylong companions. Immediately I missed them, realizing the comfort of their companionship. I was a successful housewife, mother, businesswoman and nurse, but suddenly I began to feel dissatisfied. I no longer wanted to deny the facts. The world was changing for the worse and I had an unquestionable desire to grab every morsel of truth as to why.

4

EDUCATION LOBBY DAY

The months passed quickly. Costco became my new source of books. Reasonably priced, they offered me the variety needed to begin exploring new paths of knowledge. I read when time allowed and watched the Fox News Channel. My busy daily schedule, however, began grabbing my life. It twisted and turned me in directions that took me far from the lobby day in January. I began ignoring possibilities of change I had once dreamed and by the time the lobby day in April arrived, I decided my life was too complicated. I would not attend. My decision felt good.

I awoke the morning of the lobby day uneasy with my decision. I knew immediately it was not the right one for me. Last minute changes sometimes turn out to be our mini-miracles in life. I thanked God as I slipped into my suit. Traffic was light and my destination was reached sooner than anticipated. It is not always easy to follow paths we are led to but how rewarding when we do step forward. I was happy in April of 2002.

With education the focus of the day, an enthusiastic crowd of adults and children were present. The children were from home schools and private Christian schools. I enjoyed their spirits and the innocence of youth. I sat in front this time, not afraid to be noticed. I was proud to be present and eager to learn.

Eric Hogue, a talk show host on KTKZ in Sacramento and the San Francisco Bay Area, was our guest speaker. He magnified everything I knew to be true. He was raised in the Midwest, as was I, so I immediately identified with him. He shared stories similar to mine. Being raised in the Chicago area, I remember going to school covered from head to toe so as not to freeze in the chilling winds and heavy snows that were particular to the blizzards. I identified when he told of removing our boots, known then as goulashes, when we arrived at school. Done in the back of the classroom, it was a series of complicated maneuvers to avoid getting your feet wet while trying to remove them. There was no place to sit so if you lost your balance you suffered the rest of the day with cold, wet feet. The comedy is in reminiscing the scene; the reality was the simplicity of life. I enjoyed his many tales of how it used to be. The joy of his presentation was soon overtaken by the dim reality of what our children are experiencing today in their schools. I cringed when I heard his stories of school situations that were far more serious and less comical than removing wet boots. The children of today are taught adult issues without having the maturity to sort them into the appropriate categories, while many unaware parents give silent approval for their children to slip daily in the puddles of humanist philosophy within school boundaries.

Each speaker of the day brought a new tone to the same idea. Our public schools had changed dramatically. I was confident at the time that the schools my children had attended, in the Elk Grove district, had not changed. What of the ones that had? What impact would this have on our future Nation?

Lunch was welcomed. I hardly noticed what I ate for I was absorbed in the nourishment of words. I felt strength coming into my body as I digested knowledge from the ladies who had been involved in politics for years. I shared thoughts with Orlean Koehle the President of Eagle Forum of California and Sharon Hughes Director of Sonoma Eagle Forum and the Women's Republican Club. Yvonne Ellfeldt, whom I'd met at the previous lobby day, drove up from Southern California. She never misses a Lobby Day. Education continued as our topic of conversation and the facts learned over lunch stirred my mental state. I was swirling with information that made me sick. Change was occurring everywhere and it was not for the better.

Upon returning to the auditorium, I found I was a lobby group leader. Karen knew, without me offering, I had come to know my capabilities. I walked to the Capitol with an overwhelming sense of gratitude that I could enter this beautiful building and lobby. Few choose to acknowledge this great gift. The intensity of this freedom is beyond comprehension. It's a sure way of letting our representatives know our expectations of them. Keeping our freedoms in mind gave me command of the afternoon. My words flowed freely in each Senators Office, as I was convinced of the necessity for changes in our country. Most importantly these changes needed to be made for our children.

The day passed quickly, but the impact of the information stayed permanently. The negative changes had already occurred and were connected with a slow process of *mind control* that has been working in our country for quite some time. Pictures of Nazi Germany flashed in my head and I became anxious. Racing home from lobby day, I prayed to find relief. There was none. Tolerance, diversity, hate free programs, homosexuality and Marxist thinking were everywhere. The climate had changed in America and the victims were our youth. Visions of deceptive seeds planted took hold of my emotions; they were growing quickly. I turned on the radio finding some relief through conservative talk shows. Driving into the garage and watching the door close, I began to stretch my imagination. I reached for yesteryear and the memories of those times felt good!

5

TELEVISION TURMOIL

Our little white house with it's large back yard, Mom baking apple pies, Dad coming home from work, a dog and cat, riding horses, playing Cowboys and Indians and dolls are many of my recollections of childhood. Of course it was not this perfect for everyone, not even for me, but there was an acceptable variety of the above that seemed to meet everyone's needs, even if it wasn't perfection. It was an ideal to adhere to and gave us a standard of life.

The house sometimes needed paint, we didn't have a picket fence, the yard had to be mowed, the apples weren't always sweet, Dad was late from work, our cat and dog died, I was bucked from horses, dolls weren't real and Cowboys and Indians got rough, but we dealt with it and in the process, we learned about ourselves. We learned how to deal with situations in everyday life, what to accept and what to fight for gauged by a set of traditional values and mores.

Family was an important part of our everyday existence. When TV came into our lives, it upset our family structure. Before the advent of TV, we listened to radio programs. Mom prepared our popcorn treat; we found our position in the living room and listened with our family to the radio show. From the ultimate suspense of *The Shadow*, to the pounding hoofs of Silver, the Lone Ranger's Horse, we were together sharing an unbelievable experience. We had to listen carefully or we would lose the plot of the story. A strict rule applied, no talking during the show. It would interrupt the details of the unwinding story. Our imagination was crucial to the enjoyment of the event, and we were creative in our portrayals of the story. It was a time the entire family cherished. TV changed our lives.

11

Living Rooms throughout America took on new significance. Children rushed home from school, with little time to do homework, for there was always something on TV worth watching. Parents began compromising, giving in to TV and breaking down the "homework first" principle that ruled for so long. American families began watching TV during dinner. The kitchen table was soon empty and the absence of human interaction became apparent. With the advent of the microwave oven, moms soon were able to pop in a meal that was done in a few minutes. Finding a comfortable position in front of the TV, families became lost not in their imaginations but in someone else's. It dominated the evening. With little time to discuss what happened to Johnnie at school, parental awareness of children's lives began to diminish.

The years flew by and TV took on a new moral character. There are no longer the comedy specials like *Red Skelton,* nor family shows such as *The Adventures of Ozzie and Harriet.* Today's programs bring into our living rooms and lives; a social agenda packed with liberal humanist thought designed to mold the minds of our young ones. It doesn't matter if the message is contrary to our belief system for the viewers give it their okay. It slowly crept into our lives, infiltrating all age groups. The American people could not get enough of it. It has become our fashion expert, our political mentor, our stress reducer, our therapy counselor, and even our spiritual advisor. TV is now the antagonist of traditional family values, promoting alternative lifestyles through humorous programs such as *Will and Grace.* It began to show frightening examples of bizarre families such as on the *Ozzy Osborne* show. It now takes on marriage in front of millions of American viewers. It meets people's sexual needs and pornography is rampant, even telephone sex is advertised with numbers to call available on the screen. The daily Soap Operas have rape scenes. *Sex and The City* dignifies single women searching for sex. Young women watch faithfully as their heroes continue looking for love through bed partners. Channels solely devoted to unnatural sex are available with *Queer Folk* being one of the popular shows. Homosexuality is treated as a norm. Two men get undressed, go into bed, discuss love between them and actions of penetration follow. Scenes in pick up bars, depicting men hopeful of meeting other men to initiate sexual contact, are frequently

12

seen on this show. Queer men are now trying to redo our masculine men on a show called *Queer Eye for the Straight Guy.* Showtime has a series called *The L Word,* which is about homosexual women's lives in Los Angeles. Some episodes question women's sexual orientation and whether they find fulfillment through men. They even depict homosexual women searching for male donors to impregnate them on nights of ovulation. It's interesting to note that these shows are sponsored by some of the largest corporations in America. Where have we come in 50 years? It seems like a long distance from the twin beds of yesteryear, and this morality jump has been accomplished in a short period of time. How much compromising has taken place and how much more will take place in the next 50 years or should I say 5 years?

TV producers target the young, demonstrated when an AIDS frog was encouraged on *Sesame Street. Nickelodeon* encourages programs dealing with alternative families, accepting them as normal. Television delivers messages to the youth of America; the ideas slowly infiltrate children bringing about change. TV is the babysitter of today. Moms and Dads, busy with other priorities, rarely see the content of the programs. Win the children and you will win the County.

The feminists must be happy with the depiction of the American male on sitcoms. The media's portrayal of the dumb, confused, and certainly out of authority husband and father figure represents an image undermining the man's patriarchal position in the family. Repeatedly we see the man as being incompetent and incapable of being the head of the family. How wonderful for the feminist movement. Is it any wonder why males are losing respect and questioning their identity?

Stations such as NBC, ABC and CNN are used effectively to deliver clear, concise messages contrary to traditional American beliefs. Mainstream news programs often spin the news to deliver a message far different than the reality of the situation. People, without a clue, are being *brainwashed* into accepting their hidden agendas.

The American public is the child of TV; adults continue listening to it, laughing with it and revering it as their source of life. It is easier to give in to its message, than to face the consequences of truth. Parents support indoctrination by allowing children to watch controversial programs. The adults give up authority to an inanimate object dictating how to live life.

I remember vividly, as a child, running into a chicken shed with my girl friends Mary and Camille to hide. We were escaping the torment of boys throwing rotten tomatoes at us. Most of the coop was open, with only a few choice spaces for protection. We did our best with what we had available, protecting ourselves from the horrors of being hit with rotten tomatoes. We had to be alert, ready to jump to spots of safety. Each day brings rotten tomatoes via the TV and media outlets. People, not seeking safety in truth, allow themselves to be hit repeatedly. Leaving our guard down in the shed, we were splattered with rotten tomatoes. It was very difficult to get rid of the odor, even with repeated clothes washing. The odor of society's indifference will be difficult to wash away.

Each night we turn on TV, the *Fox News Channel* and *Scarborough Country* on MSNBC. It is safe, like listening to the radio. The profound innocence of listening to wholesome radio with Mom, Dad and Brother is a highlight in my life. The truth in *Fox News* and *Scarborough Country* far overcomes the indignities of the programs that are presently on TV. The *Will and Grace*, *Queer Folk*, *Ozzy Osborne* and *Sex in The City* shows, belittle our human dignity. Only when humanity rises above intellectual depravity will we survive. I don't see this happening soon, but who am I to foretell the future. I do know with certainty, the past was good and sometimes I long for the comfort of the radio days. It is, however, a memory.

6

SILENT DAY

The phone rang at 7:30am. Usually people do not call this early. It was my husband and I could tell he was upset. Michael doesn't call me on the way to work unless it is important. He had just heard, on Eric Hogue's talk radio show that a gay, lesbian and transgender silent day was going on at the high school. I couldn't believe his words. It wasn't happening at our high school, Elk Grove High School, where our children Michael and Michelle attended only a short time ago. He said I had better call and see what was going on at the campus. I did.

The secretary seemed oblivious as to what was happening. "Do you want the people who organized it?" I didn't want someone who put it together, but someone who allowed it to happen. Eventually the Vice Principal answered my call. He answered my questions the best he could, but was not prepared for my obvious intrusion on his morning. He was cordial, but I wanted to resist his statements. The most dramatic was "What could we do?" I controlled my anger for I thought the principal and vice principal held positions of authority. I thought parents had control over what their children learned. He insisted it was not a school activity. I didn't understand this statement. The classroom is supposed to be a learning environment where students learn without pressure of outside interest groups. Instead students, who are homosexual by choice or those who support them, are allowed to stay silent in the classrooms to protest all the supposed years of being silenced. They do not have to participate in class discussions or answer questions, but instead wear badges around their necks to demonstrate their oppression through the years. Students questioning the silence were given information about the reason for silence and about the Gay Straight Alliance (GSA) club on campus. It lasted the entire day with tables at lunchtime offering further information. He "thought" notices had gone out to all parents about this day accompanied by permission slips, but was not certain. I was upset and knew I had to hang up. I thanked him and asked about it happening next year. He was uncertain.

This was my first encounter with the homosexual agenda. It was in Elk Grove. The stark reality was evident. I thought this town safe from infiltration; I was wrong. I remembered Lobby Day and my denial that the liberal agenda had reached Elk Grove. No matter how I tried, I couldn't rationalize teenagers being exposed to lifestyles that are potentially life threatening. People are dying everyday of AIDS. Were the middle and grammar schools in Elk Grove being encouraged in this direction? Was anyone paying attention to the facts? It had gone further than I imagined! My direction was uncertain as I hung up the receiver for too many thoughts jumbled my thinking. My blue chair was of no use for I couldn't relax. Bewilderment had taken over. I could not accept reality that Elk Grove had compromised our children, and for what reason I didn't know, but intended to find out. I also intended to do something about this day next year, of that I was sure.

.

7

REFLECTIVE THOUGHTS

Elk Grove had changed for it was not the town I knew 22 years ago. Following Silent Day I did not remain silent, but discussed the topic with everyone. Few seemed to care. The apathy overwhelmed me. I needed to know why no one cared and if they did, why they remained silent. Activist groups work insidiously to silence traditional family values. They are doing a great job and I must congratulate them on a campaign that is causing chaos in our country. We have now effectively given our acceptance to everything they need for their supposed secular utopia. For weeks I dwelled on organizations that support radical change in our family unit and country's moral principles.

Many modern day churches attack our family unit. Some Elk Grove churches perform same-sex marriage. Pastors and ministers welcome homosexuals into their fold with little desire on either side to reform their behavior. The message from the pulpit is one of inclusiveness and political correctness. It is far different than the religion of my time. On Sunday women dressed up in fancy clothes, hats and white gloves and men wore suits and ties to church in anticipation of a service that delivered messages of right and wrong. After church all stores were closed, which encouraged us to eat breakfast at home (or starve). Over a great breakfast prepared by mom, we discussed the sermon and its application in our lives. My brother and I respected Mom and Dad's input and listened attentively to their words of wisdom. There was unity between church and family, and the children knew what was expected of them. Indeed it made sense, and we had a balance in life that we do not see today. Now many spiritual leaders are disconnected from families because they are *brainwashed* into believing they must adhere to separation of church and state, which is really separation of traditional values being delivered to families across America. The church has planted the seed of its own demise, but unfortunately it has also affected the core of our family, and we are consistently seeing more Secular (worldly) Humanism (human interest) growing in our homes and communities. It is ripping us apart! Perhaps we should have a Silent Day so the spiritual leaders, who have forgotten their allegiance to God and family, may be awakened to their responsibility of speaking out against evil. I thank leaders who have not stayed silent.

It is ironic that one of the worst assaults on family takes place by the one who is supposed to be the heart of the home, better known today not as a woman, but as a feminist. These proclaimed free spirits *mind control* women into believing they are truly oppressed individuals that can only gain their freedom by accepting the feminist agenda. I thought of my earlier years when I didn't understand the true agenda of the 60's feminists. Many of us denied the abortion and homosexual activism of the group, focusing instead on the allure of independence. It was sad for we owned it already, but did not realize it. I thought it "cool" to be part of this radical new movement and San Francisco State University "trained" me well. I was open to their rhetoric, feeling it important to develop as a free woman not being dependent on a man. In reality, I had been involved in a relationship that did not turn out, and though I am now thankful for this outcome, I chose then to avoid the pain by believing in the feminist movement. Though I dated and liked the company of men, I continued to see them as an inconvenience. At age 27, I announced my planned trip to Europe for an indefinite stay to pursue study and travel. I told my parents not to plan on grandchildren from me. When I met Michael I knew something changed and I began to drop my defenses. Eventually we were married and, yes, rode into the sunset. It was, however, not easy for the 29-year ride had lots of bumps, but our traditional values allowed us to ride over the rough spots and my dreams unfolded along the way. Without his presence in my life, I may have been one of the aging feminists from the 60's, never finding fulfillment, only complaints about men. Instead I chose to give my life to my husband and my children and in return, I found it.

18

Young women today see their fulfillment in the allure of role models such as Brittany Spears or Madonna. They look to National Organization of Women (NOW) for their moral code. Is it because such incredible women as Ann Coulter, Laura Ingraham, and Laura Bush are hidden from them or is it that they choose to deny them as we did long ago? We allowed authors such as Betty Freidan and Gloria Steinham to mold our thinking in non-traditional ways. They convinced the average woman that she was subservient to the man because she ran the home and not the corporation. We fed into it and began to enter the workforce taking jobs away from men with decreasing salaries the result. Women thought living in an office would be more exciting than in their own home. Children became second to money and given their own keys to open the door to an empty house after school. Women really found freedom for now they have two jobs, plus raising children, all with the gift of 24 hour stress for this great independence of confinement at work all day long.

Women are afraid of being homemakers, just as I was 30 years ago. I was *brainwashed* into believing being a housewife and mother would totally devastate me with severe repercussions to my family and marriage. Women are coerced into this nonsensical thinking, actually believing we are more valuable in the workforce than at home. I knew this thought crazy, as I sat in the Neurosurgical Intensive Care bathroom crying, because I missed our baby Michael while at work. Though my schedule was part time, it still caused upheaval in our daily satisfaction in life. We made our decision and knew it best if one stays home and one works, after all it is just simple logic. We sold our red Porsche and were content with an old Chevrolet given us by my parents and our VW bug. Yes we had to give up some material things, but we learned how to conserve. I could not buy as many clothes and Michael could not buy as many big boy toys as he would have liked, but the positives far outweighed the negatives. Baby Michael ate the same food we did every day. I ground his food for it was healthier and tasted better than baby food in store bought jars. I still have the grinder, which is a reminder of the beauty of "true" conservation! We watched our money on a daily basis and soon it became easy. To live simply is refreshing!

I thank God daily that I did not have to wrap our babies in blankets at 6:00am and drag them off to a day care. They were on a schedule but it was our schedule; set with love by an intimate unit working together for a successful day. The warmth of their bodies as I held them close every morning still permeates my body as if it were yesterday. I can still see our children's smiling faces as I would take them to the park or on unplanned fun trips. Their sparkling eyes as we played and laughed together will forever be an intricate part of my rewards for staying home. When Dad came home, the dinner was ready and the house was straightened. We shared our meals enjoying the interactions of each other through all the ages of our family. We were the moral authority in our children's lives. Public education supported the parent's authority. We watched our children's lives unfold; we planted good seeds and the family tree grew strong. The branches held us strong in our convictions that we had done the right thing; one thing for sure I hold moms and housewives in highest esteem. It is the hardest, but most rewarding job I have ever held.

Why should any woman have to question her sanity in wanting to stay at home with her children? We need to stand up for our position of housewife and mother as a worthwhile job, rather than pay others to raise our children and take care of our homes. We are the home executives who know best for our families! For working single moms, I hope one day you will be able to stay home. Most other women can stay home, but must sacrifice in order to do so. I laugh when I think of the sacrifice to give up material things for the horrors of the life most women live today. I see or hear little peace in the modern day woman, so what would they give up by staying at home? I think very little. In fact they would add sanity to their lives by taking a stand for what is most important, their children and husband. It is so easy once the decision to quit work is made, and it feels so right, for women know that they belong with their children just as we know life begins at conception. We must put a stop to the degrading of the family and the ridiculing of our homemaker role in university textbooks and classes. It is very discriminatory toward the homemaker. I am sure we could legally eliminate the prejudice so predominant in the university system, but it takes time, money, and the desire to courageously face a changing world so unaware of its own indoctrination.

Can you imagine how our world would change if women stayed home? There would be less adultery with less temptation available. Divorce rates would go down. Men would have more jobs and salaries would go up as they did before the women got into the work place. Babies and young children would not feel abandonment everyday as mom drops them off at the babysitters, but instead they would sense a priority of them over material things. Families would be better nourished from home cooked meals and brown bag lunches for school. Mealtime would return to joyful family interactions where all members share their day with each other. There would be time to spend with families at night because mom got her work done during the day. Families could play together on weekends rather than playing catch up games. Children would be supervised in TV, Internet and music areas now causing destruction to them. Mom would actually have time to check out tolerance, diversity and sex Ed classes to find out what her children were learning. She could read her teenagers English books to see if the subject matter was appropriate for the student age and find out if math is really being taught the right way. She may even want to home school. Closer supervision of children could prevent association with inappropriate friends that may lead them to evil lifestyles. Spending time, not just quality time, is crucial during the teen years. I learned the most about my children when they came home from school. Best of all dads could come home and be appreciated for their job and mom can be at peace for her family is actually happy, including herself. It may sound idealistic, but it works.

How can we allow outside forces to destroy our unit and push women into deserting their families? Traditional women must stand up and fight for their *cause,* which is to be a "natural" mom. Studies now show that oxytocin, a hormone released by the pituitary gland in females, is elevated when they are in labor and delivery, breast-feeding, and during sexual relations. The release of oxytocin encourages bonding and contributes to the closeness a mother feels toward her child and her husband.[1] It is natural for a mother to want to be with her baby and unnatural to leave him or her behind as she enters the work force. This causes stress, depression, and turmoil within the family. The mother being in the workforce helps to destroy the patriarchal family.

The vigorous attack on family only confuses our men. They function daily, but are bewildered by the messages delivered them not really knowing where they belong in all of this chaos. Men and women need to recognize their roles as equally important, but of different significance in the daily organization of the family unit. This clarifies guidelines making them easier to follow with balance and peace following as a reward. A man is a natural protector; civilizations have shown this since the beginning of time. Women are nurturers and this is shown throughout history, but now women deny this part of their being to promote themselves as the super macho figure capable of everything. Why is it that police academies, fire departments and armed services must dumb down the physical tests so women can pass them? This is dangerous for citizens, and for the professional men who must back the women incapable of job performance. It is also very unfair to those applicants worthy of the position, who have been denied it because a woman has unfairly obtained it. We need to honor the differences in men and women and stop trying to make our men feminine, and women masculine, to meet the demands of the feminists and homosexuals. We must protect our children from educations promoting unisex and begin to be who we were meant to be, mothers and fathers, men and women who are proud to be their natural design. We need a Silent Day for all men and women who have been silenced about their male and female roles in the family unit and workplace.

For the last 20-30 years, homosexual activists have boastfully talked of their lifestyle as being normal. Silent Day uses deceptive tactics such as victimization to promote their unnatural lifestyle to middle schools, high schools, and college students. This Day has encouraged me to find out more about the hidden agenda of this group and other dangerous programs so frequently put into schools to indoctrinate our children into the homosexual lifestyle. Our children's innocence is at stake and perhaps their entire future is dependent on information learned in social education programs. Our family balance is challenged when little girls walking hand in hand and boys seeking male companionship are now led to believe they could be homosexual. I've heard of school counselors encouraging children into the lifestyle rather than promoting reparative therapy, which is now proven to work. Children must be allowed to grow up with parents teaching them sexual morality, not the schools. They must have freedom to be children and not be required at age 6 to learn about homosexuality. We must have a Silent Day for the children who cannot speak out for their rights to grow up in innocence.

Now homosexuals attack our family unit by saying they have no rights to marry, which inspires debate across our country. It is ridiculous to think that our precious time is spent on this type of unnatural lifestyle. If adults choose this style of life, it is their right. They also have the rights of everyone else to marry, but it must be someone of the opposite sex. This is a simple concept that my husband introduced to me that few people seem to understand. Homosexuals have every right we have, but they must stay in the guidelines of a unit that has worked for thousands of years. The natural family is proven to work, and why would we change thousands of years of success for 2-3 % of our society. We are not redefining marriage, but un-defining marriage if we allow homosexuals to marry, for every imaginable combination of people, children, and animals will follow. The family unit is on the edge of collapse, and our society will follow if we do not keep our family unit in place. Perhaps a Silent Day is appropriate to honor those who are silenced for their belief in family: one man, one woman, and children.

Assaults come from every direction on our family. People attacking our Constitutional principles continue to redefine family and individual rights on which our country was founded. Tax laws, welfare programs, and illegal immigration continue to rob not only hard working individuals of 40-50% of their salaries, but also rob the esteem of those receiving the handouts. Affirmative action programs, education reform, environmentalists, and abortion holocaust are changing individual citizen majority rights to global collective rights. They all leave the family with little to survive, and slowly we are eroding into an insignificant group, with our children now dictating when they can leave campus for emergency medical treatment (abortion, drug, suicide concerns) without parent's permission. Parents live in fear of their children rejecting them, or reporting about their home life through school counselors or nosy questionnaires.

It's pathetic as I watch intelligent people justifying the above. The morality of such issues doesn't seem to matter to the average person, and I want to find out why. How have we strayed so far as to believe it is our right to kill a baby? The right to choose takes priority over God's law and family values to preserve life. It is not very difficult to understand that a woman has the "right" to choose whether she becomes pregnant or not, and yet it seems that people do not get this simple idea. The choice made, through sexual intercourse, a human life begins and the grasping, clutching hands, evident when the hole is pierced into their skulls, are proof of life. It is cut short, by the sucking out of their brains or ripping apart of their bodies, a cruelty no less traumatic than Nazi Germany horrors. Abortion is an atrocity, 10,000 babies murdered every day, 50,000,000 in the last 30 years. America lives with these statistics. The silence and lack of public outrage is shameful! Our Nation loses pride and another woman suffers years of mental and physical repercussions every time an abortion is performed. It takes years of turmoil to come to grips with this horrific procedure, and the mental anguish is reportedly awful. Our civilization knows life begins at conception. We have been *brainwashed* to believe only birth gives the child personhood. It is a convenient way to hide the inconvenience of unwanted pregnancy. Our society pays a high price to eliminate our little citizens, but replaces them quickly with illegal immigrants who pledge allegiance not to us, but to their former country. We must have a Silent day in every school and workplace to remind ourselves of the little ones silenced by giving their lives to a Nation's arrogance in determining life and death.

Fear is at the forefront of change, and I realized instantly that this was the primary force causing change in our country. I see fear in the eyes of some friends and people when discussing politically correct issues. They move around uneasily and get a far away look in their eyes. I know they are gone, and my words are not reaching them. A chemical poisoning seems to permeate their entire body, and their lips utter rhetoric such as homophobia and discrimination. They are enveloped in fear of being called hateful if they do not follow behavior dictated by these words and many others. It is the major reason why people are afraid. They are *mind controlled* into a haze of complacency and apathy.

Weeks of reflection proved valuable for I knew that seeds of deception were being planted in our schools and institutions throughout our country. It was the only answer for the incredible speed at which this change has taken place. Seeds planted during the

24

last century have set the present climate for total destruction of our family unit. My future was set in my research to find answers as to how this happened through the last century and what programs are promoting transformation in the new century. Silent Day removed any doubts of me remaining silent, for I decided to start an organization with the focus being protection of our children and family from vicious assaults of terrorism from within.

In the weeks that followed I felt the strength of Goliath. I had reached out and it seemed as though a divine light grabbed my hand. It spun a web of confidence and I was assured in my decision. I sat in my comfortable blue chair with the anticipation of yet another new adventure. I could hardly wait to begin.

8

EAGLE FORUM

There were many different groups available, but just as you have requirements for a house, I had criteria for an organization. My decision did not come instantly.

Memories of Lobby Days at the Capitol kept creeping into my thinking. The individuals I met had a profound effect on me. Why not examine Eagle Forum? The national website was exhilarating; I was thrilled with my decision to check out this organization. The content resembled a library, with a wealth of knowledge. I read and reread the information until I felt a sigh. The mission statement jetted out from the page and I knew this was the one.

> "Eagle Forum's Mission is to enable conservative and pro-family men and women to participate in the process of self-government and public policy making so America will continue to be a land that values individual liberty, respect for family integrity, public and private virtue and private enterprise. Eagle Forum is a non-partisan, non-sectarian organization of men and women who believe in God, Family and Country. Eagle Forum members are dedicated to preserving the political, economic, and social principles upon which our Nation was founded. Our achievements have proven that citizen-volunteers can determine government policies in the United States, and effectively communicate to the public and the media the principles for which we stand."

The Organization fulfilled all the criteria that I knew would be important for success. Phyllis Schlafly's life statement is in her living. Now 79 years old, she carries self-confidence, knowledge and love of people to each person she encounters. Through her efforts, the Equal Rights Amendment (ERA) was defeated in 1982, after a ten-year struggle. She raised six children and pursued a law degree. She is an author, radio talk show host, and guest lecturer and has debated in over 500 Universities. She still finds time to write a monthly newsletter and reporter.

The application submitted; the weeks passed quickly. One day I proudly told people that Eagle Forum of Sacramento was in existence. With over 2000 state members and close to 100,000 national members, I was happy to be a part of this solid organization. I wanted to learn as much as I could in regards to the changes in our country and how we arrived in our present chaos. Finding clarity was paramount to my success of educating others to current affairs. I was certain my answers would stimulate them to come aboard and help return our country to the land it once represented. I was hungry for facts about the Homosexual Agenda. How did this movement begin? How is it connected with Tolerance Programs and Hate Free Programs? Respect of others is important; encouraging alternative lifestyles by focusing on it is not the same. I flashed on the Hitler Regime; they captured the youth through deception. How did he accomplish it? How did so much happen in Germany without people knowing? I knew that evil was a force that used deception and lies to accomplish its goal and I wanted to know more about *mind control*. I would find some answers the next day. I sat in my comfortable blue chair thinking about the future.

9

MIND CONTROL

Though Hitler was at the forefront of my thinking, I knew it crucial to understand *mind control* before doing research on Hitler's regime. A definition of *brainwashing* or *mind control* is best described by Edward Hunter in his book *Brainwashing*

> "*Brainwashing* is a system of befogging the brain so a person can be seduced into acceptance of what otherwise would be abhorrent to him. He loses touch with reality. Facts and fancy whirl round and change places…However, in order to prevent people from recognizing the inherent evils in *brainwashing*, the Reds pretend that it is only another name for something already very familiar and of unquestionable respect, such as education or reform."[1]

Brainwashing or *mind control* can be a form of control that does not involve physical mistreatment of the body, but an altering of the mind. The following is a clearer explanation of what is involved in *mind control*. Mark Dunlop, an ex- member of The Friends of the Western Buddhist Order (FWBO), gives a wonderful synopsis of the necessary requirements, which summarizes most expert's opinions on *mind control*.

    1. <u>Aspiration</u>--Personal ambition and aspiration that encourages people to improve themselves or deepen their spirituality. It can be an individual or

28

a group *cause* that aspires to make themselves or the world a better place to live.[2]
Stage 1

2. <u>Meditation</u>-- The purpose is to calm mental activity. Meditation rids the mind of preconceived thoughts and ideas, freeing it of fact, to accept other context. Westerners can usually meditate by daydreaming, looking at nature or TV, or playing music. Anything that frees the mind momentarily is useful. It is a suspension of our minds.[3]
Stage 2

3. <u>Disorientation</u>--Mental disorientation by means of irrefutable paradoxical assertions. One meaning of paradox is for "something absurd to be actually real." Dwelling on paradoxes clears the mind of preconceived notions of reality. A paradox can be set up to make a person question his or her beliefs. The idea is to disorient them and then maneuver them into a double blind situation. If the students are reluctant, they are so because they have not developed the "awareness" necessary to learn it. The students cannot dispute this, for they do not have the enlightened or superior understanding to do it. Truth can be found through the developed one who is the leader or enlightened one. The students are led to believe their own thinking is faulty, thus needs improvement.[4]
Stage 3

Paradoxes are used that hold some truth, such as below:

"We are psychologically conditioned by our race, by our class and by the work that we do...by the social and economic system of which we are a part, and by the religion into which we are born or in which we have been brought up. All this goes to

29

show we are just a mass of psychological
conditioning: a class conditioning, plus an
economic conditioning, plus a religious
conditioning, plus a national conditioning, plus a
linguistic conditioning. There is very little, in fact,
that is really ours, really our own...that is really, in
a word, us."[5]

These concepts are hard to deny. Once the individual accepts
this notion, then the leader is free to change the mind to the
intended goal.

4. Re-orientation--This takes place through peer
   pressure and false friendship. Peer pressure is a
   strong motivator to change behavior. Whether the
   person comes to the group, or the group picks the
   person, the visitor is made to feel welcome. There
   is a sense of community and loving-kindness.
   Because of the desire to be accepted and loved, the
   pressure to be accepted is strong enough to make
   them want to change.[6]
   Stage 4

A leader in The FWBO states the following.

"A lot of people feel very isolated, very alone and
they're quite desperate for some kind of deeper human
communication. And they make the point that they find
the FWBO a very, very friendly body and they find
within it a welcome and friendship such as they hadn't
experienced before in their lives."[7]

Once the person begins to accept the trust and feelings of
security within the group, it is very difficult to break the bond. They
begin to accept the group's philosophies as truth. The four points
above may be applied in different ways depending on the group. It is
a unique set of principles that can be applied in many situations. It can

be used for good or bad. The question arises as to the lawfulness of systemic *mind control* and its infringement on individual liberty of mind. The system needs checks and balances to make sure it is not misused. The people who are totally and even partially *brainwashed* work as shields to protect the group.[8] They think highly of it and hold allegiance to its principles; therefore, will defend it against anyone trying to persuade differently. If they do stray from the group, many times the depression of withdrawal is overwhelming and they return. They are resistant to consider the group not authentic. In reality, many of the groups use altruistic ideas or spiritual philosophies to present themselves in a positive light to society and newcomers. It can indeed be deceptive.[9]

The four steps gave me assurance that *brainwashing* is very possible and could be effectively carried out without anyone aware of its existence. It can happen while watching television or listening to music at a friend's house over stimulating conversation. It can be well thought out and used to make major change in education or the work force. It is effectively used in all areas of life, and I knew that schools were using it on our children. I've had a deep down suspicion for months that some programs exist that are not known to the public. This fleeting thought continues to linger pushing me to further evaluate *mind control*. I was especially interested in how it is used through evil deception, and I could think of no better place than to begin with Hitler, for he ultimately controlled a nation by lies, deceit and fear.

I sat in my comfortable blue chair remembering times when I was *brainwashed*. How easily it is accomplished unbeknownst to the believer? I felt shivers of cold rush through my body as I truly grabbed the truth of this reality! How many people haven't, nor ever will grasp this truth?

10

HITLER'S EVIL DECEPTION

R esearch on evil within the Nazi regime started early in the morning; it lasted weeks. Lies, deception and *mind control* are not easy subject matter. Many questions dominated my thinking, in particular how evil controlled the German masses and is presently controlling our country. Various authors, and past television documentaries, aided me in formulation of my ideas about Hitler and the power he held over his people. I believe Hitler's personality was formed through a series of situations that encouraged evil reactions to them. *Situationism* is the doctrine that personality traits manifested in a social situation are in direct response to its nature.[1] I studied this concept in my nursing education and also in my college psychology classes. The concept focuses more on the action one takes rather than on the character traits that an individual uses in order to make a wise decision in the moment. Without a strong moral code, humans are dominated by momentary circumstances and their reactions and decisions based on the nature of the experience. Without absolute truth, it becomes difficult to determine needs from wants. If we have a moral code but continue to base our behavior on the situation, then we can easily be evil if we define evil as that which is contrary to our alleged moral code. We have come to accept evil as being the worst possible behavior, when in essence evil encompasses all of us as we stray from moral good. Hitler was evil, but so is our society. The more we let go of our structure and our sound moral principles, the more we develop personality traits conducive to the situation which could be evil.

Hitler's childhood was strongly influenced by situations that promoted instability in his life. He never developed a solid moral code, which would give him clarity as to right and wrong. Even though he was raised with religion, stories about him indicate that he rejected the philosophy. As a child he was beat by his father, and his mother died when he was young. It is easy to see how he could react negatively to these situations. His response to his beatings became apparent in later life as he portrayed the same, even worse, brutal patterns. In his earlier years, Hitler developed a keen sense of fantasy and was able to escape into his own pretend world at will. It was a defense mechanism used for protection that provided him a safe place, structured for his own needs. The World History Channel in 2002 featured an older German woman reporting about Hitler. His delusional world included years of fantasy centered on a make believe relationship with a girl he never met. Other illusions were identification of himself as a knight and a great artist. Unfortunately he was rejected by the Art Academy in Austria; if circumstance were different, perhaps the holocaust would not have been. The History channel's documentary reports Hitler responding with anger, remaining in Austria pretending to attend classes.[2] Some scholars believe Hitler became a male prostitute for survival. These facts remain unsubstantiated. In Lothar Machtan's book, The *Hidden Hitler,* the author points out that despite massive destruction of Hitler's past records, it is recorded that he spent five months at a men's hostel known as "a hub of homosexual activity." [3] He appeared to react to situations, being moved in directions dependent on their nature. When he was young he spent time in libraries studying eastern religions, yoga, occultism, Ancient Rome, hypnotism and astrology. He studied Friedrich Nietzsche, who urged that Christian values be reevaluated. Nietzsche encouraged individuals to be responsible for creating their own values. One of Hitler's favorite reading material was Madame Blavatsky *Isis Revealed* and *Secret Doctrine.* The Theosophy Doctrines of Blavatsky, written in 1888, seemed to permeate his ideology and influenced his perceptions of the Aryan race as being the pure race to aspire future generations. Blavatsky believed in a seven–step progression of human evolution, evolving from lower to higher forms with the Aryan Race being fifth in order.[4] The beliefs are contrary to traditional thinking.

Theosophy is practiced in our country and throughout the world. The United Lodge of Theosophists exists in different areas with at least 4 being in California in San Francisco, Los Angeles, San Diego and Santa Barbara. The introduction on one of the Internet sites clearly states its position on traditional religion.

> " We live in a questioning and critical age when the religious and scientific Dogmas of the past are increasingly being challenged. The idea, for example, of a personal, anthropomorphic God, a sort of magnified image of ourselves, a God who created the universe and ourselves from nothing, who listens to prayers, grants favors, forgives sins and eventually consigns us to heaven or hell—such a God finds fewer and fewer believers. At the same time the idea of a soulless, mechanical universe governed by nothing but chance is not very compelling either. Many people are seeking a deeper and more meaningful vision of life."
> [5]

Theosophy believes in a long process of evolutionary journeys through matter. We are all bound together because we are all made of the same essence and spirit. Brotherhood is encouraged and the individual self is connected with the universal self. If dogmas are stripped from religions then people will be all alike. The Theosophical Society believes in the study of hidden mysteries of nature, including the psychic and spiritual powers latent in man. They focus on paranormal activity, out of body experiences, near death experiences and survival after death. Blavatsky believed that truth was above religion; to find truth we test ideas against our own knowledge, experience, and intuition. She looked to ancient wisdom for a philosophy of life to deal with everyday trials and temptations. Some Theosophists believe, to be a good occultist, one must become a Theosophist first. Hitler associated with these people, and this philosophy, throughout his life.[6]

In 1914, Hitler joined the Bavarian Army. He spent three years behind the lines as a messenger. In 1919, following the war, he joined the party. One of his associates, Dietrich Eckart (21 years older than Hitler), greatly influenced Hitler's life. He was editor and publisher of an anti-Semitic magazine and a homosexual occult member who carried wealth status, introducing Hitler to the Munich and Berlin society. Eckart once informed a friend in a letter.

> "Follow Hitler! He will dance, but to my tune. We
> have given him the means to maintain contact with
> them (meaning the "masters"). Don't grieve for me for
> I have influenced history more than any other
> German." [7]

Some think he was a primary force behind the Nazi movement, Hitler being the pawn in the game. Eckart introduced Hitler to the fine art of persuasive oratory, self-projection, confidence, and discursive sophistry. Hitler could mesmerize an entire audience. Thus "persuasive language" can be used to sway people; this is a great tool for deceptive evil. It promoted an agenda. Hitler won the masses in order for him to carry out his future plans.

Years later, in 1923, Hitler became involved in an unsuccessful attempt to overcome the Bavarian government. He was imprisoned, for nine months, along with his friend Rudolph Hess. Hitler and Hess believed in the occult, and some felt that Hess told Hitler he was the Messiah sent to save the people. Hitler had numerous friends visit him in prison, and one of them was Karl Haushofer, a University Professor who established the Vril Society. This Organization promoted a utopian world that was ruled by superior people possessing a super human energy called the Vril Force. The society believed in power of concentration to awaken the forces of "vril." The organization's objective was to explore the origins of the Aryan race.[8] Another friend who visited was a Russian magician, Gregor Ivanovich Gurdyev, who influenced Hitler into evil paths encouraging further his "crazy" mind. Much of what Hitler fantasized could easily be assimilated into his "real" world to meet his needs for power and transformation of the people to a pure race. His stay in prison solidified his belief in his power as the ruling force in Germany, and his delusions supported this power. Author Ravenscroft tells about an incident when Hitler viewed the supposed spear that pierced Christ's side. Dr. Stein accompanied him to the museum and told Ravenscroft his eyewitness report of the experience.

"...like a man in a trance, a man over whom some
dreadful magic been cast...He was swaying on his feet
as though caught up in some totally inexplicable
euphoria...His whole physiognomy and stance
appeared transformed as if some mighty Spirit now
inhabited his very soul, creating within and around him
a kind of evil transformation of its own nature and
power." [9]

He apparently stared for hours at the spear believing it to hold
some occult powers, and eventually he invited the powers inside of
him.[10] Some people dispute Ravenscroft's account of this incident;
the knowledge came from Dr. Stein, who is dead, and cannot back
this information. What is apparent is Hitler's personality being
shaped, by *Situationism*, into an evolutionary process of brutality. His
vivid imagination gave in to philosophies such as Nietzsche,
Blavatsky and the occult. He also associated with Guido von List,
whose creative mind fed into Hitler's. List organized the Higher
Armanen Order, allowing Hitler's fantasies to live in the world of
hierarchical priesthood, called Armanenschaft. List mapped out a
blueprint for a new pan-German empire based on revival of this order.
The plan called for the following.

" ruthless subjection of non-Aryans to Aryan masters
in a highly structured state. The qualifications for
positions depended on the purity of your race."[11]

Hitler believed occult philosophies and "magic" became true.
Fantasy was apparent when he wrote his book Mein Kempt. He
pretended to be a hard worker identifying with the working class. The
World History documentary reported that he tired after one hour of
shoveling snow. He pretended to be in the front lines fighting in
World War I; the documentary states he was only a messenger behind
the front lines.[12] The truth did not matter; the lie worked for his
purposes. His distortion of reality was in place and his life fed into a
total fantasy. He believed the following writing of Nietzsche.

"Become hard and show no mercy, for evil is man's best friend."[13]

He was trained to lie to the masses through oratory, an expert in delivering deceptive messages to the German people. He sought power; in 1933 the Nazi Party took control of the State. No one listened when Dr. P.J. Mobius warned them that Nietzsche had impaired brain function due to tertiary phase of cerebral syphilis.[14] Instead, the Hitler Regime gave thanks to Nietzsche for helping contribute to German nationalism, and eventually George Lichtheim historian wrote the following.

"It is not too much to say that but for Nietzsche, the SS, Hitler's shock troops, and the core of the whole movement would have lacked the inspiration to carry out their programs of mass murder in Eastern Europe."[15]

The people did not hear messages of evil. The 20th Century occults, that helped lay the foundation for the Third Reich, continued to grow. The Theosophical Society's influence was felt through Blavatsky's book *Secret Doctrine*, which became an important Occult reading. Her book quotes the following in relationship to God and the devil.

"Once that the key to Genesis is in our hands, the scientific and symbolical Kabalah unveils the secret. The Great Serpent of the garden of Eden and the Lord God are Identical...[16.] Thus Satan, once ceases to be viewed in the Superstitious, dogmatic and unphilosophical spirit of the Churches, grows into the grandiose Image of one, who makes of a terrestrial, a divine Man."[17]

Aleister Crowley, an associate of List, supported Theosophy. His life was evil. He encouraged sexual perversion, sending two wives into Asylums. His son died during a ritual. He transferred from a 33rd degree Mason into bizarre occult orders.[18] One of them was the

Ordo Templi Orientis (O.T.O.) begun by Freemason Carl Kellner. [19]
They practiced disgusting sexual rituals separated as follows.

" VIII O.T.O.=autoerotic practice
  IX O.T.O. =heterosexual practice
  XI O.T.O.=homoerotic practice"

He felt these rituals offered a rational basis for universal brotherhood
and universal religion.[20] The O.T.O. supposedly followed the doctrine
of Crowley. They accepted *The Book of the Law,* transmitted through
Aleister Crowley. They endorsed it as a perfect way for transmission
of the divine and a luminous vehicle of truth serving as a guide for
human behavior. [21] Quotes from *The Book of the Law* are the
following.

1. "Worship me with fire and blood; worship me with
   swords and with spears. Let the woman be girt
   with a sword before me; let blood flow to my
   name. Trample down the Heathen, be upon them,
   o warrior, I will give y Petrovnaou of their flesh to
   eat 12. Sacrifice cattle, little and big: after a
   child...[22]

2. "The best blood is of the moon, monthly; then
   blood of a child or dropping from the host of
   heaven: then of enemies; then of priest or of the
   worshippers; last of some beast, no matter what."[23]

The O.T.O. exists today. The Grand Lodge is the governing
body of O.T.O. in the United States. They have several thousand
members and 45 local bodies in 26 states as of January 2004.[25] It
remains questionable if rituals are currently practiced in the same way
as the earlier 20th Century and unclear as to the blood sacrifices.
Crowley was asked to leave the O.T.O. in 1921. He is thought
important in circles of the occult. The following is from Crowley's
Magick in Theory and Practice.

"For the highest spiritual working one must accordingly choose that victim which contains the greatest and purest force. A male child of perfect innocence and high Intelligence is the most satisfactory and suitable victim. But the bloody sacrifice, though more dangerous, is more effacious and for nearly all purposes human sacrifice is the best. In the Sacrifice, during Invocation, however, it may be said without fear of contradiction the death of the victim should coincide with the supreme Invocation."[24]

His works are available to buy or download from the websites. It is hard to imagine his wicked mind; what is harder to imagine is someone actually buying his books as a way of life. He believed in control of mind and body through sexual perversions. The occult, however, describes good as evil and evil good. Activities of chants, formula wordings, and carefully planned actions can cause devastating effects delivering a counterfeit spiritual experience, which literally transforms lives.

"...sexual perversion took a central place in Hitler's life...a monstrous sexual perversion was the very core of his whole existence, the source of his mediumistic and clairvoyant powers and the motivation behind every act through which he reaped a sadistic vengeance on humanity." [25]

Hitler was initiated into what is called, in *Pink Swastika,* a "monstrous sadistic magic ritual, which left him impotent. This impotency had a deep psychological foundation. He then only knew fulfillment through extremes of sadism and masochism..." Some feel this impotence contributed greatly to Hitler becoming a sadistic murderer. Hitler supposedly allowed himself to indulge in "black magic' routinely that involved sadistic sexual practices, animal sacrifices, heterosexual orgies, blood scourging and sodomy. It is thought he believed these practices would bring him magical powers. [26]

Hitler was deceived, believing himself the savior of a civilization. He believed a lie! Evil prevailed and its *cause* gave power for destruction of a nation. Rituals of magick, symbols (SS and Swastika), the Inverted Triangle (used to identify prisoners), sexual perversions, and philosophies we associate with Nazi Germany came from the occult. The above symbols and rituals are present in our society today behind "closed" doors, some in plain view. Hitler's regime is a vivid reminder of what happens when people ignore evil. It is a clear demonstration of living with situational decisions, which is similar to moral relativism. If everything holds relative value then we can see how evil can run wild. It will devour people and a society. Hitler played with the occult; it controlled him. The occult is deceptive, planting seeds to sprout new philosophies of destruction.

Evil *cause* is a present day danger. If evil means to promote that which is against the moral code, it is obviously present throughout our country with some groups mentioned in this chapter. My next quest would be to find active occult groups seeking normality in our communities. I became anxious to know the tactics of the group and how *mind control* was imposed on citizens of all ages. In time I would explore current pagan culture, but for now resting in my comfortable blue chair was a priority. I wanted to forget the occult and dream of better days. Instead I kept thinking of the movie *Lord of the Rings* and its content of the battle between good and evil. My return to better days may indeed be only a dream and not possible in real life.

11

PAGANISM

The research on evil deception was ugly in content, and I decided it best to have fun for a few days, perhaps even shop. Shopping leads one in many directions, especially if going for nothing in particular. Eventually I found myself just sitting, and watching people. Style of dress is particular to each person and makes people watching very interesting. There were the usual teenagers with the fat or butt "hanging out" dress that is so "hard" on the eyes. I found joy in the teens that were neat, clean and apparently had found modesty while still being stylish. Young children are fun to watch for they carry a genuine innocence that is refreshing to the spirit. I flashed on others dressed in dark clothes adorned by jewelry that gave a Gothic allure to their appearance. I thought of children growing up with this influence in their lives and its connection to The New Age Movement. New age ideas are different than normal mores and I questioned what they specifically were and how they could be used for *mind control*. My day was filled with lots of shopping but I had enough energy left upon arrival home to begin my investigation into the new age movement. I had no problems finding information. Websites loaded with information, I began my search.

Members of the New Age Movement (NAM) believe and share knowledge that our "Western Culture is currently experiencing a phenomenal spiritual, ideological and sociological shift."[1] They encourage this shift by participating in far eastern, mystical religions such as Buddhism, Taoism, Hinduism and Western Occultism. Many participants believe in pantheism, secular humanism and moral relativism. Usually they depict themselves as open minded to all faiths and other beliefs, but their philosophies are in direct contrast to

41

what we hold true. One of the goals of the NAM is to bring peace to the world upon entering the Age of Aquarius, a time of high spiritual and universal awareness. The Age is determined by cycles according to the signs of the zodiac. We are now moving from Pisces into Aquarius. In order to find out information about this group, you can't just walk into a New Age Office and find a leader and set beliefs. Instead the book Networking lists over 1200 organizations that belong throughout our Nation.[2] Every imaginable group and profession is involved in NAM, and this has an effect on our country. They each have their own *cause,* which produces power for the collective *cause* of NAM.

Douglas R.Groothuis, author of *Unmasking the New Age* and *Confronting the New Age,* gives six ideas of New Age thinking: (1) all is one; (2) all is God; (3) humanity is God; (4) a change in consciousness; (5) all religions are one; and (6) cosmic evolutionary optimism.[3] Norman Geisler writes of 14 primary doctrines of New Age religions: (1) an impersonal god (force); (2) an eternal universe; (3) an illusory nature of matter; (4) a change in consciousness; (5) the necessity of reincarnations; (6) the evolution of man into Godhood; (7)continuing revelations from beings beyond the world; (8) the identity of man with God; (9) the need for meditation (or other consciousness changing techniques); (10) occult practices (astrology, mediums, etc.); (11) vegetarianism and holistic health; (12) pacifism (or anti-war activities); (13) one world global order; and (14) syncretism (unity of all religions).[4] The influence of the NAM is overshadowing our traditional world. Change is the goal and the occult is one of the forces pushing to reach that goal.

Pagan groups are moving into areas throughout the world claiming rights of equality next to traditional religious sects. One such group is called the Pagan Pride Project. The following four statements were found on the website. They say their ultimate purpose is the advancement of religion and elimination of prejudice and discrimination based on religious beliefs. The following are their beliefs.

1. Honoring, revering or worshipping a Deity or
    Deities found in pre-Christian, classical, aboriginal
    or tribal mythology.

2. Practicing religion or spirituality based upon shamanism, shamanic or magickal practices.
3. Creating new religion based on past Pagan religions and/or futuristic views of society, community and/or ecology.
4. Focusing religious or spiritual attention primarily on the Divine Feminine.[5]

They have an Executive Director, Membership Director and a Board of Coordinators. They have regional directors also. Biographical information is available about the leaders. The Executive leader is a Wiccan priestess, who lives in a communal setting with three adults and three children. She is a columnist for Pan Gaia Magazine and a contributor to New Witch Magazine. She is quoted as saying the following,

> "The combination of the Divine feminine, the celebration of the natural Cycles of time and nature, the strong emphasis on emotion and self-transformation, and the sheer creativity in Wiccan ritual all convinced her this was her spiritual home."[6]

The group keeps a balance through the inspirations of air, fire, water and earth. Air is education, fire is activism, water is charity and earth is community.

> "The idea is to weave networking webs in our cities, in our towns, and in our rural areas. We need webs to support ourselves. The support will show others that we are growing and our faith is as valid as any other faith."[7]

Focus on nature and ecology is evident in their belief number three. The Wheel of the Year is central to pagan religion. They believe time is circular and not linear, thus through holidays, eight occurring year round, they are ever linked to life, death and rebirth apparent in nature as well as human life. The first holiday is Winter Solstice/Yule (December 22). This date is not always certain so it is recommended that a proper Astrological reference book be used for accurateness.

> " Yule is the time of greatest darkness and the longest right of the year. The Winter Solstice had been associated with the birth of a "Divine King" long before the rise of Christianity. Since the sun is considered to represent the Male Divinity in Many Pagan Traditions, this time is celebrated as the "return of the Sun God" where He is reborn of the Goddess."[8]

Examples of two other holidays are Imbolc (February 2) and Beltaine (May 1).

1. "Imbolcs is the earliest whisperings of Springtide heard now as the Goddess nurtures Her Young Son. As a time of the year associated with beginning growth, Imbolc is an initiatory period for many. Here we plant the "seeds" of our hopes and dreams for the coming summer months."[9]

2. "Beltaine is the Land represented by the Goddess now ripe and fertile, and the Young God expresses His Love for Her. This is a time of joyous reveiling as the first flowers of Summer are gathered in Their Honor." [10]

Nature is of utmost importance in pagan philosophy. People are born over and over in nature, and become their own God by being a part of it. Pantheism identifies god with earth and ecology is extremely important to the group. Many of these individuals will work with ecology groups to close down farms when they find a small fossil on the land. It takes priority over the grazing fields, cattle, and livelihood of families working ranches for hundreds of years. Society is told we are ecologically in trouble today, but in reality it is a deception. Those seeking a narrow interest agenda can use our lack of knowledge to present facts contrary to the natural law of hatching salmon eggs or rainfall patterns, and we will believe it. Pantheism takes on religion when it shows reverence for the gods of the land in the above passages by capitalization of the "g" in gods and goddesses.

Ecology is New Age, and promotes its *cause* of preservation as a powerful tool of manipulation. It teaches our children to place "earth" rights over "individual" rights guaranteed as children of God.

Another manipulative tool is the circle. Pagan groups believe time is circular, and not linear, thus the circle takes on importance in their rituals. It can be used in many ways to include, exclude, bond, and even *mind control*. The occult groups claim they hold knowledge of various "means" that give them pathways to understanding mysterious or invisible matter. The circle is used for rituals and can be a powerful force to promote power for change. I flashed on educational seminars of past and the use of positioning in the classroom, including the circle. The circle was used to calm individuals, in order for *mind control* to take place (*Stage 2*). It can also be used to make one feel welcome or unwelcome thus encouraging one to believe as the group (*Stage 4*). Is it any wonder it was used to deliver a message of rejection in an Arcata CA. High School? Children were told to sit in a circle. Brad Dacus, from Pacific Justice Institute, reports they were asked, "Do you have religious beliefs that…homosexuality is wrong"? Three girls said "yes." As a result, they were placed in the middle of the circle. It was used to label them, and silence not only them, but also other objectors. Schools increasingly are using the circle, and in Elk Grove it is reported that high school teachers are using it regularly in certain classes. The students report to parents they do not like it. Teachers use circles within classrooms to honor mother earth and father sky. Pagan rituals appear to be entering the classroom's "closed" doors where children are ripe for *mind control*. The situations above encourage inclusiveness, everyone and everything has equal merit, thus fostering *Situationism*. Strong moral values are crucial to our children, and *situational* decisions to adopt evil philosophies presented in circles, can have long-term effects on our children. Without encouragement of Judeo-Christian values, children will make life-altering decisions based on the moment.

Another core belief of the pagan pride group is reverence of the divine goddess. It is number four belief of the pagan pride project. It wraps a woman in a warm "fuzzy" of love by honoring her or other goddesses. It has an allure for women seeking to give themselves and other women assurance, credibility, value, worth and ultimately power. It does not carry the same message to all; it can be deceiving to idealistic individuals searching for meaning. Goddess love is misplaced love of God unto yourself and pagan idols. You, become the god. An article in *U.S. News and World Report* revealed a meeting of the Society of Biblical Literature, where feminine theologians discussed new interpretations of the Scripture. The article was called "The word of Eve." At a "Re-Imagining Conference" many, who are ordained feminist ministers from Christian denominations, stated their allegiance to goddesses such as Isis, Aphrodite, Brigid, and Sophia. They call themselves Christians, but deny basic beliefs such as Christ's divinity, the sacrifice on the cross and His Resurrection. They do believe in a utopian faith, based on a deity of the great mother goddess. They want to re-establish this deity.[11] Many in the feminist movement want destruction of the patriarchal God, with the great mother "goddess" worship being a way to accomplish their goal. This word is seen in New Age Programs opening across America. The word is deceptive but alluring. The seed is easily planted in the young through language "change agents" such as goddess.

Nature and goddess are central to paganism. The word magick is also central to the philosophy of paganism as stated in number two of pagan pride beliefs.

"Magick is the art and science of focusing your will and emotions to effect change in the world around and within you. It's neither good or evil, positive or negative. You determine the power and path it will take."[12]

The next definition came from Aleister Crowley, mentioned earlier in Hitler's regime. His influence is alive even after his death. Only now it's not in Germany, but in The U.S.A.

"Magick is the science and art of causing change to occur in conformity to will."[13]

Magick is spelled different than magic to differentiate it from illusion and pretend of stage performance. [14] Magick is "real" to its participants. It is growing in popularity. The websites are loaded with shopping areas, throughout our land, for witch and Wicca materials needed to perform magickal ceremonies only insiders understand. The book titles deal with the following material: death, invisibility, levitation, labyrinth walking, advanced hypnotism, occultism, conducting séances, New Age Encyclopedias, past memories, necromancy spells and vampires. Videos are available with such names as Sex Magic and Tantra. [15] Even fairies are connected to the magick of paganism. Romping fairies are cute and I felt a resistance to this material for I did not want my image shattered. I did however continue. The books were plentiful on fairy magick. The Theosophical Society, previously discussed, has written books about their experiences with fairies.[16] *Fairy Spells* by Claire Nahmad claims she has communicated with the "benign spirits who can guide us back to a knowledge or our inner selves and restore our oneness with the natural world." [17]

The natural world seems to be a part of the fairy spirit, for unknown to me, except through my research on countryside and wooded areas, nature calls to homosexual groups called "radical fairies." Harry Hay, the father of the modern gay movement, and the Mattachine Society were instrumental in developing the group in the late 70's. It extended from the Rainbow family.[18] They describe themselves as follows.

"The fairies are a bunch of fags and other queer folk
who are finding ways to know ourselves and each
other (same thing) in deeper and deeper ways. We
meet in circles and in gatherings and in sanctuaries
where we can come to know each other face-to-face.
In our explorations we...."[19]

It goes on to explain a list of things they do at these gatherings. Of course there are the everyday things such as cooking, making bonfires, tending gardens, art, and sewing, but there are such things as doing rituals, doing drag, making love, having sex, dancing naked, committing heresy, covering each other with mud, and exchanging frocks and makeup ideas.[20] I saw pictures of men dressed as women with dresses, shoes, garters and make up. Some were dressed as Fairies. The circle is important; pictures show them frequently in this formation. The first meeting in 1979 took on a "spontaneous theme of paganism." Rituals are important; some inspired by Wicca.[21] Men live year round, some stay short visits, on acreage located throughout our country. It is also International. The philosophy is a return to nature in order to develop into who they want to be. The communities in some areas accept them. I wonder if fairies come to accept their responsibilities to humanity. America's freedom allows one to live as such; my concern is for those who are lured into this lifestyle out of curiosity or dark childhood experiences. The pagan rituals can bring them further into isolation from mainstream America. The "frolicking" spirit of their behavior can lead to irresponsible sexual acts; we eventually pay for this with spreading disease, more death, and increased health care costs. A new breed of young homosexuals is now practicing the "receiver" and "donator" practice of sex. It has become the way to acquire HIV. It is by far one of the "sickest" acts that show total disrespect for oneself and another. It is a mutual decision, and the participants choose their partners carefully for the transmission of this disease. Various groups of Fairies honor the poet Ginsberg. He was a pederast (seducer of young boys). He was an active member of North American Man Boy Love Association (NAMBLA). It is unfitting to honor those who promote sex with children. We must say "No" to acceptance of this lifestyle as "normal." Their *cause* is strong and their power relentless. It is the *cause* that will push their agenda forward, and let there be no mistake, the agenda includes sex with children.

This day also marked a time of utter darkness in my life for somehow I connected to dark pagan websites. It was informational but depressing. I read about humans who so desperately need to "feel" that they resort to the cruelest forms of human mutilation for sexual gratification, energy, and mystical experiences. Homosexual women, using Sado-Masochistic (SM) techniques called "cutting" to prove they can trust another. They enjoy blood and express joy at carrying scars of wounds inflicted with sharp knifes.[22] People participate in "whipping" ceremonies, dropping from pain after reaching perverted heights of sexual enlightenment[23]. Men allow themselves to be branded, wearing the mark as a badge of courage. I once saw a movie called *A Man Called Horse*. A man in the movie submitted to a ritual called the O-Kee-Pa ceremony where he pierced his chest and put claws or horns through it, hanging from the Sundance tree till his skin ripped and he fell. Mr. Musafar does this ritual.[24] He is known worldwide for his fifty years of self-mutilation and body modification. He advocates, teaches and practices it. The young see him as a father image and he has followers throughout the country. It is a "sick" practice, but unfortunately our young participate in the process of body mutilation with cutting and piercing becoming very popular. The above is dark; it was a reminder to me of how easily people connect to evil. The websites teach how to make whips or buy them with certain outcomes in mind. Instruction in SM Technique is taught in large cities and is available at SM conferences held yearly. The mind twisted and torn can be used to justify these ritualistic behaviors. I thought of Hitler and his use of ritualistic perversion. I am sure it was similar. The *cause* of this evil is powerful. Deception, through philosophies of "equal merit" and "everything is okay," is damaging to the human spirit. It can lead, for some, to the above lifestyle and the very destruction of their being!

Of course to understand other magick, an individual can enroll in The Sacred Mists and Online Wiccan College. Just as Theosophy offers the camaraderie of brotherhood, the Wiccan College online course offers cohesiveness by online chat rooms and study groups. The quote is as follows.

> "Do keep in mind that none of this interaction is
> required, but it is offered. We have found that many of
> our students were Solitary and find it wonderful to be
> in a group-learning environment that they can consider
> a Coven home. Upon completion you will be able to
> use your talents in Healing, Health and Magick!" [25]

It appears love is again luring people into its web of deception. Novices may want to try the Academy of Sorcery. They boast beginners learn "amazing abilities including invisibility, making visions appear, high magick, curses and levitation." Most importantly I noticed the blatant mockery of the Christian Faith. Students learn to walk on water, the hidden secrets behind Moses parting of the Red Sea, and casting of the 10 plagues.[26]

I thought about Hitler and forces of evil that overtook him, the *cause* of the occult groups helping him push evil agendas forward with their power. Brotherhood and love can be deceptive. Pagan and occult groups interchange evil for good and of course are seeking normalcy through this belief. It's not somewhere else, but right in your neighborhood. Sacramento holds a Pagan Pride Harvest Festival every year. It is scheduled already for September 25-26 of 2004.[27] Author and Presenter Profiles are as follows from last years Festival.

1. *Witchcraft and the Web* by M. Macha NightMare. She has authored two books. She co-created *The Pagan Book of Living and Dying* and authored *Witchcraft and the Web: Weaving Pagan Traditions Online.* She is an initiate of Reclaiming and the Faery/Feri traditions of Witchcraft. She states her magical practice is inspired by feminism and the health of our planet. She travels on the broomstick circuit and teaches online at Cherry Hill Seminary, where she chairs the Community Interfaith and Liturgics Department. Macha is an elder in the Covenant of the Goddess and a member of many other groups. It appears she is a serious pagan, desiring to spread her enthusiasm online.[28]

2. *Pagan Writing: Beyond the Book of Shadows* by Quill Enparchment. She has been a writer for 20 years and a pagan for four years. Her editorial positions have been for *Government Technology, Claims People Magazine*, and in Elk Grove for The *Elk Grove Citizen.* She is dedicated to spreading her zeal for paganism through writing. She not only lectured at the festival, but also held a children's storytelling session. I wonder what stories she tells; our childhood fantasies are their reality. [29]

50

3. *Raise Your Voice, Raise Your Power* by Isina
    Schuyler. Isina lives right next to Elk Grove and is
    a priestess for the Caulderon of Isis in Galt. I
    recall the women of ministry giving allegiance to
    the Goddess Isis. This priestess gives a
    presentation on chanting to manipulate your mood
    and the energy in your environment. Her zeal is
    spread through the power of sound. She
    recommends bringing drums and rattle items.[30]

4. *Having Fun with Tarot* by Valerie Sim. Valerie
    has been a Tarot reader and Astrologer for more
    than 32 years. She is a published author. She
    gives hands on workshops for beginners and pros.[31]
    Her enthusiasm is spread to all ages through fun
    games with cards. We do not know the future, thus
    this is deception. Giving false information can
    destroy a person and their hope.

Other titles are *The Magic of Ritual Tools* by Raven Grimassi,
a teacher and practitioner of the Craft for 30 years. Ed Broneske
gives a class on Germanic Religion. He studied for the Baptist
Ministry, but instead chose paganism.[32] The individuals listed are
serious about paganism. The forces of the occult are real; no one
wants to take it seriously. The adults turn their heads as if it does not
exist. Children may be wearing jewelry with signs and symbols;
parents don't notice. We treat Wicca and similar organizations like
make believe with no real consequences to their actions or beliefs. We
must begin to reveal deception lurking under the guise of brotherhood
and group identity. We must alert our children to this evil.

The American College Dictionary describes evil as something
that violates or is inconsistent with the moral law. [33] The principles of
these Organizations are inconsistent with moral principles of our
country. We cannot give them equal status. The occult *cause* is
dangerous. David Spangler, Author and Holistic enthusiast, is
involved in conscious evolution into the emerging age. He is quoted
as saying in "David Spangler on September 11th" the following about
his contact with the "inner world" and the Towers Horror.

"What has taken place is an act of sacrifice and a gift given by the Soul of America to the world at large. To understand this, you must know two things. The first is that whenever a death occurs, for whatever reason, whether peacefully or in violence, an energy of spirit is released. An incarnational portal is opened, just as it is at birth. This energy is neutral or perhaps I should say, unformed. It is a gift that flows between the worlds."[34]

The thoughts are different and misleading as is paganism. Toying with the lifestyle can lead one into its den. I know; I've been there. During my mother's illness and eventual death, I sought therapy to help me through this painful experience. I connected with an incredible counselor who not only was influential in the process of mourning, but also aided me in working through control issues in my life. As a result, I connected with her Woman's Group. It seemed innocent and I wanted to better myself (*Stage 1 mind control*). I even attended astrology classes with a good friend who was also part of the group. At times, some of the material even seemed logical (*Stage 3 mind control*). Through the years, however, I began to frequent the meetings less and less for the group was changing or was it me? I continued to attend, once in awhile, because of the friendships and warm loving environment (*Stage 4 mind control*). The new age philosophy began to predominate the group. My husband warned me, but I did not listen. On a cold stormy evening, I was shook into reality when an acquaintance at the meeting was taken over by a spirit. The scene that followed made me realize these ladies "lived" my pretend, for a designated person (the counselor was out of town) led the group in a circle (*Stage 2 mind control*) through ritualized words to rid the girl of the spirit. Reality for them is the course of the planets and the energy from the crystal around their neck. Following the circle, I knew there was little to share with these ladies. As they excitedly discussed a future speaker on crystals, I left hurriedly. I no longer encourage nor attend such gatherings. I still enjoy moments of one on one interaction with them and will always be thankful for my growth during therapy, but can no longer support the group philosophy. On the night of the storm, I knew I had to leave my fantasy world forever, for reality had never been more real. It was not a comfortable evening for me.

What it did show me is how easily it can happen. I am an intelligent woman and yet I toyed and played with the New Age agenda, not even understanding that I was doing it. I, like Hitler, was led into it through my fantasy. I, unlike Hitler, have a strong moral base that shook me into reality. The occult connection with Hitler is still behind "closed doors." Society says he was evil, but our education system continues denying occultism in Hitler's life or our society. We accept terrorism and evil only in the form of blowing up buildings, but not as surrounding our own children. The *cause* of evil being good and normal predominates tolerance programs, and teaches children they must give equal respect to every form of behavior for the collective good of society. *Mind control* of our children opens the door to exploration that is dangerous. A *Situational* decision can cause destruction of mind, body and soul. It has done, just that, with many a person. It has destroyed nations. We must guide our future leaders with solid principles of right and wrong, for only then can they make wise decisions that will affect them the rest of their life.

The sun was setting. My comfortable blue chair overlooked our front yard. Our towering redwoods can be seen above eyelevel from our second story. I sometimes imagine climbing trees to reach heaven; some trees strong, some weak, depending on seeds planted and conditions. We must plant seeds wisely, for eternity is forever. I thought of evil. I thought of propaganda man uses to justify his rejection of God. The agony of this lifestyle, inner turmoil, darkness, separation, uncertainty, fear and anguish will never end. It will be to all who climb it, their eternity!

12

NAZI HOMOSEXUAL CAUSE

I awoke with a startle, escaping a powerful force. The freedom from a frightening dream makes the sudden awakening to reality welcome. My sigh of relief was followed by reflection, and I started thinking about power and how it's intimately connected to control. I thought of how a strong group *cause* can produce power capable of altering an individual's mind. In my sleepy state, I envisioned hundreds of "liberal intellectuals" smirking at *mind control*; in reality, they deny it happens to them. I am sure Hitler credited himself for the take over of Germany, with no second thought to him being *brainwashed*. He was, after all, the one who dictated the needs of the state. Our "intellectuals" claim superiority in dictating our societal needs. They elevate, to acceptance, any group *cause* they know will benefit their liberal agenda, even if contrary to the majority. These plentiful *causes* will produce change. The public eventually caves in to the pressure and gives acceptance to the *cause,* replacing it with reforms that disguise themselves as education or intellectual and social betterment. The average person, involved in the *cause* of changing our Democracy, is usually unaware of the danger inherent in its replacement. An example is the utopia promised by socialism and communism. Communism takes everything away: property, family and God. Socialism shares everything. The result is an individual with nothing and the ruling elite with everything. Radical groups use everyday people, through *mind control*, to produce power necessary for the change, but this does not empower the individual, only the *cause*. The homosexual utopian *cause* of unnatural being natural does not work, and history proves that societies collapse after accepting this form of behavior.

This collapse is bad for the individual, but meets the goal of the people promoting the *cause*, which is transformation. The homosexuals are being used, as are so many others, to produce change.

I thought of the *cause* that homosexuals seek today for it has changed from respect of the person, to normality of lifestyle. The homosexuals sought respect by not wanting to be called names such as fag or queer. Name-calling was out of line, but they proceeded to coin the word "homophobic" invented in 1972 by a psychologist by the name of George Weinberg. It is offensive and discriminatory against us, but it is now okay for them to call us names. The double standard is rather obvious. Plus to make it more ridiculous, they now call themselves queer and deem it okay. The homosexual *cause* was never about gaining respect, but about acceptance of their lifestyle as normal. This was the only way to destroy our family units. The entire façade of seeking respect was a hoax, but it's ignored by those swayed by the group *cause*. It doesn't seem to matter if lies are told or hypocrisy exists as long as the liberal *cause* is promoted, for it will produce power. The *cause* of normality is picking up speed. Legislation and our judicial courts have already swayed in the homosexual favor. I thought about how the *cause* of the occult gave Hitler power, and if so then the homosexual *cause* of "brotherhood" could give Hitlerian power to radical homosexuals. The *causes* may be different but the power is the same. The homosexuals demand attention in history and we know that to be a part of history one must take responsibility for good and bad history. This was a chance to see the power of their *cause*, if any, and how it affected Hitler's regime. I became anxious to study the homosexual influence in Nazi Germany, beginning with a brief review of homosexual history in other cultures. "Cause and Effect" produced an adrenaline rush and before I knew it, I was not in my sleepy state but jumping out of bed to begin my research.

Homosexuality has existed since the beginning of time. History tells of it throughout the ages. Greek and Roman Cultures eventually accepted homosexuality. The ruling classes, aristocracy, participated openly in homosexual activity. In Greece the relationship between a man and a boy was a higher form of contact, and a young boy was even more aesthetically pleasing and superior in communion.

The relationship was encouraged with boys 12-17, preparing them for social and political adult life. An adult male could be married, but still pursue the young male as long as he did not pay him for his services. This was considered against the law. If the boy accepted payment, he was punished by withdrawal of civil and political rights. The young men were intellectual companions, whereas women were seen inferior and strictly for childbearing.[1]

The Romans also held rigid guidelines for homosexual activity. The social code allowed insertive sex with young males, but only with his slaves. It was held highly dishonorable for a man to experience sexual penetration.[2] A rigid code of definition between two types of homosexuals existed. The warriors upheld the muscular male figure (Butch) as the preferable and deemed the feminine figure (femme) as subservient. This classification of Butch and Femmes has passed through the ages. According to a former pink triangle prisoner at the Flossenburg concentration camp, the Nazi's hated the Femme homosexuals. They did, however, revere the masculine type with the traits desired for the warrior image of a soldier.[3]

As mentioned earlier, pagan cultures welcomed homosexuality. Indeed young males in some primitive cultures go through excruciating initiations, lasting days, in order to turn boys into active homosexuals. [4] There is not much information on female homosexuals during Greek and Roman times. It was not socially acceptable and therefore not mentioned. [5] There was some involvement of female homosexuality during the Nazi Regime, but it doesn't appear the force behind their *cause* added substantial power to the movement. Sexual infatuation, however, with young boys is a homosexual theme predominate throughout history. Another predominate theme is the fact that Greek and Roman Cultures crumbled, and many authorities attribute this to the decline of moral values and acceptance of the homosexual lifestyle.

Jewish, Christian, and Muslim Doctrines held beliefs contrary to homosexuality, and their righteous attitude and religious communities were able to change the mores through the ages. It is clear that Theosophy, occultism and homosexuality were growing sources of power in Germany. This cohesiveness gave Hitler strength in taking over the State. Hitler supported these groups, which promoted unity. Hitler ridded the country of contrary influences, while encouraging occultism and homosexuality, promoting his Aryan race and allegiance to the State.

In the late 19th century, Karl Heinrich Ulrichs influenced the homosexual movement in Germany. He was molested as a child and lived as a homosexual, believing himself to carry a female spirit within. His theory attracted followers. Political activism began, and the name of pederasts and sodomites eventually changed to homosexuality. [6] A movement began to decriminalize sodomy. Changing attitudes were apparent with Germany experiencing a surge of perverted activity between 1891 and 1919. Even the ruling classes showed interest in the lifestyle. Great writers of the day and medical professionals became aware of the previously unnoticed practices surfacing. Knowledge spread through homosexual publications such as Die Freundschaft. [7] When Heinrich Ulrichs died, Magnus Hirschfeld carried on his philosophy. He became well known for his research within the medical and psychology communities. He founded the Scientific Humanitarian Committee (SHC) dedicated to "legitimizing homosexuality."

This is a powerful statement about the *cause* of groups, for "legitimizing" homosexuality became the root for the cohesiveness of the group. Hitler used the *cause* of the homosexual group within the education department of the SHC for his own means to an end. Hirschfeld devised methods to carefully implant into the minds of German people a different homosexual image than they themselves portrayed within the groups, which were indeed various forms of perversion. He opened the Sex Research Institute of Berlin housing the collections of his important research. He offered legal council and advice on abortion issues. His Institute grew in homosexual numbers and soon they had 1000 members. [8]

The homosexual movement was growing in numbers within the German Army, and its *cause* of brotherhood was used for the good of the state. Of these units, many were children. Germany is an example of youthful innocence turning into a powerful force used for one's selfish ends. A German Boy Scout troop, started by a boy in the late 1800's, called Wandervoegel (Wandering Birds or Rovers) was the introduction to homosexuality for young boys becoming part of Hitler's youth group know as "Homo Youth." The Extended-arm "Sieg Heil" salute came from this group. [9] The cohesiveness of the youth group was in the hands of Hitler. Indeed, Hitler used it to promote his agenda.

Another important man, connected with the youth movement, by the name of Blueher, had a great influence on shaping the Wandervoegel and the leaders.[10] Homosexual author Frank Rector states:

> "Blueher's case further explains why many Nazi Gays were attracted to Hitler and his shrill anti-Semitism, for many gentile homosexuals were rabidly anti-Semitic…Gays in the youth covenant who espoused anti-semitism, chauvinism, and the Fuehrer Prinzip (Leader Principle) were not so incipient Fascists. They helped create a fertile ground for Hitler's movement and, later, became one of its main sources of adherents…A substantial number of those Wandervoegel leaders were known homosexuals and many others were allegedly gay (or bisexual). [11]

Brotherhood in the German Army was a priority and male sexual bonding became accepted behavior, with a warrior mentality becoming a dominant theme. Hitler used homosexual cohesiveness wisely. Blueher became important in offering Hitler advice, as noted by Author Samuel Igra, a Jewish historian who escaped Germany in 1939. Blueher felt the following.

> "Germany was defeated in World War I because the homosexualists way of life had been considerably neglected and warlike virtues had degenerated under the advance of democratic ideas, the increasing prestige of family life, the growing influence of women and above all the Jews, based on their rejection of homosexuality." [12]

Blueher was well known through the press and his philosophies began to grow through the years, via media support. As a result the society was beginning to shape itself around the state being more important than the family unit.

The children continued training in lifestyles contrary to long-standing mores. Author Robert G.L. Waite gives a rich history of the men involved in this training. One of the men was Rossbach. He was proficient in forming groups of troopers, which eventually evolved into the Storm Troopers. He was also proficient in seducing young men. Ernst Roehm, one of them, became a top leader in the Brownshirts, which were known for their "brutality." Most of the Nazi youth had adult supervisors that were homosexual. [13]

What is clear is that the Third Reich was built heavily on homosexual bonding within military forces. The *Pink Swastika* gives in great detail the association of homosexuality within the Nazi Regime. It is wonderful reading and I recommend it to everyone. The book was to be placed in the Holocaust Museums. *The Pink Swastika* is reported not in view when visiting the museums; in actuality, it has been hidden from the public and totally ignored. Instead the homosexuals are portrayed as the victims of the holocaust. Hitler did not promote annihilation of the homosexuals, but he did promote it for the Jewish race. Homosexual militants, Hollywood and special fund raisers built an entire section of the Holocaust Museum devoted to homosexual persecution, but fail to mention that homosexuals inflicted the cruelty on their own people. Some Jewish leaders have come to the forefront supporting Scott Lively and Kevin Abrams, the Authors of *Pink Swastika*, by writing letters to the museum board. I am thankful for those who have done this act, but it appears that nothing is being done. If more outrage were shown toward manipulation of the truth, it would guarantee adequate representation of homosexuals in both the aggressive and victim status during the holocaust. Scott Lively mailed hundreds of *Pink Swastika* books to Jewish leaders, and I hope they will read them using their *cause* to bring this book into Holocaust Museums and to the attention of our Nation.

Further research showed the elite within the Nazi party were brought up in schools known as Ordensburgen, which eventually replaced many family units. They were fashioned after the Wandervoegel. The increasing numbers of these schools promoted more power for Hitler and were the foundation for the Nazi movement. The youth were being indoctrinated, and parents turned their heads the other way.

Many of our schools are becoming Ordensburgens and replacing traditional roles of parents. Nazi youth leaders dictated philosophies taught to the students. People in authority such as school superintendents, principals, school board members, teachers, pastors, ministers, priests and scout leaders are allowing homosexual activists to dictate philosophies to our children and adults. The Ordensburgens, of today, introduce these philosophies through tolerance and diversity programs. Indoctrination then takes place through seeds of deception.

Not only is it easy to indoctrinate our children, but also friends or highly persuasive leaders easily influence our adults. Frank Rector, a homosexual historian, writes about Ernst Roehm's power in the formation of Hitler's personality. Hitler was the man Roehm needed to forward his ideas of domination. Roehm encouraged Hitler to give more support to his army and working together with the Socialist group, Iron Fist, they took over the Weimar government. With intent and focus, the party became the National Socialist German Worker's Party. They began to incorporate other branches, such as the Storm Troopers, into this Party. [14]

The army was building. The Hegelian Philosophy of the State taking over as Absolute ruler was surfacing. To support this theory, Hitler needed forces to uphold the state. The people came to understand the supreme right of the people was to be a member of the State, not to be an individual. I shivered when I read this for it reminded me of the global indoctrination that is now taking place in our Nation. Children were taught that German State allegiance was more important than family, just as our youth are now being taught that global principles are more important than our Nation's sovereignty. The German people were forewarned in the 19th century, but they did not listen. John Fitche, in his "Address to the German people," said "children would be taken over by the state; told what to think and what to do." With time and implementation, it happened in Germany. [15] It is happening in our beloved U.S.A., right under our nose!

The new ideas of State took root; the German People became part of the New German Social Organization. The state replaced God. Roehm, alongside Hitler, exemplified belief in homosexuality as being a basis for world power. Roehm believed that "a society needed men who were arrogant and proud, and could brawl, carouse, smash windows, kill and slaughter for the hell of it. Straights, he felt, were not adept at this." [15] Homosexual bars reserved tables for the army elite; Roehm and his companions met to form their tactics for Nazi campaigns of intimidation and terror. [16] To qualify for some positions within the troops you had to be homosexually oriented. Hitler moved masses toward allegiance of State, and the homosexuals were used in his attainment of power. The Storm Troopers continued as one of the largest branches in the army.[17] With little interest in women, aside from his own sexual perversions, Hitler surrounded himself with male oriented individuals.[18] His Private Attorney, Minister of Justice, Minister of Economics, Financial Advisor and Hitler's second in command were known homosexuals and some pederasts.[19]

As years passed, pederast and sado-masochistic homosexuals came into conflict with other homosexuals who did not believe in the same lifestyles. The conflict began within the armed forces. At the same time that this conflict was brewing, there were favors freely given to the homosexuals in the SA branch of the Nazi party. Complaints eventually began to surface within the branches of the Third Reich causing increased concern for Hitler. The robust spirit of homosexual troopers became too much. Unfavorable feedback came from important figures in his life with one of them being Mussolini. On a visit to Venice, the conduct of some of his men was appalling. Igra, a Jewish immigrant, once again reports that Hitler was advised to rid himself of these people for his personal reputation was at risk. Hitler staged Night of the long Knives and the Roehm Purge. On June 28, 1934, important members of the Storm Troopers were massacred as they slept. Since most of the SA leaders were homosexual, Hitler justified this as a moral cleansing. It helped alleviate any public concern of moral corruption in the inner circle of power. It was, however, noted by author Igra that he did not rid himself of all homosexuality; much activity continued behind "closed doors." Hitler initiated another important step helping his career. He staged destruction of the Sex Research Institute; thousands of books and files on homosexual research were destroyed. Hitler knew these documents could damage the advancement of his goals. [20] Ludwig L. Lenz, assistant director of the Institute said the following.

"Our Institute was used by all classes of the population
and members of every political party...We thus had a
great many Nazis under treatment at the Institute.
Why was it then, since we were completely non-party,
that our purely scientific Institute was the first victim,
which fell to the new regime? The answer is simple.
We knew too much. It would be against medical
principles to provide a list of The Nazi leaders and
their perversions {but}...not ten percent of the men
who in 1933 took the fate of Germany into their hands,
were sexually normal...Many of these personages
were known to us directly through consultations; we
heard about others from their comrades in the
party...and of others we saw the tragic results...Our
knowledge of such intimate secrets regarding members
of the Nazi party and other documentary material-we
possessed about four thousand confessions and
biographical letters-was the cause of the complete and
utter destruction of the Institute of Sexology" [21]

Hitler was intent on ridding the world of anything connecting
him to his past. He killed another friend, Reinhold Hanish, who
shared his past in Vienna. It is suspected he knew of Hitler's
questionable male prostitution in his younger years. [22] His devious
behavior, in the name of goodness, was indeed a cleansing method.
The flamboyant leaders were gone. He successfully rid the Third
Reich of association with homosexuality, but continued reaping
benefits of power it generated for takeover of Germany.
Seeds of deception led to destruction of the German people
and a way of life. Hitler won the people; they were but clay to him,
pliable into any shape desired. Eventually, Hitler removed God from
schools replacing Him with pantheist gods, mother earth and father
sky. He replaced Christian holidays with pagan celebrations.
Mandatory prayer was stopped in the schools in 1935, and eventually
all religious training stopped for teachers. [23] We are doing this in our
country. Children have mother earth as part of learning circles, but
God can't be mentioned in the Christian tradition of prayer. Native

Georgiana Preskar

American ceremonies are performed in classrooms, but not Christian prayer. Muslim dress and plays, including readings from the Koran, are given clearance through Court hearings, but Christian plays are banned from schools. Christmas no longer is in schools; it has been replaced with around the world celebrations and diversity trees.

Hitler's victory also included removing guns from homes. Legislators and radical groups are trying to remove guns from our homes. They use the same reason Hitler did, in that it will reduce the crime rate. People believed the lie and Hitler confiscated their guns. The people were left defenseless and led into camps without a fight. Nationalists saw him as a savior of their people, looking to him for the glory of their nation. Some knew the truth and others continued to deny the camps. Soon everyone would know the truth behind the "closed doors."

In the year of 1933, Hitler declared himself absolute dictator of Germany. The Thule Society and Hitler began a new world order and imposing it on a nation previously a democracy, they were able to manipulate minds of the masses, seize their only protection (guns), use their aggressive military force against the people and turn Germany into a dictatorship. In 1938 Hitler began the Holocaust and in 1939 World War II. This war lasted until 1945.

Over 54 million people lost their lives in the War; silence took its toll. With over six million Jewish deaths, it is by far one of the worse tragedies our world has seen. Let there be no mistake, the Jewish people were the targeted group. There were various religious groups persecuted and some homosexuals were persecuted. It is believed many homosexual prisoners were Femmes, and warrior- like homosexuals were antagonistic toward them. Some were used for the pleasure of perverted guards, while others were used for scientific purposes along with men, women and children that were encamped. The majority of homosexuals who died did so because of poor conditions, long workdays and starvation. [24] The sufferings of humanity unthinkable. Our imaginations can't bring us to such a place of horror! The brutality promoted in a joyful spirit for the Nazi regime truly was evil!

My review of the Nazi Regime gave evidence of strong homosexual brotherhood that promoted power for the state. Heterosexuals take credit for the good and bad events in history in order for it to be accurate, and therefore homosexuals must also take credit for their past behavior and the truth of the events. If they refuse then I must question why they are living a lie? The *cause* of homosexual brotherhood gave power to the army. *Cause* can change a country, and the homosexual *cause* has changed our country. It challenged the truth of natural order. Some people have been *brainwashed* into believing their *cause* and accept homosexuality as normal. Homosexuals are being used in our country by producing power for change through their *cause*. The movement continues, but now it is moving speedily toward and amongst our children. We are raising armies of homosexuals about to take over our moral values and codes that have kept us solid for 200 years. The brotherhood will replace our traditional family unit. It will eventually destroy our society!

As I looked at pictures of Hitler and young boys in the Youth Army, I thought of their lost youth. Our young are losing the innocence we once protected, and we are losing ourselves. History will record our destruction. It will be available for those rebuilding our society. It will talk of a society that did not heed warnings from others who went before us.

Greece was a thriving society. Education, arts, warfare ability and philosophers such as Aristotle and Socrates gave Greece recognition worldwide. Greece, in their early years, held high moral codes. They did believe in moral absolutes. God, however, was not a part of their society and soon homosexuality and other immorality began. It caused chaos in the balance, unity was lost and they were taken over by Rome.[25]

Rome started in much the same way. Family structure and political organization were important in the social climate that kept the country together. Arrogance took over and morals began to decline. With the introduction of homosexuality and adultery came the beginning of its end. Abortions came to be accepted and violence in Gladiator activity increased. Rome collapsed.[26]

Jim Nelson Black in *When Nations Die* mentions ten factors that lead civilizations to collapse. He says the "United States is the first nation to have all present at one time"

1. Increase in lawlessness

2. Loss of economic discipline
3. Rising bureaucracy
4. Decline in education
5. Weakening of cultural foundations
6. Loss of respect for traditions
7. Increase in materialism
8. Rise in immorality
9. Decay of religious belief
10. Devaluing of human life[27]

13

REVISION of AB 537

T he ten points seemed to linger in my mind, and I realized that they were made possible through legislation. The legislative packet I received at Lobby Day introduced me to how narrow interest groups with a *cause* can manipulate legislation to fit their agenda. I became absorbed in the deceptive process it explained.

New age vocabulary caused me to close my eyes, desperately trying to shut out the reality of the words. I thought of times past, wondering how I passed through the "rhetoric" of the 60"s without getting its clear content. My experience helped me to better understand the easiness of *mind control*. It is a strange feeling to look back on your life and see yourself different than in the present moment.

My pioneering spirit drove me to California in September of 1967. I thought of how intellectually enlightened the "coast" would be, in sharp contrast to the "apple pie" states of the Midwest. By the time I reached this area I was primed for San Francisco General Hospital. I worked as a Registered Nurse amidst medical personnel progressive in their thinking. My return to school at San Francisco State University in Sociology was intellectually stimulating; it fostered, even further, my impression that I was part of a new generation far superior to our predecessors. I worked and went to school with a diverse group of people and wrapped myself in a warm "fuzzy" of the flower children era. Now the entire country is wrapped in this warm blanket of deception. Our education departments overflow with new rhetoric of "anti-hate" words replacing "love" words of the 60's. Our governing bodies do the same thing, replacing the assurance of constitutional rights of the past with social agenda legislation, deceptive in its wording, so the ordinary folk have no idea of what or whom they are voting for.

California usually passes bills that are liberal and contrary to conservative values. Why? We vote for immoral legislators. We must know our candidates before voting for them. Though some of the bills are clear in content, it is possible to make them worse by schemes concocted behind "closed" doors. Secrecy was Hitler's key to success. I reflected on this theme as I read the story of Delaine Eastin's task force, meeting secretly about education revisions. Delaine Eastin, California's past State Superintendent of Public Instruction, led meetings discussing AB 537, which adds "gender" and "sexual orientation" to all prohibited discrimination clauses. Also included were AB 1785, "fostering an appreciation for diversity," "supplemental resources to combat bias" and guidelines for reporting "hate-motivated incidents."

The meetings were composed of a 36 member advisory task force, which translated the new laws into state Education Codes. Though diversity claimed to be their goal, the task force was far from diverse. It weighed heavily on the side of homosexual activists and sympathizers, with some being from Older Asian Sisters in solidarity (OASIS), Lavender Youth Recreation and Information Center (LYRIC), Gay Lesbian Straight Education Alliance (GLSEN), and the National Education Association Gay and Lesbian Caucus. They met for months behind "closed" doors. No one knew what was transpiring until April 11, 2002 when the task force presented its proposals. The original bill consisted of two pages, but the new material was 21pages. Some examples of the 21-page report are:

1. Surveying children to probe their attitudes about homosexuality.
2. Integrating pro-homosexual and pro-transgender messages into "all" curricula, including sciences, history, language, arts and even math.
3. Creating new policies "to reduce the adverse impact of gender segregation related to locker room facilities, restrooms and dress."

4. Posting "positive grade level appropriate visual images" that include "all sexual orientations and gender identities" throughout the school.

5. Using taxpayer dollars to establish Gay-Straight Alliances on campuses, put all school personnel through extensive and "ongoing" sensitivity training, pay for a media blitz, "provide rehabilitation to perpetrators" of discrimination and appoint a person in each school to monitor implementation of the new programs.[1]

The Task Force gave "thanks" to Sheila Kuehl, author of AB 537 and principal consultant. She is a homosexual and primary initiator of homosexual bills that have gone through California legislature. [2]

The plan was sent to all schools. One thing missing; the schools were not required to follow any of these directives. The Bills clearly indicated that local districts were to retain ultimate control over curriculum, textbook, presentations and other material in any program or activity, and the development of any local plans or policies. The schools were under "false" impression they had to adopt Delaine Eastin's Task Force Policies. [3] The important reason for the Bill, the safety of all children, seemed to get lost in another *cause*, the acceptance of alternate lifestyles as "normal."

School districts throughout California readily adhered to the new directives. Though quietly done, force was beyond comprehension. The media backed the proposals; reports boldly printed these programs under safety, thus being good for our children. Other states adopted similar ideas. They were magnified into the "savior" of the times; they would rid the world of "hate." The *cause* and *effect* was beginning to work. The power behind the *cause* was now being implemented through networking of various groups backing it. The "agenda" had been hiding, waiting patiently to make its presence known to humanity. Just as it slowly crept in, it continues waiting patiently as each new program is accepted into our society. The "Delaine Eastins" have made their "mark." Secrecy continues with passage of bills unknown to the average person.

Georgiana Preskar

The Tolerance, Multicultural, Diversity programs began emerging years ago. They plant seeds of deception that are growing quickly and encouraging more programs. I knew our elected officials promoted programs behind "closed" doors and I suspected schools were doing the same. Everything moved me in the direction of secrecy in the schools districts, and I would follow my intuition. I needed information about the 2003 Silent Day. The first step would be to call the Principal of Elk Grove High School. This decision proved to be a very important one as did so many when I look back on the last 18 months. They seemed to connect, mysteriously drawing me, as if by design, into new directions of discovery.

14

TMD=PC
(Tolerance+Multiculturalism+Diversity=Political Correctness)

I returned the receiver to the base. Wanting my phone conversation with the principal to be meaningful, I decided to research vocabulary. Effective communication is a joy in life. Everyone knows the thrill of communicating; few attain this goal on a daily basis. We instead ineffectively communicate because of "definition confusion." A "word" according to the dictionary has specific meanings; special interest groups have "social" definitions of the same word in order to manipulate behavior. "Hate" is an example of such a word. I was taught it meant an abominable feeling of disgust and repulsion. It was the worst possible negative thought we could have toward someone or something. Hate today means disagreeing with another's lifestyle, values or morals. With two different interpretations of the same word, communication becomes difficult! Tolerance, multiculturalism, diversity and political correctness are misunderstood words. Joshua Claybourn, a junior at Indiana University writes the following in his article "Tolerating the definition of tolerance."

> "The traditional definition of tolerance in Webster's Dictionary is 'to recognize and respect others' beliefs, practices, etc. without necessarily agreeing or sympathizing." My brother's calendar, which is for middle school, went so far as to say tolerance is "accepting and even appreciating differences." The

definition on college campuses goes even further: "to accept others' beliefs and practices as equal to your own." [1]

Daniel Flynn in *Why the Left Hates America* states that

"tolerance can mean a recognition of the right of others to follow a different course. It can also mean an active support of the different course. It can also mean an endorsement of the different course. It can even mean to support laws that would punish those who were not tolerant of others." [2]

Thus tolerance becomes a word that can be used by individuals or groups for intimidating a society into accepting any behavior or value change they deem necessary for their own needs. Our country is supposed to look at other cultures with tolerance. These cultures however discourage that same trait when viewing our society. Daniel Flynn explains the double meaning of words.

" For Third World cultures, tolerance means uncritical appreciation and praise. For the First World, it means highlighting faults. Thus slavery becomes a Western invention while its popularity among primitive societies is ignored. [3]

Jessie Peterson supports this by pointing out that today in Sudan and Mauritania black men, women and children are routinely sold into slavery, yet American civil rights organizations are utterly silent about it. [4] Gregory Koukl, President of Stand to Reason, made the absurdity of the "tolerant" word very meaningful by a method he used in the classroom. He wrote two sentences on the board while speaking to a high school group. The sentences were:

"All views have equal merit and none should be considered better than another."
"Jesus is the Messiah and Judaism is wrong for rejecting it."

71

Everyone agreed with the first statement, but they did not agree with the second statement for they felt it was "intolerant." He asked again about the first statement and views having equal merit. They once again said yes. He pointed again to the second statement and said, "Is this a view?" Slowly they realized they had been tricked by the above logic and it became evident to them that the first statement violates itself. Mr. Koukl went on to explain that if all views had equal merit, then the view that Christians have a better view on Jesus than Jews is just as true as the idea that Jews have a better view on Jesus than Christians. This is hopelessly contradictory. If the first statement is true then no one can be tolerant because "tolerance" is nothing but gibberish. He then put two more quotes on the board.

> "Be egalitarian regarding persons."
> "Be elitist regarding ideas."

His explanation is to treat others with value or worth because they are human beings. Treat the ideas as an elitist; some ideas are better than others. He followed this with the fact that our society has turned this upside down. We instead do the opposite.

> "Be egalitarian regarding ideas."
> "Be elitist regarding persons."

If we reject other people's ideas we are thought hateful people. We become the "bad" guy and are thought intolerant. No matter how graciously we reject their ideas, we inevitably become the discriminatory one. This leads to an accepted attitude that we can be ill treated as a person, ignored and publicly abused for our views. The irony in this is that in order to be tolerant you must disagree with someone's views; we are not tolerant of those who agree with us for they already agree with our view. [5] Tolerance promotes equality of all ideas, people and things, which is dangerous, for without discernment we could accept others dangerous lifestyles and behaviors with death and destruction (we saw on 9/11) the final result.

72

Georgiana Preskar

I am not surprised by the power of words; Hitler showed the major impact communication could have upon a nation. Programs are put in place under the guise of tolerance; the real reason is indoctrination. Multiculturalism is one of them. I minored in Anthropology in college. Fascinated by different cultures, I studied diligently to learn as much as I could about their customs. We learned differences by comparing their culture to ours, and we were never afraid to voice praise for our culture. In the early 90's we saw an increase in popularity of the word multiculturalism. It took on traditional meaning when first introduced; many people believed it did mean learning about other cultures. Eventually we understood it was used to promote another agenda. It encouraged tolerance of all cultures with equal merit given to all. Immigrants are not encouraged to assimilate into our culture, but educated to promote and validate their culture as equal to ours. Our country is more divided today than it was years ago, with students denouncing our integrity and shunning our culture. The main focus of Multiculturalism is acceptance of other's food, language, dress, customs, and religious beliefs as equal to and sometimes better than ours. Ultimately this leads to the idea that truth is determined by the individual culture, therefore, truth is relevant to the group and not universal. If each culture is equal then all cultures have truth that is as relevant as ours and thus never wrong, even when behavior is grossly out of line with our beliefs. I flashed on the atrocities (female genital mutilation, forced abortions, rapes, honor killings, white slavery, planned marriages, etc.) that exist in other countries. Multicultural enthusiasts, such as National Organization of Women (NOW), promote a spirit of live and let live toward the people perpetrating these horrors, but indeed demand acceptance into men's golf clubs in America. Where is the tolerance or equal merit they so vehemently uphold?

I thought of words and how they can *mind control* through programs such as multiculturalism. I envisioned the Madrasas or Koran Schools in which I vividly saw Arab children being taught to hate Americans and our way of life. Multicultural enthusiasts say their culture is equal to ours, and we are at fault, causing them to hate us. The definition of tolerance, in reference to multiculturalism, can be carried to dangerous levels. Words that intimidate can be used as tactics supporting multicultural ideas of anti-Americanism, opening the doors to an easy takeover of our land.

Multiculturalism has encouraged a philosophy of "new thought." Words are used to *brainwash* people from birth, into believing ideas contrary to the truth. Children in America are taught to see our land as their enemy instead of their friend, and we are now raising our own army of traitors. We side people against each other by indoctrination through education. Do we wonder why such organizations as Movimiento Estudiantil Chicano de Aztlan (NEChA) are now on over 400 campuses? Their motto is "For our race, everything. For those outside our race, nothing." [6] The philosophy of this group is to encourage Mexicans to take over the American Southwest. They use language to slur whites and encourage Mexicans to show loyalty to Mexico and not the United States of America. An organization, American Indian Movement (AIM), criticizes American Indians who have become a part of our culture. The group says they are red apples, red on the outside and white on the inside. They encourage Indians to separate from our culture. [7]

Multiculturalism breaks down our country cohesiveness. We must keep in mind the elitist and egalitarian model of equal merit and teach it to others. Not all cultures are the same and if people do not want to assimilate into our culture then, indeed, they should not come to America. People need to come into our country to assimilate into us, not us into them. If we focus on elitism for ideas and egalitarianism for people then every individual will be given respect. Parents tell me books are taken out of schools because they don't fit multiculturalism. They are replaced with books rewritten to alter the truth of our American history. I recently had an anonymous letter sent to my husband's office about one of the middle schools in Elk Grove. She or he stated that a female homosexual teacher was working with the Principal to get *Huckleberry Finn* pulled from the reading list. The teacher felt it was not a politically correct book supporting multiculturalism. It is a racially frank book by Mark Twain, but also a traditional classic book of 19th Century America. At the same time, one of our members, Teri Lawrence discovered another book by the name of *Lupita Manana* by Patricia Beatty in her son's middle school. This story is about an illegal immigrant who comes to America. There are endorsements at the end of the book that support illegal immigration. It seems that multiculturalism, once again, is not being used to educate the children about a culture, but to serve a political agenda.

The numbers are beginning to add up to TMD=PC. If everyone is "tolerant" of everything for society's good and we give all cultures "equal merit" and diversity gives its approval for "anything," then we will have achieved political correctness. In 1978, Diversity came into vogue during the Bakke case when The Supreme Court was split four to four on affirmative action. Justice Powell used this word to brilliantly justify reverse discrimination as something other than a deliberate suspension of classic liberal principles.[8] It was nine years later that it resurfaced following the Workforce 2000 report. The report in 1987 showed that by year 2000 white men would make up 15% of the workforce. The report actually meant that the 15% of white workers were in and above those already working. It meant the work force would grow slowly upward from the already existing force. Because the public misinterpreted the facts, or were lied to by the media, businesses all over the land began pushing diversity hiring. It was about this time, in the late 1980's, that "political correct" as a term became a reality. It was also a time for advocates of affirmative action to resurface. It was a perfect time for the Powell diversity concept to come into vogue. Diversity gave everyone a new way of looking at politics, culture, society and personal identity. [9] It also robbed us of the dignity of judging, liking, not liking, and discovering our own levels of acceptance. We in essence were told how to think. If we did not adhere to these words we became homophobic, racist, and hateful people. We no longer could use discrimination to discern, for it was not allowed. Our society began to train itself to the dictates of the thought police and just as in George Orwell's *1984*, we began to "obey" or "pay" the price.

I thought of how our population honors and reveres the above words. Political Correctness has become our new god. We bend like reeds in a windstorm to its very sound. I see individuals outraged when anyone utters any disrespect of these words by a simple disagreement with one of its philosophies. I see ministers, pastors, priests and entire church congregations fall to these words before they will bend knees to God's Word of law. I see fathers of households relinquish their authority with their families for ideas of political correctness. I see mothers putting faith in the teaching of schools, rather than Godly principles. Grandparents, afraid of rejection, deny they could possibly make a difference and they do not speak out. I see principals, superintendents, school board members, and teachers sweep their long held traditional beliefs into their briefcases of old and discard them so easily into the receptacles of outdated material. I see government officials abandoning principles that elected them to office.

Indeed political correctness has become this country's god. I am aware of its power. Changes are occurring faster than we can assimilate them into our psyches. Imbalance is prevalent and people are not happy. Chaos will continue until people find a *cause* strong enough for them to want to stop this nonsense. In the meantime, I wonder if tolerance, multiculturalism and diversity will continue to replace our traditional God with flimsy words of shallow meaning?

It was too late to call the principal; the research was lengthy. Tomorrow was another day. The anticipation of communication is always an unknown. Each day is filled with the surprise of interactions we do not expect. I felt that tomorrow would be one of those days. I would not expect; therefore, I would be okay with the outcome. Each moment is precious, to be held valuable for its presence. I starred out the window and thought of the beauty of my very existence in the moment. I was suspended as if in space, not reaching for answers, but just enjoying the weightlessness of the uncertainties.

15

THE PRINCIPAL

"I will connect you." I sat nervously in my comfortable blue chair waiting to hear the verdict whether the Principal of Elk Grove High School would pick up his telephone. The voice was firm but friendly. I was happy he answered.

By the time I made this phone call, Eagle Forum of Sacramento was official. I was confident relaying who we were and how I represented Eagle Forum in our community. It was easy to explain how we stood for the political, economic and social principles upon which our country was founded by our Founding Fathers. I repeated these words many times to myself, the delivery tone important to impregnate the listener. I wanted him to remember Eagle Forum and understand that we were not going away.

We talked; getting to know each other superficially is the usual protocol for this type of call. It served its purpose. We soon were onto the Day of Silence. I found it interesting to hear his side of the story that we often do not know, but make judgments as to the behavior. I found myself enjoying the interaction, relating to him in a positive way.

His story was similar to the Vice Principal's and I listened, again, as he told me the homosexual students and supporters had the right to silence themselves. Teachers gave permission for their classroom to participate. Clarity was at the forefront of my thinking, for I always thought that children were in the classroom to learn a particular subject matter. If foreign subject matter and behavior is introduced, it may very well upset the balance of neutrality (which allows the students freedom to learn). Not all students agree with homosexuality, and yet, a narrow interest group is allowed to imprison them within the confines of a classroom. I wondered if parents knew about the day and the questionable information given their child? It was as if the principal read my mind, for his responses coordinated with my thoughts. "Parental permission had to be obtained for those participating in classroom silence, but the school failed to send home information about the day or permission slips to all other parents." He knew immediately to rectify this by promising it would not happen again. The damage was done. Unsuspecting youth, sitting in classrooms, were already exposed to controversial sexual issues via badges and handouts. Yes the damage was done and I said so.

The interaction changed. We were in debate territory. I did not want to debate; we left this arena, but remained in "social" education of today. My "word" research proved valuable for our interaction required an updated ability to converse about such topics. I felt myself drawn into his explanation of how authority had changed in the schools. I flashed on the Vice Principal's words on Silent Day when I called the school, "What can we do?" I realize they both are right, for authority has changed. Authority now carries a new age definition; everything has equal merit, including students rights to bring anything in to the classroom, with no one being able to say "No," unless everyone is appeased along the way. I suddenly realized the incredible impact of organizations such as the ACLU on principals making simple sound decisions such as "No" for Silent Day. It was not simple, but complex. The decision was not theirs to make, for it was controlled by a complicated set of new guidelines that could lose them their jobs if not followed appropriately.

We conversed of times past and how it "used to be" and how it "is now." He was honest and sincere. He guarded some words, and I intuitively knew certain issues were untouchable. Though I understood his daily struggle, it did not distract me from delivering our message of intent to make sure the classroom is not abused by Silent Days. We assured each other of working together for permission slips to go home next year, but stood alone on our ideas about the reoccurrence of this day; he thought it was scheduled for next year.

Upon saying good-bye, I was impelled to ask him if other programs were in place dealing with tolerance and diversity. He immediately answered yes. The name was SEED. He knew little about it, except teachers, parents and students participate in it. He suggested calling the District Office to find more information. I gladly accepted the advice, thanking him for his time and valuable information.

It was a good day. I would call the District Office in pursuit of SEED program information. The Principal and others like him are controlled through organizations such as the ACLU. I was anxious to find out more about this organization. I left the telephone behind and walked over to the computer. It opened its arms, once again, to more exploration.

16

ACLU
American Civil Liberties Union

The ACLU began in 1920 by Roger Baldwin. His philosophy follows.

"We are for socialism, disarmament and ultimately for abolishing the State itself. We seek social ownership of property, the abolition of the propertied class and the sole control of those who produce wealth. Communism is the goal. [1]

The group apparently struggled for recognition, but the open communistic theme was unpopular in early 20th century. The philosophy eventually hidden, years passed, and the public believed it changed. However, in writing to a friend beginning another group, Mr. Baldwin wrote the following.

" Do steer away from making it look like a Socialist enterprise... We want also to look like patriots in everything we do. We want to get a good lot of flags, talk a good deal about the Constitution and what our forefathers wanted to make of this country and to show that we are really the folks that really stand for the spirit of our institutions." [2]

The American Civil Liberties Union (ACLU) now boasts about 250,000 members; about 2000 attorneys handling some 6000 cases annually. It appears before the Supreme Court more than any other group and is the largest private law firm in the U.S., besides the Justice Department. It is made up of 51 state affiliates and hundreds of local chapters guided by a national office in New York.[3] They are on college campuses everywhere indoctrinating with rights for homosexuals, prisoners, abortion, pornography, immigration and every liberal *cause* imaginable. They consistently lobby and litigate, winning most cases. George Grant, author of *Trial and Error,* reports a budget of over 14 million in 1993. Through a Federal Program, by the Civil Rights Attorneys Fee Awards Act of 1976, the taxpayer supplies much of their money. If they win a case involving a public institution, the organization collects its full fees for the attorneys even if working without charge.[4] It is difficult to find financial information about them, but they have hefty contributors such as Ford Foundation, Carnegie, Packard, Kellogg, Gund and Open Society Institute as reported by Capitol Research.[5]

The ACLU consistently stands against the Judeo-Christian principles upon which we were founded. Though they claim the organization is no longer communist oriented, the philosophy says different. Listed below are goals of the ACLU from its own published Policy Issues, as taken from Diane Dew's article called "Revealing Facts on the ACLU."

1. The legalization of prostitution (Policy 211)
2. The defense of all pornography, including child porn, as "free speech"(Policy4)
3. The decriminalization and legalization of all drugs (Policy 210)
4. The promotion of homosexuality (Policy 264)
5. The opposition of rating of music and movies (Policy 18)
6. Opposition against parental consent of minors seeking abortion (Policy 262)
7. Opposition of informed consent preceding abortion procedures (Policy 263)
8. Opposition of spousal consent preceding abortion (Policy 262)

9. Opposition of parental choice in children's education (Policy 80).

Also mentioned is the defense and promotion of euthanasia, polygamy, government control of church institutions, gun control, tax-funded abortion, birth limitation, etc. (Policies 263, 133, 402, 47, 261, 323, 271, 91, 85).[6]

Communism not only destroys private property ownership, but also ultimately demands abolition of religion and absolute morality founded on Religion. This is the cornerstone of our society, yet the ACLU battles everything connected to solid family values based on moral absolutes. Communism eventually turns totally dictatorial and the society collapses. The ACLU would outlaw, if they could, the following:

1. The public singing of "Silent Night" and other Christmas carols
2. Displays of nativity scenes, crosses and other Christian symbols on public property
3. The posting of the Ten Commandments in classrooms or courtroom
4. The words "under God" in the Pledge of Allegiance and "In God We Trust" on U.S. coins
5. Tax-exempt status for churches [though the ACLU favors this status for certain occult groups – and themselves]. [7]

They destroy our moral character, attacking by lawsuits Big Brother of America and even our Boy Scouts. They have won over judges, professors, students, reporters, business executives and philanthropists to a liberal agenda, with successes such as Roe vs. Wade, allowing Abortion to become legal. They now want to rid us of our Judeo-Christian principles upon which we were founded. Richard Thompson, chief counsel of the Thomas Moore Law Center, wrote in his article "ACLU Aiming to De-Christianize Nation" that the intent is to "transform a God-fearing religious Nation into a pretentious atheistic culture where biblically based beliefs are banned."[8]

ACLU has money and plenty of *causes* to give it power. People "fear" the power. I knew the ACLU held enough power to change our world forever. Not sure of what to do with this thought, I sat in my comfortable blue chair, thinking of thoughts, revolutionary thoughts that brought me to another time.

17

THOUGHT REVOLUTION

It is an exhilarating experience to look back on history! Though my friendly computer brings me valuable historic facts, it is by far more exciting to have "lived" the 50's and 60's. I have first hand insight as to the correctness of the times and the blossoming of what we thought was "freedom." All taboo topics became issues of discussion, and the college campuses became havens for the new thought revolution (*Stage 1 of mind control*). We believed everything!

The youth today are like my generation; they are searching for answers. The youth are unlike my generation in that many are not taught basic moral principles. Today's education system encourages young children to develop a moral code that best fits their individual needs. By college age, students are open to radical teachings of professors and with basic moral principles missing; it is difficult to debate the new knowledge. Ultimately students want a perfect world, *Stage 1 of mind control,* and this utopia becomes their *cause.* Their *causes* give them energy that is necessary for advancement of another *cause*, destruction of our form of government in order to replace it with another. The students crave enlightenment, *Stage 3 of mind control.* The professors do the enlightening, and uncertain students and adults compromise remaining traditional concepts for new knowledge, believing it intellectual development, *Stage 4 of mind control.* Education encourages this compromise through tools, such as scientific study. The study, believed to be true, further encourages the movement. Control, meaning direction or domination, is accomplished. It made sense and it is happening now just as it did many years ago.

84

One of the books required of me in my Anthropology Minor was *Coming of Age in Samoa*. Margaret Mead, a young student of Anthropology, traveled to Samoa in 1925. She returned a year later with tales of romance and a civilization that was sexually "free." Mead felt Western moral values to be repressive, causing severe problems in our society. She thus contributed the Samoan's frolicking happy spirit and seemingly balanced life, to the sexual freedoms, including homosexuality, they had adopted. Millions of her books sold all over the world. Her research was the forerunner of the sexual revolution that began in the fifties. It wasn't until the second half of the century that Derek Freeman, an Anthropologist who studied the Samoan culture, discovered that her study was a hoax. The Culture did, indeed, have a strict code of morality when it came to adultery, homosexuality, and bridal virginity. They had a high rate of suicide and rape. In reality, Mead depended on stories from adolescents of the village who told her social untruths. They laughed behind her back. It came to be known as the Margaret Mead Hoax. She had in some instances fantasized these facts, with much of her dreamed up information coming from her instructor at Columbia University Franz Boas. [1]

Franz Boas was a German Immigrant who came to our country in 1886. He was a radical thinker who supported Marxism, believing in cultural relativism, that no culture is better than any other culture, only different. His new approach to social analysis became a reality through his teachings at the University. He taught from 1899-1942 and created modern anthropology. His name was revered in scientific circles, until a number of years ago. He too was found to be a fraud. He decided his conclusions before he finished his research, altering results to match his conclusions. Sam Francis in *Franz Boas-Liberal Icon, Scientific Fraud* wrote:

> "Not only has a giant of modern social science-and a
> pillar of modern liberalism-tumbled from his pedestal,
> but the dogma that man is merely a blank slate, on
> which state bureaucrats and social engineers may
> scribble whatever ideologies they please, has toppled
> with him." [2]

Unfortunately, there are still some schools that teach Boas's findings as truths. After Derek Freeman published, in 1999, *The Fateful Hoaxing of Margaret Mead: A Historical Analysis of Her Samoan Research,* some educational facilities continued to revere Margaret Mead, and some still ignore the factual evidence in regards to her misrepresentation of the Samoan Culture. It is a belief of some people that the end justifies the means. We saw this in Nazi Germany. They believe the "lie" does not matter, for the *cause* is the most important objective. The lie becomes the "truth"; the "truth" becomes the "lie." I was betrayed as a student for I believed the Margaret Mead study. Educators who continue teaching the lie as truth are committing Educational Malpractice and need to be held accountable. The student is being deprived of truth and paying for it! I wish for brave clients and creative lawyers willing to take on such cases.

The second study required for a psychology class was the Kinsey Report. He wrote *Sexual Behavior in the Human Male*, in 1948, and *Sexual Behavior in the Human Female*, in 1953. He surveyed a variety of people about their sexual habits. His theories were controversial, disputing commonly held beliefs about sexual activity. His studies involved premarital sex statistics, sexual patterns of men and women within marriage, masturbatory experiences (including children), and homosexual activity of men and women. His conclusive evidence was very different than previously held norms of the above categories. His statistics gave favor to homosexual activity and other forms of sexual activity, usually not acknowledged as a norm. Everyone did find the information on sexual behavior interesting. Our professor treated it like truth. We assimilated the information as accurate. The rest of society also took notice and many people read the books. The message delivered, attitudes began to change. However, the studies did not immediately change society's ideas on sodomy; laws remained in place. Society in general kept its position on the act and lifestyle being a mental disorder. The Kinsey Report, however, did have an impact in the scientific community. Changes were occurring behind many "closed doors" and the general public would see the impact of such studies for the next 50 years. A radical change in thought was taking place.

In the latter part of the Century the Kinsey Report was found to be a fraud. According to Judith A. Reisman, in *Kinsey: Crimes and*

Consequences, Kinsey was an omnisexual and he participated in all forms of sexuality, including orgies with his own staff and family. He was a firm believer in recreational perverted sex. Reisman stated statistics on "child orgasms" in Kinsey's report came from children's concentration camps in Nazi Germany where children were so brutally researched. [3] His own child research took place in a sound proof lab built to his specifications. Reisman's book discusses in depth problems of Kinsey's research, its methodology, statistical data, and general complaint's of its faults. He used a gross number of sex offenders and prisoners for his participants. He used volunteers to answer sexual questions, rather than using random sampling of the population. Abraham Maslow's comment, in 1942, about the dangers of such scientific technique, still stands as truth.

> "Any study in which data are obtained from volunteers will always have a preponderance of (aggressive) high dominance people and therefore will show a falsely high percentage of non-virginity, masturbation, promiscuity, homosexuality, etc. in the population."

Maslow and Kinsey did their own "volunteer error" research, which proved Kinsey's statistics shaky. Kinsey, however, never mentioned them in his book.[4] The entire study was a fraud and a lie, but the *cause* for normalcy of sexual perversions was strong enough to offset any investigation into the accuracy of his research for the study. Instead it helped to lift bans on sexual behavior within the law and within the psychiatric community. Though the studies were erroneous, decades of education taught our citizens the lie was truth. It eventually spread through our land and strongly influenced the sexual revolution.

We continue the lie through deceptive "percentage" studies representative of homosexual numbers in our society. The unusually high percentage of 10 % of our population being homosexual has been accepted as truth for some 40 years. This figure is highly disputed and no longer accepted as the truth. Homosexual activist Bruce Voeller has admitted in his book, *Some Uses and Abuses of the Kinsey Scale*, the 10% figure was a myth used to promote the homosexual agenda.[5] Tom Stoddard, a former member of Lambda Legal Defense Fund, said the following:

"We used that figure (10%) when most gay people were entirely hidden to try to create an impression of our numerousness." [6]

It is more accurate to say the homosexual population is somewhere between 0.8% to about 3%. There are studies to validate this information, one of them being from *The Seven Fallacies Behind "Project 10"* by Dr. Joseph Nicolosi. [7] Because the lie of 10% still is accepted as truth, public schools programs encouraged "Project Ten," and homosexual counselors are allowed to direct children toward the lifestyle. In 1990, another study by the University of Chicago stated the number not 10% but at 1.6%. [8] Despite contrary studies proving the lie, our society still encourages the 10% number of Kinsey's study. Who has time to find out the truth? People heard the lie for decades and many will continue to believe it. The "lie" becomes the "truth" and the "truth" becomes the "lie." The number works for those choosing to use it for purposes of deception, for the lie does not matter, only the *cause* for normalcy. Thought revolution has given its okay to lies.

When I was in school, I accepted validity of the Mead and Kinsey studies without question. I believed them significant and relevant to our society. I never thought about how the studies were done. The experimentation was barbaric. I am resistant to think about it, for we were *brainwashed* just as were the German people. Studies such as these are in themselves perversions and indicative of how thought revolution can affect our morality.

Our society has mistreated sex. It is a gift, but as the studies indicate above, we have ridiculed it. This ridicule has never been more apparent than in present time. A beautiful act, between a man and a woman, is clinically discussed in sex Ed classes throughout America, while teaching students how to put condoms on bananas or cucumbers. Thought revolution claims this is intellectual development. I can't imagine how the teenagers must feel during this time of humiliation, for it is depravity not intellectual. Sex education belittles our intellect and the parents and schools that encourage it.

Parents give the freedom to schools to teach this sensitive subject matter and treat it as another class in school, instead of an intimate act between a loving man and woman. Teenagers in Elk Grove see very graphic movies of childbirth as part of their family planning class. Not only is there little left to the imagination, but also it commonizes the uniqueness of that first birth between husband and wife. Sensitive personal issues need to be handled carefully, for sex can be molded into any shape to meet the needs of the presenter or program. It can be dangerous.

Parents and students need to review statistics on Venereal Disease, HIV and AIDS. Here is the time when vivid pictures would leave a lasting impression for prevention of sex before marriage. The student needs to see realistic pictures of patients dying of AIDS or of aborted fetuses. Dying of AIDS or being aborted is ugly! It is painful, devastating to families and the human spirit. People need to understand condoms are not perfect and should not be encouraged. Passion rules the moment and it is difficult to say "No" to sex. The only sure protection is abstinence. With a condom there is no sure protection from the ravages of disease, death, or unwanted pregnancy. Abstinence is the only answer. Revolutionary thought can't erase the reality of death due to alternate lifestyle choices and out of control sexual patterns.

Make sure sex Ed values are like your family values. Get out of thought revolution and in touch, once again, with traditional values. Parents need to be in control, not the schools. Parents need to check whether classes teach that life begins at conception and not birth. Question whether your child can sign out without parental permission and have an abortion. This is disrespectful of parental authority and undermines the family unit. The Supreme Court deemed parents are the final authority in education of their children; to my knowledge it did not change through the years. A parent has authority to Opt Out a child from subject matter contrary to their beliefs. The school must adhere to the parent's wishes, thus the power of parents is ultimate. They must accept the Hatch Letter or one of your own, which protects your God given right to be the ultimate authority in your child's life. In the back of this book is the Hatch letter and a copy of an Opt Out Notice. [9] Make sure you opt out with this form or one that is specific as to requests, and follow through with litigation if the school does not adhere to your wishes

All citizens and Insurance Companies suffer the consequences of disease. The *cause* of narrow interest groups continues to downplay AIDS and Venereal Disease, as if using condoms will prevent them. It is a lie and a disservice to our Insurance companies and taxpayers. We pay a horrific cost for health care of AIDS, STD and abortion victims. Insurance companies, government and local communities would be wise in saying "No" to programs encouraging behavior that contributes to this injustice. The devastating health effects on our children are outrageous! The statistics of sexual disease speak for themselves; they can't be hushed up or swept under the rug for they come from the Center for Disease Control (CDC). It is beneficial for everyone to see these numbers for I cannot help wonder why our thoughts are being directed away from these statistics. Can it be that modern day society is revolutionizing their thoughts away from scientific study in favor of social survey studies?

1. The latest estimates indicate 15 million new sexually transmitted diseases (STD) in the United States every year. Approximately one-fourth of these new infections are in teenagers. While some STD's, such as syphilis, have been brought to all time lows in the heterosexual community, others, like genital herpes, gonorrhea and chlamydia, HPV and HIV continue to resurge and spread through our population. Many women with gonorrhea and chlamydia develop serious complications such as pelvic inflammatory disease (PID), which causes severe pain, infertility (100,000-150,000 yearly) and potentially fatal ectopic pregnancy. The human papilloma virus (HPV) is the single most important factor in cervical cancer.[10] Dr. John Diggs, lecturer and author, and Ericka Harold, former Miss America, gave inspiring presentations at a National Eagle Forum Conference on the dangers of HPV and HIV. With over 400,000 new cases yearly of human immunodeficiency virus

(HIV) and 95 % of cervical cancers caused by the papilloma virus, Harold and Diggs have experienced infected and dying youth asking one question; "Why didn't someone tell us the truth?" We must make it clear that heterosexual and homosexual teens can pass on HPV and HIV to unsuspecting individuals who don't see visible signs of disease on their sexual mates, and therefore think they are safe. Many more facts are available; we must tell the facts with the passion that is necessary for our culture to believe the severity of this problem. We must tell the truth!

2. HIV is a virus that kills your body's "CD4 cells." The cells, also called T-helper cells, help your body fight off infection and disease. The acquired immunodeficiency syndrome (AIDS) is the advanced stage of HIV. If you can't fight off disease you eventually will become very sick and die a horrible death. The following are the statistics on the number of AIDS cases according to exposure and race by the CDC through December of 2001.

	MALE	FEMALE	TOTAL
Men who have sex with men...	**368,971**		**368,971**
Injecting Drug Use	145,750	55,576	201,326
Men who have sex with men And inject drugs	51, 293		51,293
Hemophilia/coagulation disorder	5000	292	5,292
Heterosexual contact	**32,735**	**57,396**	**90, 131**
Recipient of blood transfusion, Blood components or tissue	5,057	3,914	8,971
Risk not reported or identified.	57,220	23,870	81,091[11]

The "facts" speak for themselves. Homosexual activity is a big factor in acquiring this disease. This is not homophobia or a lie, but is the truth. Why would any educator or school system try and introduce this lifestyle to our youth? Homosexual lifestyles need to be downplayed, not honored on days such as Silent Day. We need an emphasis on health classes that introduce the truth about the diseases and the lifestyles that carry them. WE must let teenagers know the horrors of the "Gay Bowel Syndrome" that results from a lifestyle that promotes anal sex (sodomy). Teens need to see the ravages of death and disease caused by such lifestyles for they are not glorified on Silent Day. Does thought revolution change the course of a disease so rampant in homosexuals? Is the misplaced love, allowing this lifestyle, worth the many that will die from its effects? HIV and AIDS would dramatically reduce if we stopped the encouragement of the lifestyle, for it is the only way to eradicate it and its deadly effects on humanity. We must find individuals who are willing to litigate with school districts for introducing lifestyles that have caused their disease, or a loved one's disease, or death. Schools must be held accountable!

Cumulative cases by Race/Ethnicity of persons reported with AIDS as of December 2001.

Race or Ethnicity	# of Cumulative cases
White	343,889
Black	313,180
Hispanic	149,752
Asian/Pacific Islander	6,157
American Indian/Alaska Native	2,537
Race/ethnicity unknown	634 [12]

African Americans represent an estimated 13% of the US population, yet it is believed that they represent half of the new HIV infections. Among the African Americans, young homosexual men and heterosexual women are the hardest hit. Where is the outrage in communities over these statistics and what the schools are teaching with sex education? Deception is the rule and parents are closing their eyes to it. Blacks must get out of thought revolution and realize that conservative Americans are not their enemy, but their friends. We want to work together to stop the flagrant misuse of our children to change the morality of our land. You have the power to stop the atrocious sex Ed classes with replacement by solid moral values toward body, disease and pregnancy. We must encourage our young women to respect their bodies, which in turn will teach our young men to respect the women. We need to work together to help our young return to values that will save their physical and mental well-being.

Children, at age 12, do not have complete faculty to decide right and wrong. Education, movies, television, literature, and peer pressure promote *situational* decisions with not always a favorable outcome. Parents must take back control, but I am not sure how much thought revolution has taken over the modern day parent's sense of responsibility toward their children. Responses I hear from some parents show denial of facts, or elevation of busy life styles over discipline of teenagers. Parents think they have the right to abandon their children for other priorities in their life. I have repeatedly heard these comments and some from "supposed" Christian parents. "My child is old enough to know better," or "If I can't trust my child enough by age 12 to be able to sort what is taught, then I guess I never will be able to." In fact, children at these ages are vulnerable; they are not capable of discernment. Recent studies indicate that over two thirds of high school students having sex wished they had waited. It puts tremendous strain on their emotions, taking important energy from education and other priorities for their age group. Indeed, there is a higher rate of suicide amongst teens having sex than those who do not participate in sex.[13] Regardless of studies or disease, new age teachers continue in pursuit of your children for sexual indoctrination at the early age of six, but even worse the NEA is advocating children enter school as young as three and four. Thought revolution will now prepare our children younger and younger for new age indoctrination and humanist philosophy. By the time they reach College, they will already be *brainwashed*.

I thought about forces in play when I was in College, older smug Professors with domineering ideas taking hold on unsuspecting youth in their classrooms. I lived it, not suspecting in the least that I was being *mind controlled*. Educational tools for *mind control* were not just erroneous studies, but the attitudes of the professors during presentation of the material. The programs were introduced under the guise of love for humanity. Professors in Colleges used charm, sexual flirtations and love of the 60's to promote their agenda. San Francisco State College in the 60's had an abundance of liberal professors with "liberal" agendas appealing to both male and female. In my Sociology classes, the idea of traditional family was on its way out being replaced by a wide variety of domestic arrangements. The "working" woman was gaining status over the housewife and mother. Class struggles were winning out to positive concepts of communism and socialism. We believed it true for we elevated professors to superior status. We were in thought revolution!   These philosophies are now everywhere, but the result of an earlier time. The educators came from afar.

Educated Immigrants arrived from Europe during the first half of the Century. They believed in Marx and Nietzsche, the 19th Century philosophers that challenged the world of traditional morality and religion. These men were held in high regard, as shown by the monument that Hitler erected to honor Nietzsche.[14] Many immigrants came from Germany situating themselves in our Higher Learning Institutes. We accepted Nietzsche through his philosophies which influenced painters, dancers, musicians, playwrights, poets, novelists, psychologists, sociologists, historians and philosophers: Alfred Adler, Albert Camus, Isadora Duncan, Sigmund Freud, Stefan George, Hermann Hesse, Carl Jung, Martin Heidegger, Jean-Paul Sartre, George Bernard Shaw, Richard Strauss and William Butler Yeats to name a few. [15] Some of these names are well known in College settings and classrooms. A new philosophy reached our shores contrary to our traditional Judeo-Christian values. Unfortunately it was not staying on the shores, but moving inland to our Institutes of higher learning.   The 60's were waiting in anticipation of "new thought" teachers. Harold Rugg wrote the following in *The Great Technology:*

"A new mind is to be created. How? Only by creating tens of millions of individual minds and welding them into social mind. Old stereotypes must be broken up and new climates of opinion formed in the neighborhoods of America…through the schools of the world, we shall disseminate a new conception of

94

government-one that will embrace all the activities of men." [16]

The teachers of this philosophy were many. Thomas Mann, poet and novelist, emigrated from Italy in 1931. He joined the faculty at the University of Chicago. As a bisexual pedophile, he devastated his family with his lustfulness for young boys. He traveled extensively lecturing throughout our country. [17] His ideas reached many open minds. Bergstrasser emigrated from Germany in 1937. He taught Sociology, History and German literature at Claremont College in California. [18] He was also a free thinker. Many teachers emigrated to Columbia University as well as other well-known Higher Learning Institutes. One man of special importance is John Dewey, an influential professor at the University of Chicago and Columbia University. He played a major role in secular humanism and believed that in our great age of science we could no longer believe in a Divine Being. He believed that we could progress without a God. Through his teachings and writings he was greatly responsible for the "thought" revolution squeezing morality from our schools. He was the father of "progressive" education. It is estimated twenty percent of American school superintendents and forty percent of college heads have advanced degrees from Columbia University, where Dewey spent many years as the department head.[19]The graduated students of these professors carried the knowledge throughout our land. The climate was preparing for the 60's. Educators opened the door for revolution that had its beginning in the 50's. The *cause* of many began its push toward transformation that we are now seeing. The thought revolution began.

The modern homosexual movement began in the fifties by the official organization of two groups. Daughters of Bilitis (D.O.B.) was started in San Francisco in 1955. It was a conservative group of homosexual women. They eventually branched out throughout our country and lasted about 15 years. In Los Angeles the homosexual movement began by the formation of the Mattachine Society. Harry Hay was the founder of this group and mentioned earlier as founder of Radical Fairy. He had been molested as a teenager by an older man and was equated with the founder of Germany's homosexual party Karl Heinrich Ulrich, who was also molested as a child. Hay, however, believed in pederasty while Ulrich did not agree with this philosophy. He also became more militant than Ulrich. At age 70, Hay participated in the ACT-UP violent demonstrations in San Francisco in the 80's. Harry Hay is considered the founder of the modern gay movement in America. He stayed active until his death in the 90's. [20]

The name Mattachine goes back in time to French medieval years when a musical group veiled itself so as not to be known or seen. The Mattachine Society began with a structure like the freemasonry, a pyramid structure where cells were not known to each other. They eventually began to form discussion groups; it took hold in California with support groups growing in numbers. Eventually the cells became known to each other and the stigma of silence was no more. Many of the founders were Marxist and they saw homosexuals in terms of an oppressed cultural minority. In 1951 the Society adopted a mission statement, clearly defining its purpose to assimilate into society by merging into cultures of fellow minorities such as Black, Mexican and Jewish. Their communist leanings, however, put pressure on the group during the fifties. It was suspected that they were banning together to gain tremendous political power. The leadership feared discovery as communists and resigned their positions. New leadership was not as aggressive and meeting attendance began to decline throughout the country. In the 60's, the San Francisco Society for Individual Rights became dominant. The Mattachine failed to go along with radical militants following the San Francisco Stonewall Rebellion and eventually ceased as an Organization [21] The Mattachine group did lead the way for the "radical movement." It is, however, the radical militant group leading the movement today with shouts of "We are normal" ringing in our ears. The *cause* for normalcy is loud and often harsh.

Another important man who left his mark on our society was Herbert Marcuse. He came to America when Hitler took power in Germany. He taught at such Universities as Columbia, Brandeis and the University of California-San Diego. The writing of his book *Eros and Civilization* put him in a favorable position with the students of the 60's. The book became a sacred document for their movement. He embraced the pleasure principle shunning the labor principle. He dictated that our government and principles be overthrown. [22] His willingness to speak at student protests gave him the name "father of the new left." [23]American Universities began having marches and protests with some leading to riots. Eventually Columbia University, home to Marcuse, rioted in 1968. Though the 60's were supposed to be about love and peace, violence had its place for certain factions of society. The Black Panthers Group was one of these factions. Indeed, a well-known member Angela Davis was involved in a raid leaving people dead and included the decapitation of a judge. She was not incarcerated for her actions. Angela Davis was given a teaching position at the University of California in Santa Cruz and the Black Panthers still exist today. [24]

The Civil Rights Movement played an important role in our society, their cohesiveness was needed for an important *cause* of equal rights. The *cause* produced power necessary for a successful movement. Unfortunately the homosexuals saw this power and decided to use it for themselves. It began slowly during the 60's and its abuse is at the forefront of the homosexual movement today. Homosexuals are leeching onto a group that worked hard and lost life to attain their rights. The black issue is a skin color, which is not a choice. The homosexual issue is a by "choice" issue. It is not the same. If the black race continues to cave into this cause, it will diminish respect gained for their race. Elizabeth Wright in "Issues and Views" Spring 1996 writes about the "serious disservice blacks are doing themselves by participating in the homosexual movement." [25] She is a refreshing black author, like Jesse Petersen and Dr. John Diggs, whose insight is uplifting and encouraging to the individual worthiness of man not being dependent on his race or sexual identity.

The 60's took their toll on our Nation. In the guise of peace and love flourished new thoughts on life, liberty and the pursuit of happiness. These revolutionary thoughts, however, have not blossomed into the naïve dream of some misguided flower children, but into the dream of the true revolutionaries of the 60's. We see their dream as the chaos we are now living.

Slowly but surely seeds were planted. Morals and values began to decline. Hugh Hefner initiated Playboy, pornography flourished. Hollywood produces over 400 movies yearly, the pornography Industry 700 a month, at a minimum of $10 billion a year.[26] The image of middle class men with lots of pretty women seemed to disguise the horror of its nature and future. Just as Hitler had fantasies, so did Hefner. He says about himself the following:

> "I was a very idealistic, very romantic kid in a very typically Midwestern Methodist repressed home. There was no show of affection of any kind, and I escaped to dreams and fantasies produced, by and large, by the music and the movies of the '30's."[27]

His fantasy magnified itself in Playboy Bunnies, the Playboy Clubs and the Playboy Magazine. Hefner eventually built himself a Playboy Mansion. Our society overlooked the immorality and began condoning sex outside marriage, and sharing mates in mutually agreed upon partner swapping. Men continued producing pornography for other men's enjoyment. Feminists encouraged breakdown of the family and they elevated abortion and homosexuality. Women felt equal to men in "fooling" around outside of marriage, and the pill guaranteed no pregnancy. Family size decreased. Women took their place in the workforce, thus destabilizing men as head of households and breadwinners. We allowed the black robed idols of the Supreme Court to remove God from schools, in 1962, in Engel v. Vitale. The 60's had done their job! Thought revolution was working!

In the 70's our country became ripe for change and new ideas came easier. We lost respect for life, choosing instead support of Roe v Wade. The Nation arrogantly proclaimed it had the right to say we could take life. Professors in prestigious Universities continued transformation; young adults assimilating ideas of erroneous freedoms assured the demise of our society. Good became evil; evil became good. Our freedoms, developed from our Founding Father's principles, were in decline. The ultimate loser in the thought revolution was and continues to be the family. The radical homosexuals grew in number, gaining power through devious tactics and deceptive ideology; the goal to rid the world of Judeo-Christian values. It is the only way they could be accepted as normal. In the late 60's and early 70's, the movement began.

I remember Anita Bryant (Miss Oklahoma), a once famous singer and celebrity, who fought a long and hard campaign in Florida against the homosexual movement in the 1970's. She radiated an image of traditional America. Anita toured Viet Nam with Bob Hope, and The President invited her to the White House on 14 different occasions. She was a true lady both respected and admired.

Her political career began simultaneously, with realization of the homosexual's goal to indoctrinate our children in their lifestyle. She began a campaign called *Save The Children*. It spread across the Nation, eventually becoming known as the religious right. The Reverend Falwell went to Miami helping her and working together, under title of a domestic social issue, they were able to overturn a homosexual rights ordinance in November of 1977. However, the homosexual activists were instrumental in portraying her as a hateful person. They successfully managed a campaign against the orange juice industry that hired her under a million-dollar contract. The company fired her. Her marriage ended and her singing career suffered. The media portrayed her as an "obsessed" woman focusing her anger on homosexual victims. Few people stood behind the homosexual lifestyle, but the media managed to convince people Anita had misinterpreted the homosexual's true agenda. She became the prefabricator of lies and hate, when in reality her statements came from truth. The truth led to decades of two competing movements, the conservative Christians and the pursuit of homosexual rights by activists.[28] She, however, became the victim and they became the heroes.

My research carried me to a time of long ago. It was the beginning of a country's chaos no one knew possible. It was the end of our society, as we knew it as children, and it was the beginning of the end of our society we knew as adults. Thought revolution was winning. *Mind control* had taken its place in society. It was ready to burst forward with a speed unknown to man. Permissiveness took the lead and everyone followed in silence. I thought of the famous movie *Time Machine* and how the Morlocks *"brainwashed"* the young and led them under ground for purposes of cannibalism.

Watching decades open and close is like watching a movie, but the difference is, I lived it. Our civilization is ignoring the messages of disruptive change, instead seeing the thought revolution as the norm of a growing society's advancement. Furthermore "what can we do to stop it" is the usual excuse. Our society has made a decision. I am ashamed of our decision to ignore morality. We walk by our children refusing to protect them. We continue to allow cannibalistic appetites to devour their spirit, minds and bodies. When reminded of the evil that does exist, our hands cover our ears quickly. There is deadening silence to the injustice of our country's new ethics. We continue dying of relativism and humanism rather than listen to the voice of principles upon which our country was founded.

I turned off the computer. My body was not mine. I felt numb. Anita Bryant where are you? I thank you for your courage.

18

INTIMIDATION

Intimidation ruined Anita Bryant's life by using its powerful force to change institutions and people. Fear is at the forefront of intimidation, with its capacity to control the mind a sure thing. I wondered how homosexual activists used intimidation to promote fear and influence the "thought" revolution of the past 30 years.

From the 70's through today, the homosexual movement has spread like wildfire into every state, community and home. Due to the radical influences of the 60's, the new thought revolution was underway. Not only did our society idolize the black robed judges, but they also idolized the men in white jackets known as Psychiatrists. The homosexual activists were gaining strength in numbers and they targeted the medical group, thus the story unfolds. The homosexuals knew their redefinition by Psychiatrists was necessary for normalization. The Kinsey Report and homosexual lobbying influenced the Association's leadership to reconsider removal of homosexuality as a disorder. The American Psychiatric Association (APA) pro-homosexual activists sent out 30,000 requests to members asking a yes vote on change of status. With only one third responding, the resolution was passed.[1]

Charles Socarides an Author, Psychiatrist, and Reparative Therapist recalls the events and the reclassification. He is an authority for he lived it.

> " Homosexual activists targeted members of the worldly priesthood. (Meaning those who are sought out for knowledge, power and truth), the Psychiatric community and neutralized them with a radical

redefinition of homosexuality itself...They co-opted the leadership of the American Psychiatric Association, and through a series of political maneuvers...they got the APA to say that same-sex sex was "not a disorder." It was merely " a condition" as neutral as left-handedness." [2]

Dr. Socarides' account sounded familiar, with the force of intimidation used in a similar way as with Anita Bryant. He reports that if members did not go along with reclassification, they were "silenced at their own professional meetings. Their lectures were cancelled and their research papers turned down for learned journals."[3] They became the "bad" guy, but in reality they are heroes for they took a stand.

The National Gay Task Force (NGTF) played a vital role financially and strategically in eliciting funds for the mail outs. It was found later there was not a thorough investigation of the issue before deletion of homosexuality from the DSM. The Committee on Nomenclature had never formally approved the change. [4] This was another "behind the doors" example of how people in 1973 did not know the "truth." Four years later, 69% of psychiatrists disagreed with the vote and still considered homosexuality a disorder [5]. This "truth" also stayed behind "closed doors."

Next, "fear" and "intimidation" tactics became the focus of the movement. It became apparent that anyone or group who did not agree with their lifestyle would be harassed, ridiculed and attacked aggressively. There were many affected besides Anita Bryant and Dr. Socarides. In 1977 they boycotted Coors over alleged mistreatment of homosexuals. Coors now offers domestic partner benefits. [6] Twenty years later when United Airlines balked at ideas of same partner benefits with companies that contracted with the city of San Francisco, the activists boycotted the Los Angeles and San Francisco markets. Advertisements linked the Airlines to Pat Robertson; he was depicted as discriminatory. They proceeded to give credit to American Airlines as being the gay-friendliest airline. United eventually lost a law suit against the mandate of same sex benefits and with the huge amount of money homosexuals spend on travel, their strategy worked and United Airlines caved to them.[7] Dr. Laura,

Talk Radio Celebrity, was targeted by the homosexual radicals for her stand on homosexuality. They began a Stop Dr. Laura "public education" campaign. She was attacked furiously. They established a special Stop Dr. Laura website with support by Human Rights Commission (HRC), Hollywood celebrities like Susan Sarandon, and intense media coverage such as the Los Angeles Times and the New York Times. Each day Dr. Laura's TV show was monitored, and the Gay Lesbian Alliance Against Defamation (GLAAD) posted every anti gay statement on their Dr. Laura Watch web site. Every advertiser on her show was listed for action. Sponsor telephone numbers were listed as were the sponsors email addresses on the web site. They were sent complaints about the show being hateful. They were threatened with boycotts.[8] Eventually Sears, AT&T, Xerox, Echo Star Communications, Procter and Gamble, Gateway, Natrol, Price line and dozens of other advertisers pulled out.[9] In 2001, GLAAD proudly announced their victory over Dr. Laura after the three year public education campaign against her. [10]These tactics are ruthless, certainly not representative of American principles and the right to free speech. Research shows that nearly 90% of homosexuals said they would participate in boycotts against anti-gay corporations. [11] Is it any wonder why the common folk are caving in when we see large companies fold under pressure?

The homosexual magazine *The Advocate* featured Hillary Clinton on a past cover along with an interview inside its cover. She quoted that she "felt good when she attended a gay pride march." [12] Is it their strong moral ethics such as above that makes her want to march with them, which she has done, or is it the unnaturalness of naked and scantily dressed homosexual men and women having sex and even roller blading naked down the street that attracts her to it? I have to wonder what type of person would feel good at this parade? We have come a long way to desensitize ourselves to this type of behavior, but indeed, it is working.

I continued to research the violence of the activists. In 1959, George Lincoln Rockwell formed the American Nazi Party. It was believed the party was filled with homosexuals. It is also believed by some that many American homosexuals continue to be a "secret" of post war American National Socialism. [13] In the late 60's the homosexual activists turned militant. The climate was conducive for an uprising. The women's movement had begun, with female homosexuals prominent among the organizers. The black power movement had begun, and revolt was strong against the war in Viet Nam. There was a rebellion against the establishment on June 27, 1969. It was the perfect place and the perfect time. It was in New York at the Stonewall Bar on Christopher Street. The police were closing the bar for selling alcohol without a license. It was a frequent hangout for people with deviant lifestyles. The riot began with bottles being thrown at the arresting officers. The fire started and by morning the Stonewall Bar had burned to the ground. The rioting continued for three days. The homosexual's leaders declared the day a success. [14] It is celebrated every year in June as Gay Pride Day for homosexual enthusiasts.

After this day, the militant leadership took over the activist role. One of the influential men in this movement was Herbert Marcuse, mentioned in an earlier chapter. A theory in many of his books was counteracting the "repressive" order in our society. Stamping out the "repressive" order became a priority for the militant group. The militant leadership first developed active chapters of the Gay Liberation Front across the Nation. They then targeted the medical community, the APA, by storming their conventions in Chicago, Los Angeles and San Francisco. [15] This "fear" tactic pushed further the reasoning of the APA to change the behavior from a "disorder" to a "condition." The "fear" tactic worked following the Stonewall Bar riot. It got the attention of the Nation. The homosexual movement made a statement: they would now engage in the politics of "confrontation."

While the Gay Liberation Front was working within the medical community, there was another branch of the American Nazi Party developing called the National Socialist League. Their membership was restricted to homosexual Nazis. Membership was solicited through a homosexual magazine, *The Advocate*. Not only has it featured Senator Hillary Clinton, but also, in April 2002, featured Log Cabin Republican Patrick Guerriero, the first openly gay running mate selected by a sitting Governor in U. S. History[16]. In 1977, under the leadership of Frank Collin, the American Nazi Party in full Nazi attire marched through a Jewish neighborhood in Chicago. Collins proclaimed that all African-Americans, Jews and

Latinos should be forcibly deported. Though attempts were made to stop this March, the ACLU was strongly responsible for its approval. Years later it was discovered that Collins was a Homosexual Pederast. He molested boys ages 10-14. He was sent to prison for seven years.[17] He was released after three years and established himself as an author and editor under another name.[18]

The Skinhead Nazis leaders are predominantly homosexuals. The movement began in England by Nicky Crane who was a devout Nazi. He attempted to bring back the Nazi Borwnshirts by encouraging street fighting and fighting at sporting events. He was a homosexual porn star and died of AIDS in 1993. [19] Many of these organizations were and are still dedicated to the ideals of Hitler and his philosophy. In France the Neo-Nazi movement is closely and openly connected to the homosexual community. The Neo-Nazi movement in Germany is linked to homosexuality.[20] In the Advocate Magazine, a German writer tells of Michael Kuhnen, an openly Gay man who died of AIDS. Kuhnen linked together homosexuality and fascism. Fascism is based on the love of comrades; having sex with your comrades strengthens this bond.[21] Judith Reisman, in "A Content Analysis of The Advocate 1972-1991" found a fascist mentality predominating its issues. She states that 72% of the magazine glorified certain standards such as nazi dress, language, blonde Aryan male beauty, brutality and contempt for fems, fats and blacks, and threats toward politically incorrect homosexuals, churches and others. They romanticized fascist culture to a younger generation.[22]

In the 80's an Organization AIDS Coalition to Unleash Power (ACT-UP), began attacking Catholic churches during services in New York, Washington, Los Angeles and Puerto Rico. They stomped on communion wafers and shouted obscenities. Newspaper boxes were smashed in Sacramento, California for an Editor's views on Homosexuality. [23] This group developed into the more radical queer nation. Scott Lively saw homosexual activists' behavior in Portland, Oregon toward those who supported a bill to keep homosexuals from minority status. They threatened them with signs on poles and writings on sidewalks. They threw swastika wrapped bricks through merchant's windows that helped initiate the bill. They even put false signatures on petitions in order to invalidate them. They staged phony harassment incidents.[24] In 1991, Governor Pete Wilson of

California vetoed bill 101, which would have given minority status to homosexuals. The homosexuals rioted in the streets and burned government buildings. They threatened verbally and physically a Presbyterian Minister and his family in San Francisco because they fired a homosexual organist.[25] It was a horrible experience to read the description of his ordeal. It is even more horrible to hear it from Scott Lively who experienced once again in Madison, Wisconsin the aggressiveness of the militants. The church, where he was speaking, was taken over by a group of homosexuals who were mainly female. They would not allow Scott to speak. They used profanity inside and outside the church. They pounded the building with objects such as rocks and cans. They chanted, "Crush the Christians, and bring back the lions." My research continues to demonstrate the media giving little attention to these situations of violence. In reality it is usually kept secret. It is kept once again behind "closed" doors. What is in the open is the *cause* of the militant homosexuals that seems to illicit approval for them to do anything they want in the name of freedom.

Fear is a powerful tool and it works. Persuasiveness, through force or manipulation, can have a lasting effect on a nation. This Nation has allowed its individuals, churches, businesses and even large corporations to fold, bend and give their acceptance to groups who purposely used intimidation for their *cause*. The American people have allowed our Nation to be taken over by a small percentage of homosexuals who are relentless in their quest to destroy our family values. It will not take long before their *cause* will destroy us.

I had not anticipated the intensity of the homosexual's next step. It was the late 80's, and another important piece of writing was lurking in the shadows waiting for discovery. It is clever and revealed itself slowly through the next 25 years. Few know of it but are controlled by it. The Homosexual Manifesto is still giving the radical homosexual movement the strength needed to support their campaign.

I was no longer imagining this nightmare, and knew that devastation awaited those who followed the paths of alternate lifestyles: disease, emotional destruction, spiritual decay and lies. If our principles of God, Traditional Family and Natural Law are destroyed, equal fate awaits us all. It is certain that "fear" is the root of this change. *Mind control* is in full force. My own mind weary of thought, I rested in the arms of Absolute Truth according to God's Laws. It felt Good! If everyone felt this certainty, there would be no room for fear. His truth enveloped me in love as I drifted into sleep in my comfortable blue chair.

19

THE HOMOSEXUAL MANIFESTO

The night passed quickly and though sleep rejuvenated my body, my mind remained troubled. I kept thinking about facts assimilated yesterday, about a planned homosexual manifesto and it lingered in my mind. Following routine activities, I ran upstairs to my friendly computer anxious to begin.

In the 1980's, homosexual activists Marshall Kirk and Erastes Pill wrote an article called the "Overhauling of Straight America." Like the *Communist Manifesto*, it outlines clearly its purpose and how to reach its goals. It is a plan for homosexual behavior to not only be tolerated, but also accepted in our society. They are specific in agenda openly expressing their sentiments in the Manifesto.

> "In the early stages of any campaign to reach straight America, the masses should not be shocked and repelled by premature exposure to homosexual behavior itself. Instead, the imagery of sex should be downplayed and gay-rights should be reduced to an abstract social question as much as possible. First, let the camel get his nose inside the tent and only later his unsightly derriere!" [1]

According to Janet Folger, national director of the Center For Reclaiming America, their strategy worked; they now demand "normal" status.[2] Key points to this strategy were the following:

1. Talk about Gays and Gayness as loudly and as often as possible.
2. Portray gays as victims not as aggressive challengers.
3. Give protectors a just *cause*.
4. Make the victimizers look bad. [3]

This was written in 1987 and its implementation began immediately. In February 1988, 175 leading homosexual activists from across our land came to Virginia, near Washington D.C., to establish a four point agenda for the gay movement.[4] It was following this meeting that Harvard trained Marshall Kirk and Hunter Madsen wrote their Homosexual Manifesto *After the Ball: How America will conquer its fear & hatred of Gays in the 90's*. It proposed the following.

"...dismissing the movement's outworn techniques in favor of carefully calculated public relations propaganda laying groundwork for the next stage of the gay revolution and its ultimate victory over bigotry."[5]

"Overhauling of Straight America" and *After the Ball* were the keys to the radical homosexual thrust into society. They wanted to force acceptance, silence opposition and convert American society. [6]

Society would be changed by three strategies mentioned in *After the Ball*: desensitization, jamming and conversion.

"To desensitize straights to gays and gayness, inundate them in a continuous flood of gay-related advertising, presented in the least offensive fashion possible. If straights can't shut off the shower, they may at least eventually get used to being wet. Of course, while sheer indifference is, itself, vastly preferable to hatred and threats, we would like to do better than that." [7]

The activists strategically placed themselves in media power positions: television, movies and newspapers. They routinely slipped the homosexual message in, usually through humor in movies or television. My husband and I go to the movies often and make it our date night. It is becoming increasingly hard to find movies that don't have homosexual content in them. Alternate lifestyles are constantly in the forefront. Desensitization is doing its job.

"If you can get straights to think homosexuality is just another thing-meriting no more than a shrug of the shoulders-then your battle for legal and social rights is virtually won." [8]

I flashed on people who shrug their shoulders. They have been desensitized, slowly and with intent. This stage passed, very successfully.

The second goal is "Jamming." It is a psychological brainwashing technique involving Associative Conditioning and Direct Emotional Modeling. [9] Conditioning involves winning emotions of the straight public. The homosexual person is portrayed as a victim of discrimination, holocaust atrocities, hate murders, suicides attempts and verbal assaults. Matthew Shepard is an example of victim status. He was a 21-year-old Wyoming college student who was infected with HIV. Even though he was a carrier, he propositioned two males in a bar. He was brutally beaten and left hanging on a fence to die. It was a terrible tragedy. His case made nation-wide news and cameras were allowed inside the courtroom for the trial. He is consistently used in schools to teach about "hate" crimes. There are websites honoring him, books written, flyers for the asking and made for television movies about his story. Other malicious, violent crimes were ignored. One week later in the same town in which Shepard was murdered, it was reported that a young girl was brutally murdered because she would not have an abortion. Where were the voices of justice for her cause? No one heard about this young lady. Jessie Dirkhissing was gagged, bound, sodomized repeatedly and treated in the most inhumane way dying as a result of suffocation. This occurred within weeks after Shepard was murdered in 1999. Jessie was 13 years old. The two adult men were pederast homosexuals. I have a copy of the police report after they found his body. [10] It is quite graphic and made me wretch, almost to vomiting.

Very few heard about this young boy. In 1997, Jeffrey Curley, was murdered in Massachusetts by two homosexuals. He had been suffocated, sodomized and his body placed in a Rubbermaid container. [11] Few heard about this case. A few years ago, Mary Stachowicz, a middle aged Christian, was brutally murdered in Chicago by a 19 year old who was offended by her attitude about homosexuality. He became upset when she questioned his homosexuality. He said he became enraged; it reminded him of similar debates with his grandmother. He then punched, kicked, stabbed and strangled the grandmother of four. [12]

Each was given little coverage except the Matthew Shepard case. In the month following Shepard's death, Nexis recorded 3,007 stories about his death. They recorded in the same time span only 47 about Dirkhissing. Many ignored it completely such as the Boston Globe, The New York Times and Los Angeles Times. The New York Times did 45 about Shepard. The Washington Post published 28 on Shepard. [13] Mary had approximately five articles written the month following her death. Curly had few also. There will be no books, movie pictures or worldwide recognition for the other victims. They are instead kept behind "closed doors" with little coverage for public consumption. There will be no special laws made for protection of the Mary's of this world. They don't fit into the proper category and can't be used for "jamming" purposes. If you are a homosexual murder victim, you will be honored for your contribution to the *cause* of cultural change. If you are a Jessie Dirkhissing you will become an unknown.

Homosexual suicide cases claim "victim" status. It is another tool used for "jamming" and winning the sympathy of the public. The "individual" is no longer responsible, for now it's students, schools and outside forces that cause their suicide. It is our "hate" that did it. Dr Nicolosi, president of the National Association for Research and Therapy of Homosexuality (NARTH) states that among college students he studied there was no evidence of social discrimination, but instead rejection by a lover causing the suicide. The 30% myth of all youth suicides being homosexual is dismissed due to new and more conclusive evidence that disputes previous facts. However, school programs are still initiated for homosexuals based on the old figure. Once again the "truth" becomes the "lie" and the "lie" becomes the "truth." It is the "lifestyle" that has a detrimental effect on children. Dr. Nicolosi feels it important not to push the young into the lifestyle. Many children have homosexual fantasies, thoughts or feelings, but it does not mean they are homosexual. One study published in Pediatrics in 1994 stated that early self labeling as homosexual is one of the three top risk factors for homosexual teen suicide.[14] The power of homosexual *cause* has kept this message from reaching the public.

I began flashing on our education, which teaches our children there is no hope for homosexual reversal, once again promoting "victim" status to win sympathy of the public. This is a "lie" accepted as a "truth" for a narrow interest agenda *cause*. We have given our permission for experimentation on our own children and parents report their teens talk about "trying" it. Some of the teens are only 10 and 12 years old. Girls and guys are looking for acceptance, attention, rebellion, new things and the joy of momentary and spontaneous decisions. An article in the South Florida's Sun-Sentinel, talks about the new craze of "bisexual chic." It is the newest rage at parties; the boys encourage it; the girls love the attention. It is nation-wide and according to the youth interviewed, the parents have no idea how far this goes at the parties.[15] The youth feel it is good to share the experience with their fellow students for it is indeed a way of being accepted.

Studies that relate to reversal of homosexuality are never talked about in schools or reported in the news. This is an outrageous disservice to homosexuals who struggle with a desire to change. Instead of encouragement, they are told that homosexuality is normal and therapy isn't needed. This is a blatant lie! In October of 2003, Dr. Spitzer, professor of psychiatry at Columbia University, dispelled any belief that homosexuality can't be reversed. A 16-month study of 200 individuals showed conclusive proof their lives improved from therapy. Two requirements of participation were first they had to have a predominantly homosexual attraction for years, including the year before therapy, and secondly they had to have five years of minimal homosexual attraction after therapy. After one year the study showed that participants had successfully benefited from reparative therapy with no harmful effects. The participants agreed it was painful, but the introspection into past relationships and circumstances led them to a successful outcome. This study

112

dramatically disputes the major health organizations in their premise that no therapy can help homosexuals reorient themselves.[16] I repeatedly hear of recovering homosexuals who have success with therapy. Of course it is work, but so is all therapy if you are serious about the outcome. I greatly admire people who have undergone treatment for it takes courage, determination, and discipline to make the change. An incredible example of this is Mike Haley, who struggled with homosexuality for over 12 years. He made a total recovery, gave his life to God and is now married to a wonderful woman. They have two children. The activist homosexuals continue to send him hate mail and disgusting packages, which include fecal material. Regardless of their tactics, he continues to support the Love Won Out Conferences and has written a book called *101 Frequently Asked Questions About Homosexuality*. Melissa Fryrear led a homosexual lifestyle through her 20's, but successfully has left it. Yes it took hard work, but she was able to sort through childhood events and feelings that led her to this lifestyle and come out with an altered and healthy ability to be a woman. If homosexuals want to change, it is possible. Dr. Spitzers's Reorientation Therapy can work for those who choose this type of therapy. Few know of this information for there are no major newspaper articles, news channels or higher learning institutions dispersing this information. Very few know that Dr. Spitzer was instrumental in the removal of homosexuality from the "mental disorder" category in the 70's.[17] He would not change his mind without adequate scientific studies to substantiate his position. One thing we know for sure, this information is once again behind "closed" doors!

The "myth" that homosexuals are born this way continues to give "victim" status to homosexuals for "jamming" purposes. Seeds of deception are planted and people with tendencies have little choice but to follow the lifestyle. The "myth" holds power, for the *cause* has encouraged the lifestyle as "normal" and the public has accepted the "lie." Drs. A. Dean Byrd, Shirley Cox and Jeffrey W. Robinsons' study, "The Innate-Immutable Argument Finds No Basis in Science: Gay Activist Speak About Science, Morality, Philosophy," dispels this myth. It is published on the National Association for Research and Therapy of Homosexuality web site.[18] These authors have quoted the leading researchers in the three top studies done to prove homosexuality is inborn. Dean Hamer attempted to link homosexuality to the tip of the X chromosome, but he was quoted as saying:

> "Homosexuality is not purely genetic...environmental factors play a role. There is not a single master gene that makes people gay...I don't think we will ever be able to predict who will be gay." [19]

Simon LeVay studied the hypothalamic differences between the brains of homosexual and heterosexual men. He stated that:

> "It's important to stress what I didn't find. I did not prove that homosexuality is genetic or find a genetic cause for being gay. I didn't show that gay men are born that way, the most common mistake people make in interpreting my work. Nor did I locate a gay center in the brain." [20]

Bailey and Pillard are the researchers responsible for the famous "twin studies" used by many activists as proof that homosexuality is genetic. The study showed that in homosexuals who had a twin, 52% of identical twins were homosexual and 22% of non-identical twins were homosexual. The researchers of this study now say the following:

> "This study actually provides support for environmental factors. If homosexuality were in the genetic code, all of the identical twins would have been homosexual." [21]

Two of the authors actually claim their studies do not prove a genetic basis to homosexuality.[21] There is absolutely no proof homosexuality is inborn; another example of a "lie" accepted as "truth" to further a *cause*. The above facts make it even more obvious that behavior can be learned; instead we have planted seeds of deception that it is inborn and homosexuals cannot help themselves. Nicolosi describes homosexuality in the following way:

114

"complex behavioral and mental state which is neither exclusively biological nor exclusively psychological but results from a mixture of genetic factors, intrauterine influences, postnatal environment (such as parent, sibling and cultural behavior) and a complex series of repeatedly reinforced choices occurring at critical phases of development." [22]

These issues are addressed during reparative therapy as mentioned in Dr. Spitzer's study. Other successful programs are NARTH and a religiously oriented group called Exodus. Scott Lively's ministry has success with reparative therapy and his wife Ann has done a great job with willing participants. More and more studies prove the recovery rate is good for homosexuals. In 1997 NARTH surveyed 882 individuals who had experienced some degree of change in therapy. Before therapy 68% of the clients perceived themselves as totally or almost entirely homosexual. After treatment only 13 % perceived themselves as exclusively homosexual. [23] The medical community as a whole continues to push truth behind "closed" doors, and I don't see many "Drs." standing behind their reason for being doctors, which is healing. Instead "jamming" continues to illicit sympathy from the public and the homosexual manifesto encourages more and more forms of *mind control.*

Verbal assault is another example of "jamming." Homosexuals are made "victims" by falsely raising the number of verbal assaults beyond correctness. Hate crimes come under this category. Hate crime statistics tell the facts. The FBI statistics were taken from 11,691 law enforcement agencies encompassing a total of 237 million Americans or 84.2% of the entire population. Intimidation continued to be the most frequently reported hate crime in 2001. It accounted for 55.9% of all hate crimes. In short out of 11.6 million crimes reported to the FBI in 2000, only 1,517 involved hate crimes against homosexuals, a third of these were simply name calling according to FBI Hate Crime Statistics Report released in Nov. of 2001. [24] A 2002 FBI report shows a reduction of hate crimes by 23.3% from 2001 through 2002. [25] There is no epidemic of hate crimes directed against homosexuals. I wonder if heterosexual intimidation by homosexuals is included in the statistics, such as ones inflicted upon Dr. Laura or Scott Lively?

What is ironic is that the statistics show a high rate of domestic violence in homosexual couples. Gary Glenn, President of the American Family Association, states that two homosexual researchers estimate at least 650,000 homosexual men are victims of partner domestic violence every year. [26] *Violent Betrayal* by Claire Renzetti, gives information that homosexual women are four times more likely to be victims of violence in a homosexual household as opposed to a heterosexual household.[27] My research showed that many anti-violence organizations have a separate classification for female homosexual domestic violence. The Citizens for Parent's Rights (CPR), a Maryland-based organization, has an updated database on statistics of homosexual-on-homosexual violence. The following are some interesting facts they have listed.

1. A 1994 study of 113 lesbians indicated that 41% of them had been physically abused in a same-sex relationship.
2. One study found that 15% of lesbians engaged in torture for sexual fun that included "piercing, cutting or whipping to the point of bleeding" with their lovers
3. The L.A. Gay and Lesbian Center reported in 1998 that approximately 25 to 33 % of all homosexual relationships involve abuse.
4. Male-on-male rape constitutes from 5 to 10% of all rape.
5. A study in 1990 revealed that 9% of male heterosexuals, 24% of male homosexuals, 2% of female heterosexuals and 11% of female homosexuals reported having been homosexually raped.[28]

The "victim" classification is deceptive. It can be used and abused for extracting the public's sympathy. It is used in the marriage battle ensuing in our country. They say they want marriage, faithfulness and children, but studies show otherwise. Homosexuals have an average of 50 sexual partners and heterosexuals have an average of 4. Less than 2% are monogamous (defined as being 100% faithful to one's spouse or partner), compared to 83% for heterosexuals. [29] Homosexuals are not just interested in marriage; the agenda goes deeper. According to homosexual activist Michelangelo Signorile, in *Out* magazine, the objective is to change the meaning of marriage,

> "Fight for same-sex marriage and its benefits and then, once granted, redefine the institution of marriage completely...To debunk a myth and radically alter an archaic institution...The most subversive action lesbians and gays can undertake...and one that would perhaps benefit all of society....is to transform the notion of 'family' entirely." [30]

Their lifestyle is different than heterosexuality. Andrew Sullivan, a homosexual and a senior editor at *The New Republic*, has written a book that supports same sex marriage. He refers to marriage as a "stifling model of heterosexual normality." He says that the straight society will have to come to a better "understanding of the need for extramarital outlets between two men than between a man and a woman."

> "The truth is, homosexuals are not entirely normal; and to flatten their varied and complicated lives into a single, moralistic model is to miss what is essential and exhilarating about their otherness."[31]

Paula Ettelbrick, a law professor at the University of Michigan and family policy Director for the Policy Institute of the National Gay and Lesbian Task Force, believes in the alteration of marriage.

> "Being queer is more than setting up house, sleeping with a person of the same gender and seeking state approval for doing so...Being queer means pushing the parameters of sex, sexuality and family and in the process, transforming the very fabric of society. We

117

must keep our eyes on the goals of providing true
alternatives to marriage and of radically reordering
society's view of reality."[32]

It is clear another agenda exists for homosexual leadership,
and it is to change marriage. We are now victims of discrimination.
We are blamed for violence, assaults and discrimination against
homosexuals, when the facts speak for themselves as to who is being
discriminated against. Homosexuals have become a "protected" class
by developing a "victim" status at our cost.

Once the group gains "victim" status, then the second half of
"jamming" is ready to be implemented. Others (schools, churches,
businesses, communities, government, media) shun the heterosexual's
negative opinion. It takes a few examples of this action and soon
others get the message and are silenced. This is where the "fear"
tactics are very persuasive. Vocabulary such as homophobic,
heterosexist and diversity are useful for emotional modeling.
Everyone wants to be liked; people become silent so as not to be
accused of homophobia. It is a psychological assault on our mental
well-being. It is done quietly and people are unaware it is happening.
This was their plan.

"The bigot need not actually be made to believe that
others will now despise him, rather, our effect is
achieved without reference to facts, logic or proof.
Whether he is conscious of the attack or not, indeed,
the more he is distracted by any incidental, even
specious, surface arguments, the less conscious he'll be
of the true nature of the process- which is all to the
good." [33]

In "Selling Homosexuality To America," Paul Rondeau
explains that the last step is conversion. The *cause* to be normal is so
strong in homosexuals that it has produced the power necessary for
successful accomplishment of bringing many people to the final stage,
which is now in progress. We have set beliefs in regards to God,
Family and Country. When we come into conflict with our core
values, we become uncomfortable. Obviously the concept of same sex

relationships is unnatural and against natural law. Our discomfort determines our reactions and solutions. Eventually we want our attitudes and behavior to be consistent. To change our minds about homosexuality, the third stage of conversion is carried out with positive images of the homosexual lifestyle. It is a propaganda campaign to sway the masses. Media portrays the lifestyle as normal. The homosexual lifestyle and couples are depicted as average everyday people. Kirk and Madsen said in *After the Ball*:

> "Persons featured in the media campaign should be indistinguishable from the straights we'd like to reach." [34]

Another method of positive imaging is in claiming historical figures were homosexual. Presidents Lincoln and Washington were accused of being homosexual in some school districts. To latch onto famous political figures that are dead and cannot defend themselves is a brilliant way to add credibility to the lifestyle. Nothing negative is to be presented to the public about homosexuality. *Will and Grace* and *Queer Eye for the Straight Guy* are popular television shows that use humor, as mentioned earlier, to lighten up our spirits about this lifestyle. In my childhood we had cigarette commercials on TV. In the past years I've heard Paul Rondeau, on radio talk shows, speak about the "Marlboro Man" commercials. The Marlboro man was a cowboy depicted as a strong man riding on his horse into the sunset, and of course, the sunset was beautiful. No one associated the lifestyle of smoking with death. The rugged image along with the majestic scenery took the "truth" from the health issues.

With homosexuals being portrayed as your average every day person, it is difficult to accept the truth *Stage 3*. Once a society has gotten into the "protective" state toward a class of people, it is difficult to turn the tide. When a person enters *Stage 4* they become protective and rarely come out of this state. The average person has now gone through conversion and apathetically accepts the poor homosexuals and will even defend them. Of course they have support from the churches, which have also been undermined.

"Furthermore gays can undermine the moral authority
of homohating churches over less fervent adherents by
portraying them as antiquated backwaters, badly out of
step with the latest findings of psychology. Against
the atavistic tug of Old Time Religion one must set the
mightier pull of Science and Public opinion. This
unholy alliance has worked well in America against
the churches on such topics as divorce and abortion.
That alliance can work also for gays" [35]

It is working. Winning 53% of the vote, Susan Andrews of
Maryland was elected as moderator of the Presbyterian Church's
(USA) 215th General Assembly. She is the first woman to hold this
position; her fondest dream is that her denomination removes the ban
on ordaining practicing homosexuals. Her church members see her
selection as a way to be inclusive in today's contemporary society. An
ELCA church in Minneapolis installed, as Pastor, a practicing female
homosexual. A church in St. Paul voted to allow Pastors to bless
same sex marriages. [36] It is common knowledge that some Methodist
churches are marrying homosexuals. Episcopal churches are
ordaining homosexual ministers and Bishops. The movement
influenced other churches such as the United Church of God,
American Baptist, United Church of Christ and Congregational
denominations. The Lutheran church recently split on whether to
okay ordination of homosexual ministers. The reports are showing
the Catholic Church with at least 20% of priests being homosexual,
and some involved in secret organizations.[37] Even the Jewish religion
has been affected. The liberal branch of Judaism, the Reform faction,
can now bless same sex unions in marriage rituals.[38] Many churches
embrace the lifestyle, celebrate and compromise the "truth." This
embrace, however, leads to the kiss of death, both now and for
eternity. Their actions help plant the "seeds" of deception.
Ministers, pastors, priests and rabbis are "playing" with God's laws.
In the Bible, Matthew and Luke tell of Jesus making it clear, that "it is
better to throw one's self off a boat into the sea with a millstone hung
from your neck than to lead little ones into sin." A friend, Carol, gave
me a photograph of a millstone that she took while visiting Israel.
They weigh thousands of pounds. It is apparent that God is serious

about protecting His children from elders introducing dangerous lifestyles.

There are some homosexuals that are peaceful quiet people who participate in this lifestyle and are against methodology used by radical members of the homosexual movement. They do not agree with infiltrating schools with training in homosexual lifestyles, nor do they believe in homosexual marriage. One of them is radio talk show host Al Rantel in San Francisco, who boldly came forth on Bill O'Reilly saying that homosexuals do not want real marriage, but instead to destroy the institution of marriage. Tammy Bruce, homosexual author and radio host, has similar concerns with the radical agenda of homosexual activists and voices them publicly. I respect these individuals for their truthfulness and courage to say this in front of the nation. However, the *cause* of radical activism, deceptive judges and liberal legislators far outweighs Rantel, Bruce and others who have contrary opinions. Our *cause* to protect our children must not only overpower the few homosexual activists, but also the influential people in positions of authority. We must leave behind a moral world for our future generations.

Upon completion of this Chapter, I found an article written by Henry Makow called "Is This Behavior Sick." Makow explains that in Chapter Six of *After the Ball: How America will Conquer its Fear and Hatred for gays in the 90's* Kirk and Madsen actually tell what behavior homosexuals must change to alter society's opinion of them. They list "ten categories of misbehavior" that must be addressed. The list was compiled from interviews with hundreds of homosexuals, evaluation of their own lifestyle and from readings.[40] Unfortunately the authors are in *Stage 4* of *mind control* for they honestly believe that the lifestyle is separate from the sexuality. The misbehaviors make it clear as to why the activists feel no remorse in teaching our children to be homosexuals. The "lies," "deception," and "intimidation" do not bother them for they are truly into what they "want" with no real regard for others.

1. The authors say "a surprisingly high percentage" of pathological liars and con men are gay. This results from a natural habit of self-concealment, and leads

to a stubborn self-deception about one's own gayness and its implication.

2. They say gays tend to reject all forms of morality and value judgments. Gay morality boils down to "I can do whatever I want and you can go to perdition. (If it feels good, I'll do it!)" If a gay feels like seducing a trusted friend's lover, he'll do it, justifying it, as an act of "sexual freedom" and the friend be damned.

3. They say gays suffer from a "narcissistic" personality disorder and give this clinical description: "pathological self absorption, a need for constant attention and admiration, lack of empathy or concern for others, quickly bored, shallow, interested in fads, seductive, overemphasis on appearance, superficially charming, promiscuous, exploitative, preoccupied with remaining youthful, relationships alternate between over idealization and devaluation."

4. As an example of this narcissism, the authors say "a very sizable proportion of gay men" who have been diagnosed HIV positive continue to have unprotected sex.

5. They say the majority of gays are extremely promiscuous and self-indulgent. They must continuously up the ante to achieve arousal. This begins with alcohol and drugs and includes such "forbidden" aspects of sex as wallowing in filth (fetishism and coprophilia) and sadomasochism, which involves violence.

6. They say many gays indulge in sex in public bathrooms and think it is antigay harassment when it is stopped. Many think they have a right to pursue straight males, including children.

7. Many gays are "single minded sexual predators" fixated on youth and physical beauty alone. When it comes to the old or ugly, gays are "the real

queerbashers." Disillusioned themselves, they are cynical about love.

8. "Relationships between gay men don't usually last very long." They quickly tire of their partners and fall victim to temptation. The "cheating ratio of 'married' gay males, given enough time, approaches 100%."

9. Even friendships are based on the sexual test and hard to sustain. Unattractive gay men find it nearly impossible to find a friend, let alone a lover.

10. The authors say gays tend to deny reality in various ways: wishful thinking, paranoia, illogic, emotionalism and embracing crackpot ideas.[40]

A homosexual revolutionary by the name of Michael Swift offers a challenge to straight America in his writings in the Boston Gay Community News. The article written in February 1987 is entitled "Homosexual Manifesto: An Essay on the Homosexual Revolution." Below are two quotes from his article:

"We shall sodomize your sons, emblems of your feeble masculinity, of your shallow dreams and vulgar lies. We shall seduce them in your schools, in your dormitories, in your gymnasiums, in your locker rooms, in your sports arenas, in your seminaries, in your youth groups; whenever men are with men together. Your sons shall become our minions and do our bidding. They will be recast in our image. They will come to crave and adore us."

"All churches who condemn us will be closed. Our holy gods are handsome young men. We shall be victorious because we are fueled with the ferocious bitterness of the oppressed." [42]

I was motionless. The *cause* for normality would use lies of oppression to ruin our children's innocence. Children are mentally threatened as carefully manipulated programs grab their thoughts and twist them into perverted lifestyles. The schools are *brainwashing* our children and I was certain that my intuition was correct. Delaine Eastin paved the way for secretive school agendas, and schools throughout America are experiencing similar change with diversity programs lurking in the shadows. Programs in schools and Institutions are pushing agendas so fast we can't keep up. I was sure, in time, they would reveal themselves.

Though I didn't know the answers, I felt secure in the power of truth. The truth made me realize that our organization was more vital than I ever imagined. Eagle Forum of Sacramento's mission statement would be to "Protect our Children for Survival of our Great America." The words were boldly imprinted in my memory and I knew that Eagle Forum would make a difference.

20

SUMMER SURPRISE

S ummertime was fun and a special time we always looked forward to as children. A carefree spirit unmatched by anything else when we knew at last it had arrived. This spirit crossed into adulthood and anticipation of the season continued as a critical part of the joy. Summertime anticipation was different this year, for it was not carefree nor would it be again; I knew it for sure.

Following my talk with the Principal I tried finding information on SEED. I found nothing on line. Summer was approaching fast; our first Eagle Forum meeting would take place. I had much to do and put SEED on hold. This time of year should be relaxed. I wanted to have fun. I especially wanted people to enjoy the first meeting in June of 2002.

The evening arrived quicker than anticipated. I was happy I had researched and kept abreast of current news, for my words seemed to flow freely and I knew people were listening attentively. My knowledge was apparent as I delivered information about Eagle Forum and its importance in our changing world. Karen England from CRI gave a spirited talk on legislation and how we can make a difference if we participate. Once the facts were delivered it was an individual decision; the attendees were responsive and they became members, eighteen to be exact. It was a great first meeting. New acquaintances Tammy and Wendy, who had pre-school children joined. I was happy my long time friend Diane became a member. New friends Cliff, Carol, Mary, Marguerite, Teri, Bill and Chris, and Joe and Dee became members with some eventually forming our board. My family gave support to Eagle Forum by joining our local group. Our son's girlfriend, Josilyn, and her family Mark and Gloria also became members. I was thrilled with everyone's enthusiasm and knew that our group would contribute in a meaningful way in our community. Within a few weeks we had more members: Henryne, Nita, Renee, Gilbert and Unadella, Ray and Jacque, and Al and Sue. Our Co-Director, Secretary, and Research Director positions filled and we continued to grow in numbers. Things seemed to fit just the right way; my worries over a treasurer disappeared when Linda, a special friend and competent businesswoman, took the position. It, indeed, had been a good night!

The rest of the summer reached out to me with previews of things to come. I held tight taking advantage of what it offered. Two very distinct messages came into my life. The first message came soon after this meeting. While sharing Eagle Forum with a friend who is a teacher, I suddenly asked her if she had heard of the SEED Program. She was quick with a response. It had been in place for a while. It was a different type of program not having clear content or standards. It took place in people's homes or after school in various locations. The participants were students, parents and teachers. The teachers were given school credit, which then allowed them to move up the salary scale. She however did not partake. She was uneasy about it and its origins. It was suggested that our group might want to look into it.

I planned to do research that evening on diversity and decided to check again for the SEED Program. Once again I could not find it. How unusual and I finally decided to call the school district office in the morning to obtain information. The next day was a positive one; I was referred to one of the SEED facilitators. Our conversation began positively in that I finally found the meaning of SEED, which is Seeking Educational Equity and Diversity.

We conversed at length with the usual introductory "small talk" making it easier to assess the other's personality. When we got to the real substance of the call, my worst fears were confirmed. Everything my friend told me was true. There was no content and no set standards for the course. My mind was swirling with questions, but no matter how I worded them the "facilitator" responded with rhetoric that was illogical. Teachers getting credit for classes having no content seemed unusual. I decided to ask about the student's SEED Program and if diversity covered homosexuality. I intuitively knew the answer but needed confirmation. She was hesitant and weighed her words carefully. SEED did not push it on anyone, but instead explored lifestyles by allowing the boys and girls to explain how it felt to develop into a boy or a girl. In other words they explored how they came to be homosexual or heterosexual. I realized how far this topic could carry a group of inquiring children. I proceeded to ask if they discouraged homosexual behavior based on dangers of AIDS. She said no because the disease was as prevalent in heterosexuals as in homosexuals. I knew after this response that she was in *Stage 4* of *mind control*, ignoring factual evidence about AIDS. My mind was anticipating the next question and before I realized it, I was asking if I could sit in on a group session. She flat out said "No." I was stunned but questioned why. She said interactions were personal and it was not good having people other than the group hear such private things. I knew instantly it was behind "closed" door therapy with intent to change one's mind. My heart was racing and I was beyond being able to be quiet. It was time to say thank you and hang up before my upset spirit released on this woman. Before I said goodbye, however, I had the foresight to find out how to get more information on line. It was through Wellesley College. I heard this name before. Of course it was the Women's College back east that Hillary Clinton had attended. It was a liberal college promoting feminism. How appropriate, finding its origin in such a setting! I found the site instantly. With little time to explore, our board meeting in a few minutes, I downloaded some of the information. I also found the application form an interesting document, and showed this information to Cliff our research director. He is very knowledgeable in such matter; I was grateful for his presence in our organization.

This was the second message of summer. Cliff reviewed it with great focus. The word Pedagogy on the information sheet immediately grabbed his attention. He explained it could be used as an educational tool controlling people's minds without them knowing it. Cliff instantly affirmed my suspicions about deceptive school programs in the Elk Grove School District. No wonder schools across America are changing so quickly without an outcry of concern. Parent, teacher and student groups everywhere are being drawn into this program. I knew I must act quickly and begin to explore this program.

The Eagle Forum meeting seemed endless. I kept flashing on SEED, the effect on our future generations. Everything seemed insignificant in contrast to the majesty of what I had just digested! Schools allowed this to take place behind "closed" doors. For just a brief moment I hoped I was imagining it. Cliff reassured me of reality. The meeting was over. I was thankful for the meeting, but anxious to begin my research and I was upstairs in a flash.

The information revealed a well thought out tolerance program with clear intent to change and reform. It was far reaching, stretching into not only our country, but also throughout the world. The emptiness within seemed unexplainable. It finally came to me, that nagging awful feeling that accompanies you when you are about to take a test, it was called fear. The fear was not for me, but for the lost innocence of youth. Summertime was here and I was not having fun.

21

PEDAGOGY

My schedule, as usual, was full. I was busy finding speakers for our summer Eagle Forum meetings; Sharon, Santa Rosa Eagle Director, would speak on the U.N. and Orlean, State President of Eagle Forum, would speak on the Influence of Education on our country. With the flourishing of activity, I knew I had to make time for research on the SEED Program.

One morning while working on scheduling, I flashed on a previous luncheon engagement with a friend and school board member. Mentioning the SEED Program and Eagle Forum's concerns as to content, she assured me it was a new program in place due to "racial" issues. She was certain it did not contain sexual material. I accepted her answer; unsure as to why she had little knowledge about its content. It was a pattern, people know of its existence but not content. She also had no idea as to its funding. The Principal didn't know, the School Board Member didn't know and my friend was also vague as to specifics. SEED's secrecy became my motivator. I saw what happened behind "closed" doors in Germany. In every free moment I researched the SEED Program. It became my passion. The pieces of the puzzle were beginning to fit.

Cliff was right about the word Pedagogy. It is defined as the art or science of teaching. When the word is used today it usually refers to teaching methods. It encompasses multiple philosophies and stretches its influence in educational systems nation-wide. Critical pedagogy is meant to methodically criticize and make new that which it criticizes. I was uncomfortable when I read the information about SEED on the Wellesley College website; others would read it and perhaps feel comfort. In the very words that give others comfort, I saw destructive forces at work. Pedagogy is mentioned on their information sheet.

"multi-cultural pedagogy, curriculum
and institutional change"

Pedagogy, curriculum, and change appear to be the focus of SEED. The Program, in existence for "18" years is taking hold in learning communities evidenced by its growing numbers. It uses words of acceptance and love, welcoming participants with education agendas and encouraging change through philosophies that are not clear. It was difficult finding detailed information, with Wellesley College being the only source. I was at the mercy of the website, but was able to find some information about the workshop's cost.[1]

Teachers must sign an application form for the summer workshops that are a weeklong.   A $3000.00 per leader participation fee is payable by school or district to the SEED Project based at Wellesley College Center for Research on Women. There is a cost of $1000.00 provided by a school administrator or Board of Education to be spent by SEED leaders on books and materials for seminar members to keep. This project is also supported by grants and gifts. The curriculum content is non-specific, but as mentioned, they do provide materials such as books, videos, articles, etc that would enable the individuals to better understand multi-cultural pedagogy, curriculum, and institutional change.

The rhetoric connected with SEED Programs is unusual and not to be understood in the context of traditional education. Words and phrases such as " 'windows and mirrors,' 'textbooks of our lives,' 'inner and outer work,' 'curriculum revision,' 'know thyself,' 're-construing,' 're-situating,' 'vertically oriented,' 'laterally oriented,' 'transform the curriculum,' 'intellectual and personal faculty development,' 'cultural realities,' 'shaping school curriculum,' 'passive recipients,' 'lens of gender,' 'leveraging the gender,' 'change agents,' 'systemic inquiry and transformation,' 're-open,' 'creators,' 'co-creators,' 'empower,' 'shaping,' and finally 'transformation.' "   The examples are representative of new age wording that sparked my attention. The vocabulary was definitely used with a "different" agenda, rather than showing respect toward all citizens of the classroom, transformational thought seemed to be the agenda.

First and foremost is that change is very important to the program. It is mentioned frequently. The above words and phrases are used to explain some of the methods used for this change. The methodology is important for a successful journey. Information, given on the website, encourages the student to find what is important for his "own" education. Pedagogic teaching is a series of interactions between the teacher and student. The teacher no longer gives information to the student, but provides avenues for him to find his own education. The participant utilizes these avenues and through introspection based on his life experiences (the textbook of ones own life), race, culture, disability or sexual orientation, he decides what is appropriate for him to learn. Most people who use Pedagogy today use it in the context of Critical Pedagogy.

> "It signals how questions of audience, voice, power
> and evaluation actively work to construct particular
> relations between teachers and students, institutions
> and society, and classrooms and communities.
> Pedagogy in the critical sense illuminates the
> relationship among knowledge, authority and power."[2]

It appears that "truth" is not central to the philosophy of Pedagogy, as seen in the following passage:

> "The Critical Pedagogy tradition begins from a very
> different starting point. It regards specific belief
> claims, not primarily as propositions to be assessed for
> their "truth" content, but as parts of system of belief
> and action that have aggregate effects within the power
> structures of society. It asks first about these systems
> of belief and action, who benefits? The primary
> preoccupation of Critical Pedagogy is with social
> justice and how to "transform" inequitable,
> undemocratic or oppressive institutions and social
> relations. Indeed, a crucial dimension of this approach

131

is that certain claims, even if they might be "true" or substantiated within particular confines and assumptions, might nevertheless be partisan in their effects. Assertions that African-Americans score lower on IQ tests, for example, even if it is a "fact" that this particular population does on average score lower on this particular set of tests, leaves significant larger questions un-addressed, not the least of which is what effect such assertions have on a general population that is not aware of the important limits of these tests or the tenuous relation, at best, between "what IQ tests measure" and "intelligence." Other important questions, from this standpoint, include: Who is making these assertions? Why are they being made at this point in time? Who funds such research? Who promulgates these "findings"? Are they being raised to question African-American intelligence or to demonstrate the bias of IQ tests? Such questions from the Critical Pedagogy perspective are "external" to or separable from, the import of also weighing the evidentiary base for such claims."[3]

Valid testing determines whether a student is equipped with knowledge to move forward in his present studies or if he needs further instruction to "successfully" move forward in subject matter. Many multicultural education supporters believe the "testing" methods must be changed, even the SAT and ACT tests for College Entrance Exams. Some feel that tests are slanted toward whites. Despite these opinions, two recent studies showed that high-stake testing brings about academic gains and better performance on testing for all people.[4] There are organizations questioning the importance of entry requirements and bar exams for those interested in practicing law. I read of medical instructors disagreeing with "make up" requirements to "catch up" people from poor backgrounds; they felt it unfair to keep them behind a year. I would not want someone "slipping" by to become a nurse if they do not understand "math principles" when they are pouring my medicine. Some parents don't believe children should be tested. A recent example is in Florida.

Many students tested, prior to graduation, did not have passing grades of basic knowledge in order to graduate. The parents were upset with what they thought was poor education. They, however, still wanted their children to graduate and not be held back. The same parents are against standardized testing to gauge student's progress. We do a grave injustice to students by allowing them to graduate if they do not have the necessary tools to "make" it in our world beyond high school.

Critical Pedagogy does "open" the door to change, but it appears this change is meant to accept "everything" as being "okay," including a false sense of knowledge that can't be tested by traditional testing methods. The new "change" is for no set standards; it is dependent on the individual and what he deems necessary for himself. Teachers of this philosophy promote our society as oppressive, thus stirring feelings of discontentment and encouraging radical empowerment ideologies. Change is their focus for improvement of our institutions.

The Journal of Pedagogy Pluralism and Practice gave special recognition to Paul Freire who was a Brazilian philosopher and educator. His picture was shown above Peggy McIntosh in one of the magazines editions.[5] Peggy McIntosh is the lady who began the SEED Program, along with Emily Style. They were featured in the fall 1997 issue of the above Journal for contribution of "The National SEED Project on Inclusive Curriculum: Developing Teachers as Sources of Systemic Inquiry and Transformation." It was a surprising discovery to find them in this Journal, but indeed they do share the Pedagogic philosophy. Paul Freire had a rich political career and taught at Harvard University, as did Peggy McIntosh. He was a controversial figure for his views on societal reform. He was arrested, with a short stay in prison and exiled from Brazil for 15 years as a dangerous political pedagogue. His ideas on society made me take notice. He felt few human encounters were free of "oppression" from one form or another, by virtue of race, class or gender. People are either "victims" or "perpetuators" of oppression. This oppression, he felt, was also in religious beliefs, political affiliations, national origin, age, size, and physical and intellectual handicaps.[6]

This is the philosophy we are teaching our children and adults today. Our oppressive economic, political and social principles are responsible for what happens to other people. If there is a discontentment the government, institution, business, school district, family or individual is held accountable for the other persons discomfort or unhappiness, for it is obviously the fault of the other. Growing up for children today means they take responsibility for the "common good," not for themselves (which is focal to our "individual" concept in our Declaration of Independence). The "common good" takes priority, especially in the public school system. Paulo Freire died in the late 90's, but was honored repeatedly for his recognized pedagogy associated with progressive *causes* of the educational left. Two of the main theoretical and methodological innovations resulting from his work have been implemented in social studies and curriculum studies not only for adults, but also for secondary and higher education. It has been used in teaching of mathematics, physics, educational planning, feminist studies, educational psychology and more. His school curriculum, teacher training, and school governance influenced social movements with the state. [7] "Change" was a focal part of his methodology.

The philosophy of "oppression" is indoctrinating our children. It appears there is an automatically "supposed" oppression taking place in our country without factual "truth" to document it. It is affecting children of white, middle class America. People who have worked hard for their position in life are made to feel guilty for it. We are supposed to feel ashamed of being white and Christian. Paul Gorski, author of the McGraw Hill Multicultural Supersite, in November of 1999 stated that

> "the cultural landscape of the United States continued
> to become less visibly white Christian and more
> visibly rich with cultural, racial, ethnic and religious
> diversity, underscoring the necessity for everyone to
> develop a set of skills and knowledge that the present
> system was failing to provide all students."

The idea is to develop a new culture, but not based on our Judeo-Christian Ethic. Instead of allowing others to filter into our "way," there is a push to try and make every culture predominate in our society. It will not happen and we will lose our heritage in trying. I

134

see separation and a country that will grow weak in time. This is very serious for our national security is at risk. Lastly I see a lack of concern for factual knowledge that has kept our citizens educated for centuries. Without a solid background of knowledge (accurate history and civic classes) that each student has a responsibility to learn, we will lose our solid cultural heritage, falling prey to communism and/or socialism. It's what the perpetrators of such programs have in mind. It is hidden in the new age rhetoric that sounds so warm and loving that few can resist it. The SEED Programs are using *mind control* to manipulate a new society, a society far different than the one our Founding Fathers had in mind. The *mind control* begins with the parents, teachers, businesses, church leaders and the very communities in which we live. Slowly, like a repeat of Nazi Germany, we will be taken over by our youth, children who are being molded and manipulated to become co-creators of their own education. This education process is being carefully manipulated to move our children in directions far different than the traditional grammar, middle and high school students of yesteryear.

Each year, teachers are being initiated into this new way of teaching. In 2004, the New Leader's Workshop in San Anselmo, CA., will have over 40 new attendees. The SEED leaders return to their communities after the weeklong summer workshop, encouraging participation of other teachers, parents and students, initiating meetings each month for three hours behind "closed" doors. This enables the participants to become in "touch" with each other's inside experiences in life to help them better understand the "windows" of each other's souls. It is a dangerous agenda for it is secretive, manipulative, and has as its goal transformation.

The SEED teachers return to the classroom and direct this creative education scenario into any path that seems appropriate for the student. When a child's mind is "caught" at an early age, anything is possible. We saw it with Hitler, and we are seeing it again in our youth of today, for humanist ideas prevail in their ideologies. Leaving the learning up to the child, dependent on what he deems valuable to his own education needs, is inviting every imaginable interest to infiltrate our traditions. The words I found in regards to the *SEED 101 For Students Kick-Off August 2003* flashed in my mind. I reviewed these words and realized its implication; the "seeds" were being planted for "change" and it was happening faster than I imagined.

> "SEED 101 for Students will provide youth from across all cultural and socioeconomic backgrounds, the opportunity to engage in positive and supportive environments where attitudes and behaviors are clearly the important roles in "shaping" young peoples' lives. Current attitudes and multicultural programs do not adequately prepare young people for their leadership roles as multiculturalists. While schools understand the importance of young people in their community, too often youth are relegated "passive recipients" of information instead of active "co-creators" of knowledge. In order to "empower" students to realize their potential as "change agents," they need opportunities to experience first hand with mentors who will help form, educate and affirm their roles as active "full creators" of their education." [8]

22

SYSTEMIC INQUIRY and TRANSFORMATION

Peggy McIntosh, Ph.D., Associate Director of the Wellesley College for Research on Women and Emily Style Co-Director, are the founders of SEED. They now have a third partner, Dr. Brenda Flyswithhawks, who works in the Santa Rosa school district in California. The SEED's Program rhetoric is not only believable to those eager for "change," but also capable of *brainwashing* unsuspecting individuals into believing they are in need of it. "The National SEED Project on Inclusive Curriculum: Developing Teachers as Sources of Systemic Inquiry & Transformation" makes its own statement in regards to its purpose. Systemic and curricular change is accomplished by bringing into the classroom of our lives issues of race, gender, class, and ethnicity. It is clear in intent to transform our systems of education through critical pedagogy and *mind control* behind "closed" doors. There are five faculty development education phases of this program which are listed below:

1. "Unless we as teachers re-open our own backgrounds to look anew at how we were schooled to deal with diversity and connection, we will be unable to create school climates and curriculum which more adequately do this for and with students." [1]

The first assumption is that teachers have not had adequate training to handle the complexity of diversity in the classroom. I immediately thought of *Stage 3* of *mind control*. This is a paradox that is crazy, but believable and capable of changing minds in the appropriate setting. I can imagine the mind of a traditional teacher thinking that perhaps this could be true and opening her mind to its suggestions. Miss McIntosh and Miss Style say the following.

> "We ourselves had very debilitating schooling in matters of gender, race, culture, manners, money, power and belonging and not-belonging."[2]

They were not trained in the above; therefore, they know other teachers are not able to teach in a meaningful way in the classroom. It is only through serious "soul searching" and "reopening" their own backgrounds that a teacher is competent to "create" school "climates and curriculum" satisfactory for students to learn.[3] They claim the program takes time, time to change "all" one has learned in order to be a good teacher. The 9-month SEED Program begins by "undoing" previous thought patterns, slowly developing a new "formulation" of ideas "better" suited for all. This is the perfect example of *Stage 3* and *4* of *mind control*. It is used to change minds and reverse thinking. Are they saying the former education received was "faulty" and therefore teachers are "ill equipped" to teach correctly? If so then it is discriminatory in nature and I find this rhetoric degrading toward teachers and the Institutions that taught them.

As a child, I experienced fantastic teachers working hard to teach us. I learned reading, writing, and arithmetic, and in history and geography classes I learned about different cultures. We had a diversity of students in our classroom, and they also learned. Our society educated "everyone" for hundreds of years and successfully. In the last decades, we see declining test scores. Scores worsen the further we stray from traditional teaching. We can see this in Reading. In years past everyone used phonics and a set Reader and people learned to read. At a cost to tax payers and time to teachers, new Reading Programs are introduced frequently to school districts. Scores are not substantially improving and in most areas still a problem. We need to change and return to traditional ideas of learning.

2. "Intellectual and personal faculty development, supported over time, is needed if today's schools are to enable students and teachers to develop a balance of self-esteem and respect for the cultural realities of others."[4]

In order to develop self-esteem and respect of other "cultural realities" the Authors believe there must be intellectual and personal faculty development. Do Miss McIntosh and Miss Style feel schools do not encourage intellectual and self-knowledge? They seem to feel teachers are encouraged to form personal opinions, but not to develop an awareness of where they are situated in the following:

"...situated in the worlds of power, knowledge-making, agency, possibility, creativity, resources, people, places and things."[5]

I once again find this demeaning to our teachers who took their jobs seriously and did not need group "therapy," behind "closed" doors, for "personal" development guiding them through an understanding of their positional status. They are claiming this experience gives teachers a "new" sense of self esteem allowing them to approach students in manners more conducive to understanding them, thus contributing to the "common" good of the classroom. Are teachers being manipulated to believe that dignity of the student only comes through a complete understanding of them by their cultural or sexual realities? Does this not elevate the group above the individual? The children are now exposed to group math, group reading and group writing. Individuality used to predominate our society. It made America Great for 200 years! We now have a "global" concept, promoted by programs like SEED. The individual must "change" in order to "open" a new way for people to learn; one that is more conducive to who they are in light of their culture, gender and every sexism you can imagine. This does not elevate an individual but gives self worth through "collective whole" or the "group think" mind. As for "cultural realities" being necessary to respect others, we learned to respect people based on who they were. We were not forced to do it because they were black or homosexual. We learned it the natural way by developing personal character traits and following the Golden Rule. Our teachers and parents taught us daily and we took responsibility for our own learning and not each other's. This is indeed taking "responsibility" for our lives. The above is an example of another paradox perfectly worded for parent, student and teacher participants who thrive on self-esteem gained through the condoning of every imaginable status, rather than earned status through hard work and study of traditional subject matter.

3. "Teachers and other school personnel are the authorities on their own experience. Only if teachers are put at the center of the process of growth and development can they, in turn, put students' growth and development at the center of their classrooms." [6]

From reading material on the website, once again the only source of SEED information available, it appears the authors feel teachers pretend to be competent in the classroom, but do not have an understanding of classroom dynamics. Miss McIntosh and Miss Style feel a new kind of discipline, unknown to the common teacher, helps them in their times of "need." It is an understanding of the "playing out" in the power divisions of classrooms; learning to exercise a degree of constructive control which fosters and insists there be balanced learning for all.[7] The education for learning this new process comes through materials they use in monthly seminars. Materials are given to facilitator's attending summer workshops at Wellesley College. The leaders are free to use whatever materials they think will most benefit the group. These could be videos, books, readings, journaling and discussions. They are also encouraged to read each other's journals. No two sessions are alike. Miss McIntosh and Miss Style offer some of their own writings to be used along with a list of suggested readings. I began sensing an overwhelming arrogance connected to this program. They are telling other teachers they are inadequate in classroom dynamics and incapable of putting students at the center of learning. Another paradox offered for teachers to think, "perhaps it is true." *Stage 3* of *mind control* sets up the mind for *Stage 4*, which converts the person to a new way to teach or learn new materials.   In reality, there is only one thing missing in classrooms and it is authority of the teacher to perform as a teacher and teach what needs to be taught. Simple, easy and it works. No extra money needed and students know what is required of them. Students know security by actions, similar to a toddler who has "no" said to them by enforced actions that show the parent means it. The classroom might be compared to the family. Individuals remain unique, but must adhere to a necessary "set" of rules in order to give balance to the unit. The unit then works for its purpose, which in some schools is still to learn reading, writing and arithmetic.

> 4.   "Group discussion of interlocking systems of over-
>   advantage and oppression and of the research on
>   'separated knowing' and 'connected knowing,'
>   can support teachers and administrators in shaping
>   the school curriculum to become more gender-fair
>   and multiculturally equitable."[8]

 The authors believe recognition of "power inequities" in society is necessary to compensate for the "scattered and incoherent state" of much teacher training. Most teachers, according to these authorities, are not trained to see inequities in our schooling and in the general society. The SEED Program offers teachers and students a seminar existing outside of school that breaks down, through candid conversation, what was "done" to them educationally causing them to not understand inequities in our system.[9] Of course this is all based on their "authority" of us being an "oppressive" society. According to Webster's Dictionary, oppression means to burden with cruel or unjust impositions or restraints. It is an intense word. I flashed on fear and hate. Just as we can teach children to be homosexual, we can teach our children that our society is hateful and oppressive. Participants eager to become better individuals, *Stage 1 mind control*, attend meetings that are behind "closed" doors providing relaxation, *Stage 2,* and interjection of paradoxes to cause questions, which is *Stage 3*. New ideas are introduced to the prepared individual and after nine months of acceptance into the group the individual is trained and truly believes he is oppressed, *Stage 4*. This program is a nightmare of injustice toward our individualism and our country's belief in it. The fostering of a "false" belief that our society is largely "oppressive" is promoted in SEED and can introduce chaos. Chaos dictates change, thus the supposed need for Tolerance programs. The programs take over schools, with tales of future contentment and a misguided journey to obtain it. Humanity will have difficulty reversing it, for once in *Stage 4* many do not come out.

    5.   "Without systemic understanding of gender, race and class relations, educators who try to transform the curriculum will lack creative flexibility and coherence when dealing with the scholarship of the last twenty-five years in specific disciplines." [10]

With systemic understanding, teachers are able to develop "new" ways of working with the classroom by learning "better-informed ways of being." We must learn what it is like to be everyone else. Social education is put above academics. The teachers become students and the students become the teachers. Mutuality exists, and teachers and students welcome and embrace daily encounters in school. The institution of schooling is fundamentally "transformed."[11] Everyone becomes the co-creator of his own education. This is the ultimate step, a radical transformation of traditional school. It is here; it is happening. People are not seeing it for it is behind "closed" doors.

We have placed our children in the hands of educators who look upon the SEED Community as their home. They find solace, love and support of "all" views, ideas, morals, religions, and governments through group identity. The power of the group connection gives permission to "change" our past identity of traditional beliefs, replacing them with "new age" philosophy. I have personally experienced bonding in women's groups; the cohesiveness is very strong. The exchange of your soul can take place during these encounters. You give your soul for the acceptance of the group's

142

approval. The positives are very addictive and become "agents" of change.

I kept thinking of the Hitler Youth. Through slow but methodically planned programs of desensitization and retraining, the state was able to win the allegiance of the youth. God, family and individuality were no longer important, for the State had become the new god and freedom disappeared. Collective whole became the focus of the new generation and their input had a profound effect on daily life. No longer could people think independent of the collective whole for it was not acceptable. Children reported on their parents if they did not adhere to the rigidity of state supremacy. We are close to this in our society. Children are given surveys in schools, without parental permission, asking personal questions about family life. Parents are accused of child neglect if they do not give their overactive child daily Ritalin. Fear, tolerance, diversity, multiculturalism, political correctness and now "oppression" can be added to the words that are helping with this "slow" manipulation of not only our children but also the world.

SEED is a dangerous program. The secrecy tells of deception with the above philosophies reeking of paradoxes preparing unsuspecting individuals for transformation, which to them is and will bring acceptance and love. A Program behind "closed" doors with a loose philosophy, shouts danger for participants and our future.

The facts are real, though I wanted it otherwise, fantasy didn't work for me. Seeds of deception are planted everyday through SEED and similar programs, and it is a big reason for the rapid change occurring in our land. I had my answer; I knew further exploration would reveal more. For now I had to rest in my comfortable blue chair for tomorrow was another day.

23

WHITE PRIVILEGE

Exploration can be tedious, but I was determined to find as much information as I could about the books used in the programs. I began by downloading the names of the books given in summer seminars to the facilitators. I planned to look at the books content and the author's biography. First on my list was Peggy McIntosh.

I am continually amazed at the status one receives when they have a Doctorate in the Social Science areas of education. They become a god unto themselves. I remember how we felt when we were in class with our PhD teachers, for we revered their knowledge. It was of course the "truth." It is easy to look back in life and see the realities of what we thought was truth.

I decided to return to the information on Pedagogy with Peggy McIntosh's picture below Paul Freire's picture. The information proved to be valuable, for I discovered links that made me turn cold. It was called "White Privilege." I had read about people advocating interracial marriage to rid the world of the white race; I wondered if this was the same mentality. My conclusion was correct.

The articles on these sites described the white man with language and attitudes that not only made me nauseous, but also fearful. The main philosophy of the writings is that we are "somehow" privileged because of the color of our skin. We of course are not aware of this because it has been carefully taught to us without our ability to recognize it. One particular group called The New Abolitionist Society declares, "Treason to whiteness is loyalty to humanity." They have publications and events to support their beliefs. In a 1996 radio interview with Dr. Noel Ignatiev, who is trying to abolish white skin privilege, he is quoted as saying:

> " In our view, the country needs some reverse oreos: a whole bunch of folks who look white on the outside but don't act white. So many, in fact, that it will be impossible for those in power in this country to really be sure who's white merely by looking. When that happens the value of the white skin will diminish."[1]

What caught my eye, once I recovered from shock, was Peggy McIntosh's name; she was involved with a panel discussion on White Privilege. I next realized she was the author of a paper called "White Privilege: Unpacking the Invisible Knapsack." I sat still. My intuition about this woman was correct. She is promoting a philosophy of "transformation" and "change" based on oppression by the white race and by doing so is discriminating against us on skin color. It is indeed racial discrimination. Her five points in SEED were beginning to make sense. It appears she based them on her own life experience, her own misconceived ideas of her own privilege. Some people cannot accept their own life. I don't claim to know her reasons for her discomfort with her past. She has, however, successfully transformed her own feelings about her alleged privileged past into what she "feels" is the truth for all "white" people. I continued to read. It contained 26 conditions that Miss McIntosh felt are connected to skin color. She felt, with certainty, these conditions were met by being white, but not by being another skin color. I examined her assumptions.

1. I can, if I wish, arrange to be in the company of people of my race most of the time. [2]

When I worked in San Francisco, there were many days I did not work with white people, but only blacks and Hispanics. I did not think "color privilege, where are the whites?" My Dad worked in the Steel Mills in Chicago; many days he did not see a white man. He did not think "black privilege" because the blacks were the predominant race. Does her above assumption take into account that each race

145

makes up a certain percentage of our population? How can one be in the presence all day of their own race when the black race makes up approximately 12 % of our population?

2. If I should need to move, I can be pretty sure of
    renting or purchasing housing in an area that I can
    afford and in which I would want to live. [3]

I shopped for apartments many times when I was single. I distinctly remember being turned away, but I never knew the reasons. It appears that Miss McIntosh never had this happen to her, so she assumes it does not happen to white people. It happens to everyone! I believe that "some" people of color automatically assume that everything that happens negative in their life is based on their skin color. My whiteness, for sure, did not get me the apartments of my dreams.

3. I can be pretty sure that my neighbors in such a
    location will be neutral or pleasant to me.[4]

The receptiveness of people to us is complicated by so many other factors that this statement has no merit. I have lived in areas where my neighbors never talked to me. Some of my neighbors have been rude to me also. This was not due to my skin color, but the circumstances and the individuals involved. It is everyday "stuff" that most people learn how to adapt to by either accepting it and moving on with their lives or else continuing to search for paranoid reasons for the rudeness. My whiteness has never protected me from rudeness or isolation.

4. I can go shopping alone most of the time, pretty
    well assured that I will not be followed or
    harassed.[5]

As for harassment, I was robbed at knifepoint in the middle of the day in Sacramento. I have been harassed many times in my life. My whiteness did not protect me; in fact it may in deed have attracted my assaulters to me. More than 90% of interracial crime victims are

146

white.[6]   A black man is 64 times more likely to rape a white woman than a white man is to rape a black woman. [7] Blacks murder whites at 18 times the rate that whites murder blacks.[8] "White oppression" being taught to students through SEED, perpetuates ideas like Miss McIntosh's above; this can only damage society. It is a contributing factor to growing anger that many people of color feel toward us. In reality people are taught anti-white by the very ones who are promoting peace and love. How ironic! I have many friends that have been robbed and assaulted, in home and out of home. There is no guarantee because we are white that we will be spared.

> 5. I can speak in public to a powerful male group
>   without putting my race on trial.[9]

All of her comments were amusing but this one really made me laugh. This deals with the paranoid thoughts of a speaker. Every speaker has their own issues of focus when speaking, how the audience reacts to them is not just dependent on race. I do believe this is very arrogant. Does Miss McIntosh really think that men care so much about the color of skin that they would make it a priority when listening to speakers such as Colin Powell? Any person speaking to any group puts their "own" identity on the line based on the presentation. It is the paranoia of the speaker that would make them believe her statement above. Interesting that this paranoia can be taught, for it appears her material and the SEED material deals with teaching everyone how much is being done to "him or her" by "us."

> 6. I can be sure if I ask to talk to "the person in
>   charge" I will be facing a person of my race. [10]

This statement is totally out of line with present day facts, just look around. The people in authority are not just white. In fact there are more people of color in "power" positions than whites in many areas of life. In families where both parents have college educations, the black family tends to make more money than whites.[11]   From 1982 to 1987, the number of companies owned by blacks increased by a third and their gross income more than doubled. During this same period, non-black owned businesses increased by only 14%. [12] Among black, white and Hispanic Americans with the same age and IQ, annual earning is comparable within $1000.00 of each other. [13] With these statistics, I find it hard to believe the credibility of the above assumption.

7. I can choose public accommodations without fearing that people of my race cannot get in or will be mistreated in the places I have chosen. [14]

With the public awareness of political correctness, there is a preferential treatment toward people of color. We see it in housing, we see it in job security based on skin color and we especially see it in our University systems of admittance. Her premise is out of touch with reality. However, this idea is perpetuated in programs across our country such as SEED. It is convenient for some people to have reasons to shirk responsibility for their lives; we can be their scapegoat. I see people of color being used. They are but pawns in the general plan to redo our society. How sad for the very "freedom" they want is right at their doorstep, but they don't see it. They have instead "chosen" to not see it.

8. I can be sure that if I need legal or medical help my race will not work against me. [15]

In 1968, I was amazed to see the fantastic care that people of color (in the lower income bracket) received in San Francisco's hospitals. I could not get that care because I was not of lower income. Did my white privilege help me? Not at all for I had to pay very high premiums for a plan that only gave me minimal coverage. Race did not enter the picture. It was pure economics for everyone. People who had no money received fantastic medical benefits. L.A. County's health department estimates it spends some $340 million yearly to treat illegal immigrants who seek emergency and follow-up care. [16]

The rest of the 26 points are mere repeats of loosely put together rhetoric that can be countered with factual evidence to disprove her assumptions. I had read enough. I knew immediately that this paper gives Miss McIntosh recognition from her peers. It is one of those "elite" education wonders that all the pseudo scholars buy and will say "How enlightening" or "How insightful." In reality, if she truly believes her own assumptions, then her writings and SEED are not significant for they have only been accepted because she is white. Her own philosophy has degraded her own work. She states in one of her 26 points that she could be pretty sure of finding a publisher for white privilege but because she was white.

The paper proceeds with all the complicated definitions of New Age words and phrases that Miss McIntosh and Miss Style seem to exemplify. Earned and unearned privilege, earned strength and unearned power and male privilege are but a few. Her philosophy is clearly stated:

> "I have come to see white privilege as an invisible package of unearned assets that I can count on cashing in each day but about which I was "meant" to remain oblivious. White privilege is like an invisible weightless knapsack of special provisions, maps, passports, codebooks, visas, clothes, tools and blank checks." [17]

She proceeds to talk about the oppressiveness of white males and white females; they are unconscious about it. She says, "Her schooling gave her no indication of herself being an oppressor, as an unfairly advantaged person or as a participant in a damaged culture."[18] I wonder if Miss McIntosh ever thought that perhaps she might have these privileges because she lives in America. A country wrought from Judeo-Christian ethics, by white men, guarantees her the right to express herself the way she does. Her education may have contributed to her status in life; of course she herself must see that her status is unearned for she only got into the University because of her "white privilege." She is against the white privilege getting her into positions of authority or into universities and yet she is promoting this same philosophy for people of color. Where is the consistency in her philosophy?

The real danger comes in the promotion of SEED and White Privilege. People are attracted to it for many reasons already discussed. Her words put reality into a new light; the "white privilege" theory is being used to uphold the "oppression" theory in order to promote the change in our "social system." The change will take place through the SEED Program. I heard her words as if she were present.

> "To redesign social systems we need first to acknowledge their Colossal unseen dimensions. The silences and denials surrounding privilege are the key "political tool" here. They keep the thinking about equality or equity incomplete, protecting unearned advantage and conferred dominance by making these subjects taboo. Most talk by whites about equal opportunity seems to me now to be about equal opportunity to try to get into a position of dominance while denying that systems of dominance exist."[19]

I sat in by comfortable blue chair. I sat out of necessity; my body was weak. It was drained of my reserve strength to counter such assaults. I had to restore my energy, but first I had to digest what this really meant. There was no longer doubt in my mind that SEED was a well-planned, slow, methodical plan to take over the minds of our children with the ultimate goal to change our society. Only worse is that the *mind control* begins with the parents, teachers, businesses, church leaders and the very communities that are buying into the above rhetoric. It is a repeat of Germany, with God, family and Country being sacrificed, yet no one noticing. When will we wake up? Michael Savage's words resonated in my ears. It is only when the "men" in our society become "men" again that we will take back our Nation. Where are they? Please return to us. The intensity of the moment brought me to thankfulness for my husband's presence in my life. His influence in our family, as a man of principle, has been a steady force in our daily lives.

I felt anger, but knew it was good and more than justified. I would reach out to everyone with the facts for I was certain seeds of deception were being planted for our destruction. It was happening right in Elk Grove and I could do nothing to stop it or could I? I would think more about this question as time went by, but for now I was happy to be white just as others are happy to be red, yellow, black, or brown.

24

SEED MATERIAL

(Seeking Educational Equity and Diversity)

Miss McIntosh's article motivated my search for materials used in the SEED Program. I was clear on her writings on White Privilege, but wanted a representation of other books recommended in the SEED program. I was able to locate a sampling of the books and articles distributed to leaders the past few years.

The first name on the list was Marjorie Agosin. The name sounded familiar to me from past readings. Finally, with more research, her name was found. She was connected to another author by the name of Rigoberta Menchu who wrote The book *I, Rigoberta Menchu* an autobiography about the Guatemala Civil War. David Stoll, a professor of anthropology at Middlebury College, examined her book finding oversimplification of the war, misrepresentations of feelings of poor Guatemalans and outright "lies" about her personal life. Rigoberta says in the January/February issue of *Ahora* magazine "Ciertas mentiras hacen bien," which means, "Certain lies are good."[1] The individuals who support her book also support this statement. Margorie Agosin is one of the supporters of this book. She says in *The Chronicle of Higher Education* Jan.15, "Whether her book is true or not, I don't care."[2] This is the philosophy of Margorie Agosin, a tenured professor at Wellesley College and listed author on the list of SEED books. The "truth" becomes the "lie" and the "lie" becomes the "truth."

The next author is Bill Bigelow. He has co-edited four books: *Rethinking our Classrooms, Rethinking our Schools, Rethinking Columbus* and *Rethinking Globalization*. He is a teacher of U.S.

152

History, Literature and his favorite class is Global studies. His focus being "socially" oriented, he attempts having his students think about the impact of social class and gender in explaining the development of America. He feels our society is stratified based on race, class, nationality, language and gender and because of this, he says our history is bad and it is bad sociology to assume a common past. He therefore chooses not to use facts but uses skits in his classroom. He does not believe in fact-rich and idea-poor curriculum; he feels skits will support learning of small sections of history. He also feels poetry and personal narrative can link student's lives to curriculum. Mr. Bigelow feels Fact-rich teaching is only useful for standardized testing which he says pressures teachers to promote conventional facts and conservative shallowness. He feels the best classes are ones with lots of "pedagogical" diversity.[3] He has taught at high schools in Oregon and Ohio.

In November of 2003, the National Assessment of Educational Progress (NAEP) reported that public school children have made no gains in reading.[4] I addressed this in the Systemic Inquiry chapter that despite money and new programs, reading skills are not improving. Teaching methods, such as group study and skits, have devastating effects on children. Disciplined learning is disappearing. Children are not made to memorize timetables. Everything should be fun. I see results of this fun when I watch people in jobs struggling with mathematics. It is not fun for them when they cannot read or understand our country's history and form of government in order to vote appropriately. We have traded basic education for New Age learning.

Gregory Cajete is next on the SEED list. He is a Tewa Indian from New Mexico and his book introduces us to Native American practices. He shares tribal legends and stories emphasizing the importance of education connecting people to each other; thus, finding our place on earth. Dr. Cajete believes we are interwoven with each other and must respect rhythms and patterns of nature and ways these are expressed archetypally, both culturally and through individual psyche. Social ecology is important, how we relate to one another, the physical ecology, the land and resources. Education must be used to deal with relationships. He uses slides for his education in order to open the "window" into the Tewa Pueblo's world.[5] The phrase Pinpe obi means, "look to the mountain." Indigenous people orient themselves to the place and the space with referencing seven directions: north, south, east, west, earth, sky and the Centre of the self. This is the starting point for relationships. The spiritual understanding at the core of their ceremonies is essential to relationships necessary to mobilize the world into solving problems. He proceeds to talk about Kokopeli, a figure from their culture who represents a pro-creative force within humans and the "Great Turtle," who teaches us how we must see ourselves in relation to others and to the natural world.[6] He may be quoted as saying, "Education is not seen as a technical process to be managed by "specialists," but as a heroic journey, a challenging quest that each individual undertakes with support and guidance of community."[7] Nature, ecology and community are the focus of his teachings.

The next book is by Susan Hoy Crawford. It is called *Beyond Dolls and Guns.* I could find no information on this woman. The description of her book told me immediately what I needed to know. Her theme is "Don't Let Your Child Be Sex-Stereotyped!" Her book offers ways to detect and combat gender bias hurting your children. Transformation is the theme; unisex is the goal. These topics include:

1. How can I tell if my child's school is gender biased.
2. How can parents look for "linguistic bias" and change it to "inclusive language."
3. How can parents get schools to recognize the unconscious ways they promote gender bias.
4. Why is gender bias so pernicious?[8]

The list is alphabetized. I decided to go down a few spaces to Mark Gerzon. He is included in writings that are a part of a service given at the First Unitarian Universalist Church of Columbus Ohio. Mark Gerzon's Book is titled, *A choice of Heroes: The Changing Face of American Manhood,* also included was, *On Being a Man.* I read some of the articles. The predominate theme; they did not believe we could categorize any one trait or characteristic as being typical of male or female. The writings indicate we should not raise our boys to believe any behavior is typical of men. The Ministers sermon talked about the ridiculousness of Mars and Venus systems of classification. His ministerial language amazed me as he talked about the form of "garden-variety ignorance and human insensitivity, something not one whit different from the ignorant statements which routinely froth out of the mouths of Laura Schlessinger or Phyllis Schlafly."[9] I had hoped to find some element of conservative thought, but soon realized that this minister was New Age.

Jean Baker Miller was the next author. She wrote *Toward a New Psychology of women.* She is connected to Wellesley College for Women; she is indeed the Director for the Miller Training Institute. Her program deals with the Relational-Cultural Theory and how it opens the way to a new beneficial "paradigm" for understanding human experience. It is about "transforming" and making changes focusing on dynamics of relationships. It is about mutual psychological development. She believes "growth fostering relationships" are essential to home, community and workplace.[10] Her priority is workplace and within the labor movement. Mutual empathy and mutual empowerment are crucial to needed change. Mutual empathy is the ability to "be able to feel what other people feel," thereby enabling mutual empowerment to develop. There are five results of the mutual empowerment philosophy.

1. Zest or high energy by feeling connected and feeling apart of the world.
2. Next comes empowerment in order to feel motivate to act beyond the relationship.
3. Clarity about your feelings allows you to provide a stronger feeling-thinking base, which motivates actions.
4. Sense of Desire.
5. A desire for more connection. [11]

This is what the SEED Program uses for their base. Both of these programs come from Wellesley College and with the same philosophy. We must feel as the other feels. It is "feeling" that allows the power. The *cause* to feel is producing the power. The above information was gathered from a lecture given by Jean Baker Miller and Kris Rondeau in order to explain a theory for the functioning of a new kind of labor union with expansion into other workplaces. Union organizers used some of these methods following a loss of the 1977 Union Election at Harvard.[12] They believed in order to promote Union Organizing in the workplace, it would be important to get to know the people first. The Organizers stopped using old methods to attract people and began to implement ways to connect people to each other. The sharing of lives, jobs, families, and outside interests allowed for a creation of a community spirit. Once people became connected they were more easily swayed into believing in the formation of unions.[13] It sounded very familiar. Once students, parents, teachers in SEED become connected behind "closed" doors then they are more willing to make changes in their traditional values and morals. Change agents are at work even in the workplace. The name may not be SEED, but the philosophy is the same, transformation.

The next writer is Liz Whaley. Her book is titled *Weaving in the Women: Transforming the High School English Curriculum.* She believes that we need more role models for young women in high school texts. One of her suggestions was to read Aphra Behn.[14] I looked up her works under her biography. She was born in 1640 and perceived to be the first woman to make money as a writer. Little is actually known about her. She died in 1689. This is what is said about her writings:

> " Aphra's opinions were unconventional and because
> she openly expressed her viewpoints in her lifestyle
> and through her writing, she was seen as scandalous.
> Her poetry remarks on romantic relationships with
> both men and women, discusses rape and impotence,
> puts forth a woman's right to sexual pleasure and
> includes scenes of eroticism between men." [15]

Liz Whaley recommends this author as a role model for teenagers. Her unconventional life and writings supports the SEED theme of everything has equal merit.

I continued skipping to random names; my next was Zora Neale Hurston. Her book *Their Eyes were Watching God* was very controversial. It is about a black woman who marries one man, realizes that she doesn't care for him and runs off with another man. After he dies, she marries within a week. This man she eventually kills, but is acquitted of his murder and returns home.

The author, in 1907, traveled with an acting tour when she was 16. She eventually began working for a wealthy family that saw her potential for writing. They helped her attend Morgan High School. She then enrolled in Howard Prep School where she graduated with a two-year degree. Miss Hurston went to New York and enrolled at Bernard College and received a scholarship to work with Franz Boaz in Anthropology. [16] She went on to graduate from Columbia University, and began publishing her poetry and fiction. She became involved in Voodoo incorporating it into her writing; eventually her work lost popularity. Miss Hurston was arrested for molesting a ten-year-old boy and, though acquitted, the reputation stayed with her. She became depressed and died penniless. Her works were revived in 1970 and are studied in literature classes, women's studies and black studies.[17] It is on the SEED list.

I searched randomly thinking that perhaps there may be one book with traditional subject matter. I went to May Sarton. She wrote *The Education of Harriet Hatfield*. This book is about a married female homosexual couple. One of them dies and the other opens a female homosexual bookstore to provide a "meeting and gathering place." The book attempts to parallel homosexual and heterosexual couples. It discusses homophobia and the fear of AIDS. [18] According to Eagle Forum member and concerned parent Teri Lawrence who read the book, it portrays Christian women in a negative image.

Cathy Nelson and Kim Wilson were next to review. The Book *Seeding the Process of Multicultural Education* seemed to jet out at me. This is the description given about this book.

> "While so many of us were academically trained in a canon attributed to our field (Science has its Newton as English has its Shakespeare: Theology has its Aquinas, as History has its Revere). In Seeding The Process of Multicultural Education, we have finally received a canon for our Enterprise. For this canon,

we can be grateful. For Nelson and Wilson we owe praise." [19]

Cathy Nelson is responsible for beginning the first state branch of the SEED Program in Minnesota in the early nineties. I rummaged through the material on the site of the Minnesota Inclusive Program. I notice under Resources websites a section devoted to Articles by Tim Wise and available through MIP. There were 36 articles; 15 were directly related to "white prejudice." Some of the titles are:

1. "White Denial and School Shootings"
2. "Membership Has Its Disadvantages, Whiteness and the Social Entropy of Privilege"
3. "Lecturer attacks White Supremacy"
4. "White lies, The Assault on Affirmative Action"
5. "Some Folks Never Felt Safe: The Truth Behind National Unity"
6. "Membership Has Its Privileges: Reflections on Acknowledging and Challenging Whiteness"
7. "Breaking the Cycle of White Dependence: A Call for Majority Self-Sufficiency"
8. "Chickens…Home…Roost: School Shootings and White Denial"
9. "Fear and Loathing in Suburbia: Crime, Panic and the Irrationality of White Racism"
10. "Riots of our Own: The Invisible whiteness of Majority Mayhem"
11. "Bill of Whites: Historical Memory Through the Racial Looking Glass"
12. "Misremember When: Whiteness and the Recollection of History"
13. "Rebels Without a Clue: Neo-Confederacy and the Ironics of white Supremacy"
14. "Dreaming of a non-white Christmas: Santa, Jesus and the Symbolism of Racial Supremacy"
15. "A Call to Take a Closer Look at the Culture of Whiteness"[20]

The above is "white" discrimination, more prevalent than imagined. I continued reading about the Process of Multicultural Education. Ann M. Tighe says, "stories told and lessons are passed along as if we were all sitting together around a campfire." [21] The warm "fuzzy" which predominates the SEED Program is apparently an important aspect of the education process; more specifically I see the warm fire as certainly meant to burn our past for it was changing fast. I decided to skip down to articles; some grouped together and distributed in packets. The first was a packet with three names and called the *Anti-Homophobic packet*. The word homophobic is discriminatory. I am anxiously awaiting the first person to file litigation for false accusation ruining their reputation. Homophobic accusations have gone far enough and now we have an anti-homophobic packet. I could not get information on its content, but I did look up the names associated with the packet.

The first name is Audre Lorde (1934-1992). She was a black, homosexual, poet, activist and mother. She was an originator of the Audre Lorde Project. The Group works for community organizations focusing on the New City Area. They work for social and economic justice. They actively work against our "War on Terrorism" and wrote an Open Letter to LGBTST Communities Opposing War. The letter was first released in January of 2003. The message is that they do not believe in "the War on Terrorism" and that the "real" intent of it is to silence the minority. [22]

Jane Spahr is the Rev. Dr. Jane Adams Spahr and she describes herself as a lesbian, feminist, Presbyterian minister committed to justice issues for the lesbian/ gay/bisexual community, pursuing connections for wholeness with other oppressed communities claiming their freedom. She travels throughout the United States with her message of inclusiveness to Presbyterians and others, and she is involved with many other groups standing for the concerns of homosexuals. [23]

Harvey Milk was the third name. In 1979 in San Francisco, Dan White, a fellow council member, killed Mayor George Mascone and Harvey Milk. Homosexuals elevated Milk to a hero status; the reality is that he was not killed because of his homosexuality. Next year in San Francisco there will be a museum dedicated to him; he is called St. Harvey by many of his followers. Last year media attention was on a special homosexual school for 100 children in New York; it is named after Harvey Milk.

The next book is by Carol Gilliganm. It is called *In a Different Voice: Psychological Theory and Women's Development.* My associate Teri Lawrence reports on this book. It is a book about three different studies. It shockingly portrays one study wherein 29 subjects are interviewed. The book portrays the women who aborted their unborn children as "very mature and responsible" while the girls who did not as "selfish." The utter lack of respect for the unborn made me realize the perpetuation of this program is no less than giving support to the Nazi Regime. My research on reading material was done.

The SEED tools of manipulation are behind "closed" door therapy, books, suggested ones and otherwise, articles, visual aids, journaling, and infiltration into colleges of "White Privilege" classes and seminars. I found pages and pages of suggested videos. The videos teach the "victim" lesson to the students. Most of them deal with race and sexual orientation.[24] I cannot imagine being a student today and taught this negative knowledge. The Minnesota SEED Exchange, under the Media Center writes the following.

> "Looking for a good way to connect with and teach high school youth? Using "film" is an effective and powerful tool to create discussion of many issues, especially areas we are learning in SEED." [25]

They use video parties promoting movies to SEED facilitators. Chosen videos are then taken to seminars for attendees to watch and discuss.[26] Journaling is very important in the SEED sessions. Participants have opportunity for thinking on paper if they lack the chance to openly express themselves in-group. It encourages participants to reduce responses and clarify, since they cannot write all thoughts. Serial journaling is encouraged; individuals pass their material to each other.[26] Reading others personal thoughts is like reading another's diary. It can be dangerous and backfire. Liability can become an issue for individuals and the school district if they support this program.

160

One of the more powerful tools is the promotion of the philosophy through on going education in colleges. Miss McIntosh travels to different Universities and gives her seminar on "White Privilege." It is promoted on websites such as Equity Network. The article is described as:

"...short, powerful and easily readable, her 1989 article has centered our thinking about race (and other variables) on the notion of privilege like nothing else."[27]

Carleton College in the Fall of 2002 has an Educ 338 class under Multicultural Education. The texts used are: *Seeding the Process of Multicultural Education* by Cathy Nelson and Kim Wilson. Another text is *Rethinking our Classroom* by Bigelow. [28] These books are on the SEED Reading list and mentioned earlier. Other Universities are taking on "White Privilege." The University of Utah addresses Whiteness Theory and Education. They believe that "whiteness" gets in the way of being able to teach in the classroom. The class is not addressed by the color of the skin but once again by white privilege.[29] The Santa Rosa Junior College in Santa Rosa CA. has Dr. Brenda Flyswitthawks, a Director of the SEED Program, working in their Education Department. The College has a catalog of resources; there are approximately 43 SEED Resource Titles. Over 15 of the authors I reviewed are on this list.[30] Dr. Flyswitthawks has been honored with many awards. She has a Doctorate and a "name" in the community. She will promote SEED as a wonderful loving program and because of its "fuzzy" appeal; everyone will believe it is good for the community.

I was weary and tired, for the journey of discovery was tedious and disheartening. I finished and sat in my blue chair. My thoughts reached beyond any branches of logic. There seemed to be no logic; there seemed to be no hope. The SEED Seminars have stretched into 30 US States over the past 15 years and Buenos Aires, Hong Kong, Jakarta, Kuala Lumpur, Manila, Singapore, Taipei, Tokyo, Toronto, Vancouver and Dar Es Salaam. Many of these seminars continue for years. The enrollment of approximately 40 new facilitators in the summer of 2003 and approximately the same in

2004, weighed heavily on my mind.[31] They return home teaching more group leaders, continuing to perpetuate the program. I envisioned the innocence of youth being destroyed by advocates of the above subject matter. I wanted to save them before it was too late, but I didn't know how.

25

DECEPTIVE SKITS

The discovery of this information was vital to the outcome of many lives. It came to me for a reason and I took this responsibility seriously. I was in a contemplative state when my friend Teri, and Eagle Forum associate, called. Her son attends an Elk Grove Middle School. She questioned a last minute Assembly the School had in September of 2002. She did not receive a permission slip for him to attend, nor did she know the subject matter. I immediately became somber. Her son was non-specific, just that it was funny. She questioned him again. His response the same, we knew something was wrong. Teri did not stop questioning; a few days later the truth was revealed.

Michael Fowlin performed 8 one-man skits that humorously portrayed 8 different situations. The scenes involved overweight people, race discrimination, handicaps, women, rape and homosexuality. Her son expounded on the skit about a homosexual football player. Michael portrayed the youth as being "born" this way. He also asked if anyone in the crowd was heterosexual. Her son said the kids were confused and did not know how to react. Teri was angry. She had a right to be upset; the school overstepped their boundaries. I referred her to Brad Dacus from Pacific Justice Institute. Not only had her right been infringed upon, but also her son had been told a "lie." Seeds of deception were planted. I wonder how many would hear the message and make *situational* choices based on this incident.

I knew this program was connected to SEED in some way. I ran upstairs to check on this man. Michael Fowlin has a Doctoral Degree in Clinical Psychology. He travels the country with a mission of unity through his skits. [1] He also receives a hefty sum of money for each skit performed. His fees are as follows:

1. $2000.00 / Performance Outside New Jersey
2. $1500.00 / Performance New Jersey Only
3. $4000.00 / Performance Colleges and Universities
4. $5000.00 / Performances Non-School Affiliated Business Organizations and Corporations
5. Rates do not include out of state travel
6. Rates may vary under the following conditions:
   a. Multiples shows in schools
   b. Multiples shows in school districts
   c. Workshops
   d. YES Inc. Trainings[2]

Money signs flashed. Our children ask for lockers for they carry heavy books back and forth to school. School officials say there is no money. Children wash cars to make the money and parents work at school carnivals to make money for all things that the district can't support financially. Somehow money was found for Michael Fowlin, and it took precedence over anything else such as tutoring programs that may be a little more relevant to education. Michael Fowlin is also involved with a Program called YES. The purpose is to give a "training" session to pre-selected students before his skits are performed. These students then lead smaller discussion groups when his performance is over.[3] I discovered YES in some schools in Elk Grove. Michael uses humor and student backup as agents of change.

The following weeks passed quickly, litigation was at the forefront. Two more parents came aboard and Brad Dacus, President of Pacific Justice Institute, accepted the case. The Institute is nation-wide, has over 1000 affiliate attorneys handling more cases on the west coast than any organization of its kind. Brad Dacus is recognized on national television and radio, standing for religious freedoms, sanctity of life, parental rights and other civil liberties. Parental rights were violated. In California, parents hold ultimate authority in their Child's education. School districts are required, at the start of the school year, to inform parents of controversial

164

assemblies or education planned for the year.   Parents can opt out their children by signing an "opt-out" form. The school then must excuse the child from the activity and provide them with an alternative learning experience. The schools did not notify parents, thus litigation proceeded.

In October Brad Dacus spoke on Parental Rights at our Eagle Forum meeting. The meeting moved fast; the room was full, for the information was valuable. Brad Dacus announced he would be on the local news that evening. It was about the litigation. The excitement, apparent in the room, went home with concerned citizens. We watched proudly as Brad explained reasons for this litigation. Courageous parents struggled to make this decision, and I am honored to have Teri, and Lori, and their families as my friends and representatives of Eagle Forum.   The journey is long and sometimes perilous, but they were willing to take a chance. They believed in a *cause*. Finally, people brave enough to take a stand!

Under the guise of humor, a very serious message was delivered and innocent children heard it. They did not hear that the lifestyle could be dangerous, with possibilities of physical, emotional and spiritual repercussions for participants. Eagle Forum began to speak out; my first radio experience was on KFIA radio with John Stoos. It was top on my "fear" list. All the signs and symptoms of fear were present, but I controlled them for I wanted our message concerning parental rights heard by listeners. The evening marked the beginning of radio encounters that became easier with each one. John made the encounter a smooth one, as do most radio talk show hosts. I give thanks to them for their ability to make us feel comfortable when we know thousands are listening. I also thank Rush Limbaugh who popularized talk shows for conservatives in the 80"s.

We began a series of writing letters and making phone calls to people in authority positions within the school district. We wanted answers to questions, but we were met with resistance. *Mind control* in the form of "run around" was used. They believed we would eventually go away but we didn't. Our letters continued until finally I was able to schedule a meeting with the Chief of Staff in the District. I appreciated the session, but left unsatisfied for my concerns about SEED were not answered. We stayed focused on finding the facts about the SEED Program, Michael Fowlin skits and their funding. Until we found answers, we stayed busy in other ways.

We continued to learn. In September 2002, many attended Eagle Forum National Convention in Washington D.C. It was an experience beyond my expectations! I was fortunate to share it with our daughter, and we enjoyed combining it with a memorable tour of Washington. This tour made the conference even more important in learning knowledge and ways to preserve our liberties.

Sean Hannity, author and Fox news show commentator and Pat Buchanan, author and advisor to three Presidents, were our feature speakers. The excitement of meeting such people comes in the moment of recognition of all they do for the people who so desperately need truthful representation of the facts. I admire people who dedicate their lives to the pursuit of a truthful *cause*. Both of these gentlemen deserve our respect and recognition. Powerful topics and speakers were the Maple River Coalition on Outcome Education, Michelle Malkin author of *Invasion,* Joel Mowbray columnist and Steven Camarota on topics of Terrorism and Immigration. Elaine Donnelly covered military issues and Janine Hansen talked about private property rights of citizens. Other topics included UN propaganda, abortion, health powers, nosy questionnaires, and litigation. I met many of the State Presidents, such as Eunie Smith (Alabama), Bobbie Patray (Tennessee), and Cathie Adams (Texas). Many of our state leaders have served in Eagle Forum for years, but their energy for our *cause* has never ceased. Phyllis Schlafly completed the weekend with an incredible celebration of the 20th Anniversary of the Defeat of the Equal Rights Amendment. All age groups were represented giving the meeting a variety of input crucial to the real meaning of diversity.

The impact of the weekend further encouraged our belief in protecting our children to guarantee survival of America. We returned to little news about SEED or Michael Fowlin. Pat Rousch was our speaker in November and she told of her children being stolen some 20 years ago into Saudi Arabia by her ex- husband. She continues to look for them with hopes of one day being reunited with her children. Her courageous battle for their return made us even more grateful at Thanksgiving for our children. In December, Scott Lively, President of Abiding Truth Ministries and Director of Pro-

Family Law Center, spoke on the Homosexual Agenda. He is passionate about defending the natural family; it is uplifting to hear a man speak who gives his life to protect our young. We are thankful to Scott for his well-researched books, informative presentations, and always-positive presence in our lives. His children appear to be following in his footsteps and I know they will make a difference in our world, just as Scott and his wife Ann have done.

The Christmas Season passed quickly. It is my favorite time of year. It was different this year. I knew a part of me was changing. My joy in the birth of Jesus would never change, but my perspective of the world had changed. I knew more than I wanted to know. Perhaps this is why some turn their backs. Perhaps this is why people deny the truth. They can't bear the heaviness of the sorrow that sometimes accompanies it. The branches of our Christmas tree, however, held bright sparkling lights that seemed to send me a message every time they twinkled. They seemed to wink at me, alive with encouragement for our future. I knew that Eagle Forum would make a difference in 2003. My comfortable blue chair became even more comfortable during Christmas of 2002.

26

BOARD MEETING

A New Year brings the promise of change, usually for the better. This year was not unlike the others, and 2003 began with a new focus for Eagle Forum. We hoped to make a difference by educating the board and fellow citizens in Elk Grove about the SEED program. Teri, Lori N., Lori M. and I decided we would attend the School Board Meeting in January as the district was addressing diversity and multiculturalism programs. My friend on the school board told me SEED was a new program and we thought it best to inform the Board of our concerns. Perhaps they would consider eliminating it from Elk Grove. Teri researched some of the books and found them to be offensive and necessary for the Board to be made aware of their content. Behind "closed" door philosophy, along with lack of traditional content, was our concern. The time constraint would not allow all information to be divulged, but we would be happy to be heard.

We entered the room with the excitement of introducing it to the Board. The room was packed. I knew two people aside from our Eagle Forum members. One woman originally from our neighborhood (our boys grew up together) is the Assistant Director of Student Affairs. I wondered if she would understand our concerns. The other person is my friend who is a School Board member. I mentioned her earlier when we met in July.

The meeting began. The School Board members sat in chairs high above our heads, it was intimidating, but not enough to suppress my enthusiasm. We waited patiently as department heads reported on diversity programs and their progress or lack of it. It became apparent board members were not happy with the rate of crime in the district and the statistics were not dropping as promised by the programs. Eventually it was our turn to speak. They opened the floor to questions and answers. It was my first meeting and I was unsure of the rules. After a few mistakes, I understood my time was close. My heart was pounding with anticipation. Though it was January, my hands were sweating and my body felt warm with the intensity of the moment. I called it fear but controlled it. I walked proudly to the microphone. I stated my name and who I was, then began to speak to my concerns. There was an uncomfortable quietness that overcame the room. I did not feel support or camaraderie. Questions were asked of me; I was able to answer. Eventually the SEED class "content" came up followed by the behind "closed" doors philosophy. This statement received the attention of one of the Board members. He said to me, "You obviously do not know what you are talking about. We will have to talk to you later about what is really happening." It was difficult to find words; I thought I might lose composure at his belittling remark. The flash from the town newspaper reporter's camera distracted me from the irritation. Before I knew it, I was boldly saying, "Excuse me, you say I don't know what I am talking about; well I do know what I am talking about." I proceeded, with time left, to explain the dangers of secrecy and unclear content to students and community. Teri went next. She did a wonderful job presenting material regarding the books and their subject matter. Her charming southern accent, clearly describing the books, gave us hope that at least a few would hear us. My attendance at seminars taught me to know immediately the room atmosphere. It was antagonistic toward us and it never got better.

Following Teri, numerous ladies spoke in defense of the SEED Program. Their rhetoric was filled with the warm "fuzzy" of the SEED program. A black woman, with a baby in her arms, spoke of how she came to love herself feeling part of the community of SEED. I could not help but wonder at whose expense. Other's moral values were compromised so this woman could receive therapy behind "closed" doors to love herself. My thoughts were not harsh, only reality. After a number of teachers and parents spoke, a youth pastor spoke. I was thrilled; surely he stood for moral absolutes. He had already compromised. I heard his message of plea to the board, making sure that if Christians accept other programs that this would guarantee Christian Club representation in the school system.

The meeting soon ended and I was happy it was over. People rushed to us; some ignored us. I understood their plight. I escaped them momentarily as I distributed large envelopes to the Board Members. Enclosed was a letter of introduction about Eagle Forum and concerns over the SEED Program. Also enclosed were Scott Lively's booklets about The Legal Liability of Homosexuality in the Public Schools. I asked them to read the enclosed material, if only one responded I would be happy. An Education department representative gave us his card saying he would meet with us to inform us about SEED. Though I appreciated the offer, I did not have the time or inclination to learn any more than I already knew about SEED.

A few walked with us part way to our cars, attempting to give us a "better" picture of the Program. I flashed on *Stage 4* of *mind control*. Defending the group was a priority. The ladies were doing this now and when they spoke at the microphone. Feelings of belonging, acceptance and love were the words they heard, not ours. I saw this in their eyes as they tried desperately to make me understand the true intention of SEED. I thought I was back in the 60's. The focus was not on continual increase in crime in schools, not on horrible test scores in the district, but on false hope the Programs would somehow "save" everyone. The "village" would take care of everyone and we would emerge as a loving community ready to take care of everyone. It was a "commune" spirit; I have been there and it does not work. Approaching my car, I thanked the women for their time. I wanted desperately to reach out and say "There are better ways to find love than to sell your soul." Silence was best. I knew the issue too complex to begin a debate.

Everything exploded following this meeting. It was on the front page of our town newspaper. We were horrible, unloving and even hateful people. Letters to the editor were frequently written about Eagle Forum and the ugliness of our group. I kept number 4 of *mind control* steps at the forefront as I read the letters. Many came from attendees of the behind "closed" door sessions. We became the focus of the New Year. The paper wanted to interview us. Our story would be told again. I was happy, for it was a second chance at the truth. The first story had facts incorrect; we were misquoted a number of times. When I asked the man who wrote the story if he would retract them he became indignant; he clearly indicated we should be grateful for what we got. I flashed on "lie" subject matter, what difference does the truth matter as long as the message gets out. He never did retract his statements about the inaccuracy. The next article was written in truth of our beliefs and concerns about SEED. Mary McIntyre, the reporter, did a fantastic job of interviewing me; I felt at ease. She called following the interview to make sure her facts were correct. I liked her and her attitude. She was good at what she did, with the final result a great article about our concerns of SEED, honest facts about our beliefs and our position on homosexuality and abortion. The SEED side of the article was presented by two of the SEED Facilitators. Mary did an amazing job of combining the two without showing partiality to either. It was advantageous for readers to compare our thoughts and ideas. Letters to the Editor continued to pour into the newspaper; many of them were open letters of disgust toward us. Of course, the media push to publish liberal ideas rather than conservative is always apparent. In defense of the newspaper, there may not have been conservative ones to print. Many conservatives are fearful of writing letters. I received a few emails and letters written by former teacher friends now advisors to Homosexual Clubs. The messages were derogatory in content. It amazed me that people preaching tolerance are intolerant of us. It is like a community gone mad! Eventually positive comments began to offset the negatives. People on the street, recognizing my picture, stopped me and said thank you. It is an uplifting moment. People called and said thank you. People emailed and congratulated us on delivering information to the community. My friend Al taped 25 minutes of SEED content that aired on his valley radio station. I thank Sue and her husband for giving me the chance to talk; I didn't want to stop. What still catches my attention, however, is noticeable absence of conservative male input in our community. It is hard accepting men stepping down from authority positions both in family and community. In days of old, men would show up at schools saying "No" to this program. I long to reach out and find more "men," the ones who portray strength of male spirit, necessary for the stability of our Nation. No wonder some of us still love Cowboys!

I did not receive "one" board member response to our packets of information. The Superintendent, Chief of Staff, nor the Assistant Superintendent of Student Services responded to my SEED concerns. I wrote a letter to the Youth Pastor, hoping to work with him but he never responded. The information given me by my school board friend, as to SEED being a new program was erroneous. It is obvious SEED has been in place for a long time in Elk Grove. I needed information as to the facts surrounding its formation and why so many know so little about it.

Information on SEED was hard to come by. Whenever I inquired, the first question asked was "Do you have a child attending school in the district?" I didn't have a child in school, thus doors closed to me. My friend Cliff informed me of The Freedom of Information Act giving me the right to request and be granted information. I began to understand the power of citizenship. Eventually Teri and I met with the school authority responsible for the SEED program and Michael Fowlin's skit presentation. He was solid in his belief of the programs for he too had been *brainwashed*. In conversation, he wreaked of vocabulary particular to SEED. He was good at what he did, but I was aware of vocabulary control. It did not work with us. We stayed focused on our questions and wanted to know when we would receive answers. I left the meeting marveling at how easily someone can be swayed from his platform, if unaware of it happening. This same man will be a new Principal at one of the Elk Grove High Schools in fall.

In January I received a call from Sharon Hughes, our Sonoma Chapter Director. She had a special speaker coming to her meeting in February suggesting strongly that we have him to ours. She knew his information would be helpful in our dealings with the school district. Due to the excitement surrounding the SEED exposure, I hadn't thought about a speaker for February. Sharon indicated the subject matter was "deep" and some people may not be ready for it. This immediately got my attention. What topic could possibly be that shocking or at least alerting? I was drawn into wonder and very excited about our guest speaker Dean Gotcher. His topic was The Dialectic and Praxis.

27

THE DIALECTIC and PRAXIS

If there is a defining moment in time, it was mine in February of 2003. Perhaps you have experienced such a moment, you simply have a "revelation" that pulls everything together changing your life forever. When we are ready for the moment, it is an uplifting experience! Dean Gotcher is the Founder and Director of Authority Research Institution. Dean and his wife Karen travel ten months a year giving presentations on Dialectic and Praxis. Dean was our guest speaker in February of 2003. His dedication apparent; I became anxious to hear his presentation.

He stood behind the long table beginning with prayer. The table was filled with interesting books, many of them very old, with a few being new. I was intrigued as to how he used them in his presentation. He knew exactly where they were placed on the table; he began using them immediately following prayer. The presentation moved quickly; I knew I had to take notes, but also think quickly if I wanted to follow his teachings and understand the specifics. His messages were strong in content, but I did not want to hear them. I longed for the days of "old" when reading, writing and arithmetic was the focus. The Training manual for Goals 2000 states the following.

"They, the American community, may not yet recognize that there is no "going back to basics" in Education."[1]

Mr. Gotcher explains that the new age ethic for life long learning is transformation. It deals with how people think rather than how much people know.

> "The dialectic is a way of thinking used by "intellectuals" to evaluate both personal and social "felt" needs. The first consideration is how people relate to each other. It is not on "what" we think about when we think about others (monodimensional thinking), but on "how" you think about others (multidimensional thinking). This transformational thinking includes not just ways we think about friends, family, everyday events, community, established ideas etc., but must include strangers, enemies, foreigners, innovative ideas, daring behavior and new or different ways of doing things. The so-called experts in dialectic thinking must collect this information from you in order to predict or estimate the "best" ways they can "help" you resolve your personal-social relationship needs."[2]

Once the group or facilitator knows your need or anxieties, which we all have, the facilitator will then bring you back to the authority conflict that supposedly caused it.   A contrary idea or belief is introduced. Your position, the thesis, is then discussed in the group with the antithesis, opposite view. The praxis is the process of discussion, which usually introduces ideas to cause further confusion. We talked of paradox introduction in *Stage 3* of *mind control* to keep the individual in confusion. The facilitator is very important through all of this for they can control the mood of the room by manipulating emotion and relationship importance to sway people into transition. Once the individual comes out of his moral absolutes, he is then capable of being led into compromise and transformation. With each new compromise, comes more conflict and thus the process starts all over again.

The Dialectic and Praxis is the process whereby the Marxist theory of Hegelian Marxism is introduced to change a society. Hegelian is a process of evolutionary thought. It is the basis for helping people to reach consensus or compromise on subject matter that they disagree on. The Dialectic is now in governments, businesses, churches and in schools deceiving all who believe its premise. The program comes equipped with a trained change agent, the facilitator, who successfully guides you through transition from tradition thinking to new beliefs. It is a deceptive method carefully plotted to rid our country of authority "rules" and traditional "values." It manipulates the person's chaos through emotions and cognitive dissonance to changed ideas supported by group acceptance and love.

The new compromise has erased an element of authority in one's life that is connected with right and wrong. You become the ultimate determiner of your life and what is good for you. It is based on what you feel and not on what you know is the truth. The dangers in supporting such humanist philosophy are seen in a recent case of cannibalism in Germany. A man was on trial for eating another man alive. The female judge said the murderer did not mean it maliciously, but was only living out his fantasy. She gave him a light sentence. Who determines the truth when there is no longer a higher authority? If it is to be another man then we see what can happen with this philosophy.

This type of thinking was not prevalent in the early 20th century. It began to surface in the 1930's, when praxis (the process) became part of an intellectual circle of men including some who were discussed in earlier chapters. Societal changes began to take place. These changes, as I learned, became evident in universities, government, churches, small businesses, corporations, private and public schools and even in our family unit. The dialectic is a way of thinking and behaving dependent on compromise, which then produces tolerance toward ambiguity. It seeks to overcome differences by the agreement through compromise. The solution does not have to be the truth, only that it is acceptable as a solution that should be tried. Thus there is justification even in a "lie." [3] It certainly explains why so many people are willing to accept lies without a second thought about the act.

Mr. Gotcher's presentation was rich in knowledge of men such as George Lukasc, Karl Korsch and Antonio Gramsci who were famous transformational men that applied Hegel's dialectic to Marxism. Gramsci called this reactivated Marxism, "The Philosophy of Praxis." Instead of focusing on one position such as Marxism or a dual position such as Marxism vs. Capitalism, it would focus upon process. Gramsci spent the last part of his life in prison and wrote 21 notebooks on the process. After his death these books were found in Moscow and are now the foundation for most societal change. This change is referred to as the "Paradigm Shift" a change in "how people think, feel, behave and interpret the world" they live in. The transformation Marxists use environmental control, language, face-to-face encounters and informal situations to change people.[4]

Throughout Dean's presentation, I applied the knowledge to my findings on the SEED Program. The language such as "change agents," "restructuring" and "paradigm shift" are particular to the SEED Program. All programs in the Dialectic encourage individuals to give up their identity for the collective whole. The group assurance of love and acceptance is then given the person. Man's desire for acceptance takes precedence over tradition but the compromise only causes chaos, which brings more chaos each time he compromises. As mentioned above the process is ongoing continuing to repeat itself. L.J. Lebret describes this as "evolution through tension" in "Marxism as Humanism."[5] The Dialectic process thrives on small interactive groups; they provide the environment for change. Mr. Gotcher explained the breakdown of the Dialectic and Praxis.

1. Dialectic: Using dialogue as a means to resolve conflicting positions.
2. Praxis: To practice the experience of speculating, conjecturing, and theorizing.
3. Diaprax: The dialectic driving for unity through the "controlled" use of cognitive dissonance, within the environment of social praxis. [6]

"**The dialectic** is the merging of opposites. Praxis is the experience, practice or habit of, in this case (diaprax), the merging of opposites and the compromising of each original position. For the dialectic to function there must be at least two or more opposing positions on an issue. Each position is called a thesis. The condition of differing or opposite positions is known as antithesis. For the dialectic to arrive at its final stage of synthesis some condition

176

must be established which encourages or allows the differing theses to put aside their differences long enough to merge on one or more issues. Thus, each thesis must compromise part of his original position for the sake of relationship. Synthesis must therefore include this "rational" experience of justification. Cognitive dissonance is the condition produced when one must be willing to put aside important parts of his original position. Diaprax requires both opposing positions to build relationship or partnership as part of their resolution of a need, a need both positions have in common. This requires both positions to justify or rationalize the compromising of their original position. Thus praxising the dialectic eventually changes a person's paradigm or his way of thinking.[7]

It takes a long time to understand the realities of this process and the overwhelming impact on our society. Dean Gotcher's paper called "The Dialectic & Praxis: Diaprax And The End Of The Ages" is valuable information, along with my other readings. His introduction includes an honest appraisal of the difficulties he and his family encountered during research and delivery of this material to people such as myself. He read over 600 books and spent five years in his research. His dedication is remarkable and I thank him and his family. Mr. Gotcher's presentation proceeded with the following examples he calls "global village." It helps clarify how the process works in the different stages of its development. There are three sub-phases under each main category.

I. <u>Thesis Interrogation</u>

1. Stating your position - An absolute, established fact or position to the compromising-feelings.
2. Defining the meaning of your position without offending anyone. This is the cognitive dissonance; it causes the confusion and mental upset. Dean calls it micro-terrorism.

3. The self-realization that we will never be able to properly defend our position and that we are not the cause of it.

II. Antithesis or Climate or Environment Control
(Relational Building)

1. (Negation of Negation) is saying no to restraining command by Authority. This is rejection of the "Is" and "absolute."
2. Conflict or chaos where obverse values are experienced. The facilitator helps in this area.
3. Mediation or Conflict-resolution training. All are willing to seek common ground for the good of the whole. The fear of rejection is so great one cannot refuse to participate.

III. Synthesis-Life Long Learning

1. Determination is to always live in the process and to propagate it where it is not used.
2. Necessitation is always to be aware of another and to expose their lack of self-determination. One helps them to think for themselves.
3. Causation is always helping someone to accept compromise as a way of life in a "rapidly changing world." [8]

It is complex, but when broken down makes sense. The environment is important. SEED, behind "closed" doors, gives comfort necessary to put aside "authority" of rules, standards, parents, church, government and even God. The security of environment gives the individual the ability to confide in members within the group. The authority must be "absent" for the process to work. This

178

is why I am not allowed to visit SEED, behind "closed" doors. I represent an authority figure. Also the leader of the group (a facilitator) must not teach, only assist.

The environment must be dialectic if everyone is to experience group life (communism) and develop group-think (socialism). The facilitator questions standards set by authority, and it works best if the leader is also questioning the standards. The learner is then indoctrinated with new absolutes and previous beliefs are replaced. The dialectic facilitation is the method of teaching used for this process.[9]

The facilitator takes control and teaches, without participants knowing it has occurred. He stays hidden in the process. The facilitator is able to elicit feelings; therefore, he has power to shape each person's position in the group. No matter the position we take, the facilitator will influence it. Our position usually will change once we are out of the absolute. This is why we do not debate our "is" or "absolutes." This type of teaching is very dangerous and can introduce philosophies contrary to parent and church teaching without the student's awareness.

In our schools today, new age teachers introduce conflict into the classroom such as homosexuality, occult practice, euthanasia, suicide and religious views contrary to most student's beliefs. It causes shock to the students thus producing confusion. The student groups dialogue, which then weakens the traditional beliefs. The teachers are trying to broaden the horizons of thought, for according to Marc Tucker, the mastermind behind school to work programs, "the objective will not be met unless there is a change in the prevailing culture of attitudes, values, norms and accepted ways of doing things." [10]

We are now using what the USSR, China and other Communist Countries used to *brainwash* their children. Each day children would confess their thoughts and feelings to their group. The facilitator would guide the children through a pre-determined consensus. Opinions and ideas, thesis and antithesis were mixed together into an evolving higher truth. The students were trained and *mind washed* into abandoning their prior beliefs for the Soviet understanding of issues. The individual never learned to think for themselves, but for the collective whole through group work. This education system was brought into our country in 1985 when we signed the U.S-U.S.S.R. Education Exchange Agreement. It put our technology in their hands and we received the education of psychosocial strategies that was used to indoctrinate their children. The National International Education system now requires students to follow these guidelines.[11]

1. be open to new ideas.
2. share personal feelings.
3. set aside home-taught values that might offend the group.
4. compromise in order to seek common ground and please the group.
5. respect all opinions, no matter how contrary to God's guidelines.
6. never argue or violate someone's comfort zone.[12]

In Iowa, it is reported that students learn through integration of subject material, such as ecology, economics and science, which is then discussed in multicultural context. The context is then integrated into the Native American Cultures and they role play the tribal life and religion of the imaginary shamons.[13] They then discuss this experience with the facilitator-teacher who guides them through their feelings. This process is being taught to our teachers in such programs as SEED, where role-playing is important. They return to the classroom well prepared to follow through with Peggy McIntosh's program of indoctrination. The little ones so innocent of the content are unknowingly led into the secular humanist teacher's hands. "Group learn" is everywhere with the whole "group think" being more important than the individual and our American way of life. Marxism is doing its job transforming our citizen's way of life from absolute truths to humanistic ideologies that will lead to destruction of our Nation.

Mr. Gotcher's presentation brought *mind control* into total understanding of what I knew to be true. Dean's teachings magnified the reality of how "change agents" such as "group *cause*," "language," "studies," "legislation" and " narrow interest programs" are accomplishing their goals. The Dialectic and Praxis is the glue that holds the web of transformation together as it stretches throughout our world. People are unaware of their own *brainwashing* for most are in (*Stage 4*) of the process and totally transformed. I flashed on the Board meeting when Teri and I were so frowned upon and it makes sense, for everyone was in the "feeling" territory of heart and had already compromised. It didn't matter if we told the truth for they saw it as a "lie," but they can accept their "lies" as long as they benefit their *cause*. Therefore it was perfectly acceptable to shun us and rebuke our character through any means necessary to save their identity and belief. We were deemed as not understanding, hateful and lacking appropriate knowledge of SEED.

Dean's message lasted three hours. In order to grasp the knowledge, strict attention was paid to his presentation. I was exhausted and eager to relax. Dean and Karen returned home with us and following a brief relaxation period, we exchanged more ideas about the praxis. When everyone retired for the evening, I thanked God for the gift given to me this evening for I would not waste it. During my months of research I was continually plagued with writing a book, but it remained a dream. Finally, after repeated suggestions by my husband to write my book and get started, I took my dream seriously. I wanted to make it real and I knew that tonight made it possible. No longer do I have to ask "How did this happen?" I know the process and why our country has changed. My book will share it with others. I sat in my comfortable blue chair remembering when I began and before I knew it, the next day arrived. I was waving good-bye to Dean and Karen thinking about my next adventure, writing a book for the first time.

28

PURPOSE DRIVEN INSTITUTIONAL CHANGE

Dean Gotcher's material was very informative. I wanted to understand everything about this process. My reading branched out to other authorities in the Diaprax. I was fascinated when I began to read about the "centering" process that is core to the dialectic process. The "centering" and "wholism" of the "new age" movement is a priority in many religious sects, not stopping at eastern mysticism, but continuing into demonic territory whereby individuals seek demons advice. [1] I paused thinking about the occult and Nazi Germany. Influential members of the party were involved with the demonic, as discussed in my chapter Evil Deception. Today we find influential leaders that lean toward New Age philosophy. Some of these people are listed below:

1. Ervin Lazio is associated with business and global communities and is also an important member of the UN. He is author of the book *Choice Evolution or Extinction*, and Director of the United Nations Institute for Training and Research. His organization studies paranormal activity. He discusses in his book *Choice* religious paradigms and is considered to be a change agent in "Systems Theory."

2. Shirley McCune is involved with education policy and promotes "Outcome Based Education." She co-authored a book, *The Light Will Set You Free*, with Dr. Norma Milanovich, a well-known spiritual channeler who is a consultant for large

182

      organizations. The book documents Miss
      McCune's demonic activities.

3. Peter Senge, who authors *The Fifth Dimension,* is a
      guru in the current movement of "corporate
      change" and is involved in the "new age"
      movement. His book encourages group dynamics.
      He believes in a new economic age where
      collective aspirations are set free.

4. Rick Warren, who wrote *The Purpose Driven
      Church,* includes the dialectic change processes
      used by businesses and schools.[2]

     These are but a few of noted authorities involved in New Age
ideology. I was amazed when I saw Rick Warren's name connected to
the Dialectic. Fortunately I never read beyond Chapter 4 in *The
Purpose Driven Life* by Rick Warren. Something kept pulling me
away from the book and now I understand why for it is human driven
and not God given content that permeates its program. Few realize its
ability to change God's law to human consensus through compromise
of His word. Dr. Schuller (Crystal Cathedral), Rev. Bill Hybels
(Willowcreek Community Church) and Rick Warren (Saddleback
Valley Community) promote purpose driven change in the church.
When they began their churches, they based them on community
needs (God never bent to the will of the unbeliever, but wanted His
disciples to prepare believers for ministry).[3] Purpose driven churches
focus on increasing the number of members. Next the church is set
up with ways to allure people to them such as drive-up windows or
preferred parking for newcomers. Newly built churches are free of
religious décor in order not to offend anyone who may be a potential
member, for they usually will decide within 8 minutes of visiting a
church if they want to belong.[4] Pastors are encouraged to preach to
the needs of the people, for Rick Warren says that " the pulpit is the
ultimate tool for church growth."[5] The message is usually watered
down with sin and judgment left out entirely. Indeed, scriptural
passages contain the positive message, but eliminate God's all
powerful statements that those who sin will be punished unless they
seek His way.[6] Once the individual decides to be a member, they must
sign a covenant saying they will obey the church and its authority. It

does not allow them to gossip or evaluate leadership in light of Biblical Scripture, but God clearly stated we are not to sign covenants and are to question non-biblical standards. Regardless of this, they must sign and are then profiled for their talents to be used within the church, even though God made it clear our weaknesses are supposed to lead us to our strengths. These strengths, however, are used for social ministries that keep people connected to the church. It is not God, but the ministry that becomes the bonding glue. Small group interaction is required of the new member and each group has their own facilitator. [7] This is where the people confess their sins, confusion, and discontentment and are held accountable. The group eventually takes on significance above God for participants fear rejection by their fellow man more than God if they break a law. It is within the small group that compromise takes place.

I will use the concepts of Dialectic to explain how individuals can be swayed in biblical beliefs by this program. If an individual comes to group with concern that someone in the church is homosexual and has no desire to change, then it would be discussed. The (traditional) ideas would be presented as number 1. Then the (dialectic) would begin and lots of discussion would ensue about the love of Jesus and what it really means. This causes confusion and thoughts of change. This is number 2, which is the transition period, for already the group has come out of the absolutes of the biblical truth. Eventually through dialoging, the group decides it is better to be accepting of the person for this is what Jesus would do and perhaps the person may change in the future. They have now compromised and are in (transformation). Lastly they will evangelize about this new thought on love and acceptance. It becomes (consensus) that it is okay to have diversity in the church and they will defend it to the end.

Here in lies the downfall of our churches as we knew them years ago, for our moral absolutes are breaking down from within, not from without. The change is happening because of purpose driven agendas of the Marxist Hegelian Dialectic, which seeks to promote humanism and not God. The paradigm shift takes place by God no longer being the top of the hierarchy, with pastors underneath and men under them, but the famous circle now exists with men inside it and God noticeably missing.[8] It is fascinating reading about the men

184

who support purpose driven change one of them being Peter Drucker. He is an incredibly educated man, author and business entrepreneur held in high esteem by the corporate world for his contributions to purpose driven transformation. It appears the men who support this change believe as Mr. Buford from The Leadership Network.
"The new paradigm is not centered in theology, but on structure, organization, and transition from an institutionally based church to a mission-driven church." [9]

The 21st Century corporate world continues the practice of purpose driven policies, in order to bring about a productive workforce. All workers must be a part of the whole or group effort, and management and worker programs insist on dedication to the group. Unfortunately in many cases the companies suffer financially with devastating results, for we see individuality peeking through and some workers are not able to adjust to the group process. Our children are being trained to work in a "group" spirit called "cooperative learning groups" rather than learning individual responsibility. It teaches dependence on the group, rather than on self, and the collective group is the *cause* promoting power. For the companies that have compromised the individual worker, these future workers who are students of compromise, will be welcomed. Total Quality Management (TQM) stresses the need for consensus process, but it is not possible to consensus and stay in your absolutes of truth. The "group" and "man" takes the place of our Absolutes and God, and this makes some people very uncomfortable. Large companies, however, ignore the individual in exchange for the desired outcome of diverse groups using the "Delphi Technique." Facilitators use group dynamics, peer pressure and sometimes unethical methods to accomplish desired outcomes.[10] Those who compromise and work well within the collective whole are rewarded, thus consensus becomes easier. Those who don't will feel the rejection. I see this with my friends who are battling unions within their workplace. Fellow members ostracize them if they disagree on contributing dues to abortion or homosexual programs. Groupthink, through Dialectic *mind control*, promotes the *cause* of collectivism.

Researching further, I found incredible evidence of Marxist influence within corporate arenas encouraging the Dialectic. It revealed Marxist Intellectuals responsible for supporting an organization that now reaches into some Fortune 500 Companies, Hollywood and the Media. It began when the Immigrants I reviewed earlier, who wanted to celebrate the "intellectual life of Germany," decided to commemorate the bicentenary of the birth of Goethe. This man's philosophy encouraged realities of "this world" and not the next, challenging foundations of morality and Christianity. The year was 1948; it took place in Aspen, Colorado. The men involved in the celebration believed in Marxist praxis for making the student not learned, but capable of learning. I thought of the increase in role playing in classrooms, indeed one transformational style Marxist immigrant, J.L. Moreno, was the father of "Role Playing" and some of Abraham Maslow's projects were done with him.[11] Role-playing is an example of making one capable of learning, but not being learned.

I read on about how the celebration organizers composed a wide circle of intellectuals who believed in a cultural order controlled by an academic elite. It appears they stood strong in belief of the Hegelian dialectic. The group, adopting the dialectic, became the Aspen Institute. One member Hutchins, the President of the University of Chicago organized a two-year Great Books seminar involving the dialectical form of subtle *brainwashing*. [12] The attendees responded well and as a result Hutchins began "The Fat Man Seminar" at the Aspen Institute. It eventually turned into The Aspen Institute for Humanistic Studies, where Supreme Court judges, congressman, senators, CEO's, and international political figures were welcomed into the executive seminars. Its educational mission was to make a single discipline of the physical and biological sciences and the humanities. The environment of the seminar offered only a few chosen books to read, but ample time to think, imagine, love and feel. Some of the class curriculum consisted of 5-6 speakers, with their lecture material given equal merit by the Institute.[13] The sessions were geared to illicit human emotional responses.

Between 1951 and1964 more than 400 corporations had participated in the Fat Man Seminar; more than 2000 alumni held positions of authority in government, education and business.[14] Money poured into the seminars from Coca Cola, Sears, General Mills, Rockefeller, Goodyear, etc. Supporters of "Change Management" such as theTavistock Institute have been involved with the Fat Man Seminars. It continued to grow through the years and by

1975 the Institute was receiving money from not only the above names, but from the following:

> City of Berlin, German Marshall Fund, the National Endowment for the Humanities, Carnegie Foundation, Henry Luce andrew Mellon, Rockefeller Brothers Fund, Rockefeller Family Fund, Russell Sage, Atlantic Richfield Foundation, Edna Mc Connell Clark, Commonwealth Fund, Danforth, Spencer Fund, North Star, Charles Kettering and Lilly Endowment, ABC, CBS, NBC, IBM, Thomas J. Watson-head of IBM, Sperry Rand of Chicago, Ford Motor, Smith Barney, Motorola, Container Corporation of America, Bristol Myers and Borg Warner.[15]

Through the 60's, the Institute targeted every imaginable group. In Hollywood they promoted humanistic views and teachings to writers and directors. Hollywood at that time still portrayed traditional values and beliefs. The Institute organized an Aspen Film Conference in 1963 in order to promote serious self-examination of the movie industry. It promoted Hollywood as being capable of producing movies that appealed to tradition, but challenged this standard by interjecting creative and contrary ideas, not determined by a set standard.[16] Radio Broadcasting became important as did TV and Cable. By the mid-seventies, The Aspen program had teamed up with MIT Communications Policy Research Program. It had drawn over 500 leaders in the communications field that had an interest in promoting humanistic ideas through their media outlets. [17]

The Institute's Environment and Quality of Life Program held summer workshops starting in June of 1962. These were geared toward high school teachers (it appears that an "environmental crisis" was created) in order to promote these yearly seminars. Teachers then returned home and became the community leaders that set up workshops at the local and state levels. Following these seminars there appeared to be a leap in interest in the "environmental issues." [18]

The Institute stretched its arms into our Government through their past 1969 President, Joseph Slater, who believed it was important "to create a network of institutions and people who can generate and transmit tremors that will ultimately 'change things' in an orderly way." [19] He indeed, did make a difference. He was responsible for establishing many departments within our government and within foreign countries such as Germany. He eventually joined the Ford Foundation in New York as Deputy Director of its program in International affairs. He encouraged joint bio-medical efforts with foreign countries. He was responsible for drawing up a five-year plan that specifically focused on "social change." The seminars were trans-national and trans-societal in nature, which also had profound humanistic implications. The "change and needs" became the focus of the Institute. [20]

> "...to the endless pursuit of freedom from outmoded dogma (Christian beliefs and values), freedom to go beyond convention, freedom of the imagination and the will, freedom from materialism, 'freedom also to be in conflict with oneself."[21]

Slater explained that the social, moral and aesthetic values of our culture must be formed by the roles of those involved with the Institute. Members such as William Benton, who co-founded UNESCO, United Nations Educational Scientific and Cultural Organization, contributed to this *cause*. He played a major role in economic and social development of the masses worldwide.[22]

The Executive Seminars helped in the work of social change. The Aspen Institute stretched into every area of our country, including women's groups, artist's villages and the University System. Far Eastern and Japanese seminars were begun and readings by Chinese, Indian and Japanese authors were routine in regular sessions.[23] Summer study groups were implemented to examine critical problems of humanistic concerns requiring solutions. Thought to Action Programs, were implemented with titles such as " Education for a Changing Society," "Science, Technology and Humanism," "Justice, Society and the Individual," and "Environment and the Quality of Life." [24] I knew these programs must have influenced our education system. I decided to research further Outcome Based Education.

It was IBM that was responsible for and conceived The Business Roundtable Participation Guide: A Primer for Business on Education. It contained the "agenda for educational change" written by Rand Corporation and providing the "blueprint" for the nation's Outcome Based Education "restructuring" movement.[25] Last year at our National Eagle Forum Conference the Maple River Education Coalition presented the facts about "Outcome Based Education." With three bills, the Federal Government took over Education. It took place under Clinton. The bills passed in 1994 and Clinton signed them into law. The bills were Goals 2000, the School to Work (STW), and the funding bill for most federal education programs HR6. These bills stole the power from local and state governments to determine the curriculum of their own schools. This is apparent in the ability of HR6 to dictate one organization called NGO, to be the sole determiner of Civic and Government education taught throughout our country. No committees were allowed to review the material *We the People: The Citizen And The Constitution.* It's the source of information for our children for all civics and government. The new program dictates that education should be civic centered rather than education centered, and all classes must restructure to include the new curriculum. This happened even though our tenth amendment states, education is reserved for "state and local" government. Tests are rewritten to adhere to the new Federal curriculum, thus other books being published must follow what is taught in the new Civics Book. [26]

The new civic books present themselves in a reader friendly manner with fun illustrations and easily read material. *We The People* is for middle schools and *We The People: The Citizen And The Constitution* is for high schools in our district. At first glance they appear to support our traditional government. Upon careful inspection and reading of other critiques, I found it the opposite. The word "idea" was used consistently rather than "truth" or "right." Repetition of "idea," meaning notion or thought, poorly represents our Constitution and Bill of Rights. It does not dignify its strength. This is the way our Foundational Principles are presented in the High School text.

"This unit provides an overview of some important philosophical *ideas* and historic events that influenced

the writing of our Constitution and the Bill of rights.
The first and second lessons in this unit introduce you
to some basic *ideas* of the natural rights philosophy
and theories of government. These *ideas* were of great
importance in the development of our government.
The remaining lessons in this unit examine in greater
detail the historical background of these ideas." [27]

Our Declaration of Independence does not talk of ideas, but
says of our principles, "self-evident," "truths" and "unalienable
rights." The principles are ideas, but they represent truth, that which
is actual and verified fact. Our principles of truth have kept our
country free for over 200 years, there is no other document that has
done this; it is actual and verifiable. It is solid, but not depicted this
way by the consistent use of "idea."

The next quote is on page 207 of the High School Civic Book.
I thought of my previous thoughts on Multiculturalism. I read Alan
Quist and Orlean Koehle's review with them having similar views on
this quote. After 200 years of success, the Bill of Rights is presented
in the following manner:

"As fundamental and lasting as its guarantees "have
been," the U.S. Bill of Rights is a document of the
eighteenth century, reflecting the issues and concerns
of the age in which it was written....Other national
guarantees of rights also reflect the cultures that
created them. Many of these cultures have values and
priorities different from our own. In many Asian
countries, for example, the rights of the individuals are
secondary to the interests of the whole community.
Islamic countries take their code of laws from the
teaching of the Koran, the book of sacred writings
accepted by Muslims as revelations to the prophet
Mohammad by God." [28]

It is presented as an archaic idea, of a past time. Alan Quist in
critiquing the Federal Curriculum says the "National Curriculum
Standards for Social Studies are emphatic in promoting the post-

modernist view that what passes for truth is really the social "constructs." [29] Multiculturalism dictates equal merit to all government systems changeable upon the culture climate. Multiculturalism is "anti foundational" to the principles of our country. The Civic Book presents multiculturalism concepts as true, but our concepts as "ideas." This concept is carried throughout OBE and is the shift that has taken place in traditional education and our new standards. We now look to the U.N.'s Declaration of Human Rights as worthy of any society[30]. This is contrary to our absolutes on which we were founded. We have "freedom" because our government was founded on Judeo-Christian Principles, which did not allow anyone or anything to dictate otherwise. It is an incredible system; unfortunately, many people still do not "get" it. When we take God out of our world and government, we open our land to every imaginable take over that will rob us of our freedom. There is one indisputable fact that has shown this to be true, proportionate increase in crime and moral decay since God is being removed from our country. David Barton in *America To Pray? or Not To Pray?* outlines clearly the national problems (child and sexual abuse, illegal drug abuse, increase in AIDS, violent crimes, increase in divorce and pregnancy rates, and voluntary abortions) that emerged after God was removed from the schools in the early 60's.[31] When people live with absolute truths, they live with internal values. They do not need external forces to control them. The more we eliminate our solid historic principles, the more we need external forces to keep us in line. This is why we continue to add more and more social programs to make the world a better place, but they do not work. Mark Matta, at Preserve Liberty, has information that explains more in depth the principles of the above[32]. He is a spirited man dedicated to bringing back these principles to preserve our freedoms guaranteed by them. He holds weekly classes that are geared to teaching people these principles and voting in God fearing leaders. Some of these principles are from the following verses in the Bible.

1. The Law of Nature is in Romans 2:14-16
2. That our Creator is the Author of life is seen in Genesis 2:7

3. God, not government, grants liberty is in Galatians 5:1
4. Pursuit of happiness is in Ecclesiastes 3:13
5. Second Amendment found in Luke 11:21 and Luke 22:35
6. Fourth Amendment comes from Deuteronomy 24: 10, 11
7. Eighth Amendment originates in Deuteronomy 15: 2-3
8. The constitutional form of government with three equal branches legislative, judicial and executive comes from Isaiah 33:22. [33]

I found it interesting that Bible passages are used in discussions of Capitol Punishment in the Civics Book, but not in reference to other rights and truths. Documented evidence, to numerous to expound upon, show the Founding Fathers' belief in God. *Original Intent* by David Barton is an informative book on this topic. The Fathers' intention was to institute Godly Principles in the Documents, thus indisputable. God is all-powerful, having ultimate authority over man. Our law system is based on a 1500-year history of law from the Bible and Exodus. The principles keep us free of evil but only if we adhere to them. We are in chaos because we have strayed from these truths.

The children need to learn the facts about all the amendments. Tony Nassif, an Author and lecturer, brought these facts to my attention. The 6th Amendment guarantees a person a speedy public trial with witnesses against and for him. Our unborn children are murdered for a capital crime they have not committed. The 8th Amendment is in place to protect a person from "cruel and unusual punishment." This Amendment is broken everyday by burning and tearing apart the bodies of our unborn. The 14th Amendment guarantees protection by due process. We clearly deny our unborn citizens rights of "equal protection of law" that includes the protection of life, liberty and pursuit of happiness.[34] The Civics Book does not mention the rights of the unborn. The 2nd Amendment is ignored. Our most precious freedom, to protect ourselves, is not discussed. The 9th Amendment, which states that individual rights not delegated to the

federal government by the Constitution are reserved or retained, by
the people, is briefly mentioned on page 211. In order to keep power
in the hands of the individual states and people, we have the Tenth
Amendment. It states that rights not delegated to the federal
government by the Constitution are retained by the states of the
people, respectively. The 10th Amendment is not discussed, nor
mentioned. The 1st Amendment however is covered on 16 pages.[35]
Free speech and assembly as well as the separation of church and
state will be discussed, I am sure, at length. The Civic Books weigh
heavily on critical thinking. Facts, however, do not appear relevant to
learning as stated on page X of the Introduction.

> "The primary purpose of this textbook is not to fill
> your head with a lot of facts about American history
> and government. Knowledge of the facts is important
> but only in so far as it deepens your understanding of
> the American constitutional system and its
> development.[36]

Since facts are not relevant, class discussions can easily be
used for Diaprax. Facilitators can manipulate our principles to meet
their agenda for change. Parents need to recognize the new standard
of learning. It is a disservice to our future citizens. In Outcome
Based Education, reading, writing and arithmetic are not important;
facts do not matter. Mathematics is not factual; 2+2 does not always
equal 4. Many answers are acceptable for what "we know" is truth.
Education focuses on smaller classroom communities that "train"
students for future specific jobs; these jobs are determined by the need
of the area. The student chooses a "career" pathway by 8th grade;
states are assigned career clusters. In Minnesota, it is Minerals and
Minnesota's students are then encouraged to go into mining. The
students are awarded a job certificate upon graduation, not a diploma.
This certificate is good in other Countries. It is not a new idea; other
countries have done it for years. I know Georgia and Minnesota's
citizens are battling this very system, and Virginia and Utah have said
"no" to federal funding so as to avoid the new curriculum. Jane
Lesko is a courageous Eagle Forum leader in Idaho,who is battling
revisionist, socialist, history curriculum textbooks in her state and the

Nation. A horrible abuse of education takes place in her school district, for some students tests are sent to Switzerland to be graded. We are moving backwards and joining socialist countries in forming our new Nation. We are preparing our young well with new education programs and the Marxist Dialectic.

I found Allen Quist's book *Fed Ed: The New Federal Curriculum and How It's Enforced* excellent reading.[37] The following is also useful in determining if OBE is used in a particular school. To recognize OBE, listen when your children talk about the following:

> using calculators to learn math
> incorrect spelling is okay
> getting someone else's grades
> grading system changes
> checking someone else's work
> no books come home
> whole language (guessing at words when "reading")
> role playing in class
> helping others with work
> teachers monitor
> class is a "family"
> re-taking test until it's passed
> can't talk about schoolwork
> multi-age grouping
> work groups, pairs or partners
> group answers must agree - right or wrong doesn't matter[38]

It is important to find Legislators who support your position against OBE. Senator Michele Bachmann from Minnesota is working to stop it in her state. The Maple River Coalition gives incredible presentations on the subject matter. Encouraging speaking engagements is a positive action. Michele Bachmann, Michael Chapman, Renee Doyle, Dr. Karen Effrem and Alan and Julie Quist are dedicated to this work. I thank them for their endless hours of research and fantastic presentation of their results.

The ability to implement a program, without people knowing, is a Hitlarian tactic. It is *mind control* and is taking hold in our country. It is the tactic of transformational Marxism, taking over a society in a democratic way without the people knowing where it is going or that it's even being userped.[39] Judy McLemore's well-documented account of the Aspen Institute was another defining moment in time. Her research and well-written information helped me to better understand how our country has changed through the last Century. Seeds planted at the Aspen Institute have flourished and grown into every avenue of our lives. I mourn a country that is no more, reminding myself to hang onto what is still good, pure and innocent. *Lord of the Rings*, my favorite movie series, is a story of the battle between good and evil. Throughout the movie, a recurring message is given in that one cannot go back to the way it was, once you see the results of evil. Our society will never go back to the way it was, we can only hope to save but a little of what we were.

29

SILENT DAY "2003"

Silent Day was in April. Writing my book sidetracked my attention to coming events, and I was thankful that I remembered this day. The event left a lasting impression from last year, in that it honors people leading unnatural lifestyles. It is dignified and respectful toward other people to keep our personal sexual behavior quiet, so why are we supporting a day that apologizes for us silencing them? It is yet another ploy victimizing homosexuals, but in reality they victimize the other students by disrupting their rights in the classroom. We believe it is proper to keep sexual issues out of schools making "Sex Free Schools" just as important as "Drug Free Schools." With limited time, I had to move fast and develop a plan of action.

First and foremost, I had to examine my motives and attitudes. Protecting our students was my priority, and I was positive we could formulate our goals and reach them. I began by learning the history of the day and how it has evolved through the years.

The Silent Day was founded in 1996 at the University of Virginia with 150 participating. By 2001, the Gay, Lesbian, Straight, Education, Network (GLSEN) had become its official organizational sponsor. They developed a Leadership team to give support to high schools nation-wide and joined forces with the United States Student Association (USSA) to support colleges and universities nation-wide. It is now in over 1900 middle schools, high schools, colleges and universities throughout our country. The modeling instructions they have on line are specific in content. They include information on how to persuade a school or principal to participate, and they have tactics to use for media coverage. It is clearly outlined how to have a successful day with the handout materials, signs worn around their neck and end of the day ceremonies on campus. It stresses using the day as a tool to promote further changes in the school. It even suggests that it is a "good" tactic to affect negative press coverage and discourage enrollment to private Universities that do not allow Silent Day. Teenagers reading the site are reminded that conventional ideas are misinformation, but GLSEN and USSA are the educated ones. The young are drawn into *Stage one of mind control* believing that by showing love and acceptance of this lifestyle, they will make the world a better place to live. Reading the material made me feel very uncomfortable. It was not right for all students to be submitted to this in the classroom and I knew this to be the truth. It is the American way to protect our students in the classroom! We began a series of steps that shaped the course of the next five weeks to rid the classroom of this content.

It was best to begin where it all began, with talk show host Eric Hogue and my memories of a year ago when Michael called me on his way to work. I called Eric and left him a message as to our desire to stop this behavior in the classroom. My next goal was to find others within or without our group who wanted to become "active" in this *cause*. I contacted our State Eagle Forum President, Orlean Koehle, for support in emailing and sending out information about this day to our State members and Chapters. Karen England from Capitol Resource Institute agreed to help. My Bible Study group offered to help with distribution of educational material about Silent Day among their group of friends. We contacted the schools to find out which ones were participating; last year two, and this year all six high schools in the Elk Grove area district were participating. It was not easy obtaining this information for the schools were reluctant to releasing any information about the day. We found a list on the Silent Day Website of participating schools, which gave us information as to some of the Sacramento High Schools involved. We, for sure, knew of two. Our next step was to contact two well-known lawyers Brad Dacus and Scott Lively to let them know our goals in regards to this day. Within a week the above had been done.

Eagle Forum began to write letters to newspapers and began to contact radio talk show hosts and TV news shows. I repeatedly emailed noted "celebrities" in the TV news, but to no avail. We did however have great responses from Eric Hogue and Joe Pursch, radio talk show hosts. They invited me on their shows to discuss the homosexual movement, the dangers of this lifestyle for our children and traditional family values. Other Eagle Forum members made calls alerting the public to the silent day agenda. It was educational for listeners, as well as for us, to be able to exchange ideas. We recommended parents signing an "opt out" form, which would require their children to be excused from the classrooms participating in this day. The schools are required to provide a location and alternative lesson plan for them. We recommended parents and concerned citizens call schools and write letters of protest to schools, school board members and newspapers.

People began to understand who we were and what we stood for; some gave us support and some despised us. This was apparent through emails, phone calls and nasty letters to the newspapers. It bewildered me to read letters written by women who proclaim to be Christian teachers but support this lifestyle. Some shared a common background with our family by having our children in their classroom or by having our children involved with sports together while growing up. It was amazing to see the people who preached "tolerance" being so intolerant of us. They were "intolerant" in a very critical way; their letters were abusive to Eagle Forum and us. The more they lashed out at us the more I knew we were making a difference.

Our support came in various ways. One friend, Linda, brought me the name of the Superintendent of Assembly of God churches, Reverend Cole. She knew he would be interested and she was right. I thank her for her concern. Within a few days of contacting him, he composed a letter to his entire Northern California Association asking their support. He gave me the name of another Pastor, Dwight Burchett, President of the National Evangelical Association. He emailed requests of support for us. Though I always hope for a good Christian response, there was little and the majority was silent. At least the messages of these brave men reached the people and informed them of the day. People usually need to hear something 7 times before they decide to act on it. Perhaps by next year they will be ready.

We have a branch of Eagle Forum known as Operation Noble Eagle (ONE) begun by Sharon Hughes. It provides current information to churches on civic matters such as voting guides, abortion and education issues. Marguerite Hall, Co-Director of Eagle Forum and Director for ONE, has great patience in her quest for acquiring new churches to join in. She has consistently encouraged churches to participate and trains other ladies in the principles of ONE. I applaud the churches that are beginning to accept responsibilities toward the promotion of Judeo-Christian principles in government. Marguerite remains positive in her efforts and was able to educate people as to the specifics of Silent Day in the schools. We are thankful for not only her dedication, but also the example she sets for others to follow.

Our next goal was to reach out to parents and students. Scott Lively suggested passing out flyers and information at the schools. It included a newspaper about the homosexual movement and a flyer indicating that real Americans do not "push" homosexuality on children. It gave dates and times for Scott Lively's presentation of the "Natural Family verses Homosexuality." Our plan was to distribute handouts after school at two of the high schools and we scheduled four ladies for each school.

We contacted the principals once more, hopeful of them canceling the day. We were met with heavy resistance and it was clear the day would go on. I assured the Principal of Elk Grove High School we would be present on Silent Day to protest it. We were strong in our position.

We began passing out material at Elk Grove High Schools approximately 14 days before the silent day; some guards on duty questioned our appearance and our actions. I was happy for their concern for the students; we readily answered any questions. Our interactions were positive and we were able to continue with our information pass outs with students being receptive to the material. Our daughter Michelle came from U.C. Davis and helped pass out material. Having a young student with us encouraged other students to accept the information. One elderly lady, Cay Chandler, helped us also. She is close to 80. She appealed to the parents and was an asset to our *cause*. Most parents were accepting of the flyers and information. Our first day was successful.

The second day we went to Laguna Creek High School. It was a beautiful day and everyone was receptive to the brochures. We split into one group with two ladies; the other two ladies went out individually. Angry aggressive students suddenly surrounded my friend Chris Warmby and me. At first the number 25-30 seemed like a 100. They were aggressively shouting and screaming how horrible we were and it didn't stop. When we passed out literature, they would push our arm away and hand out a yellow sheet with their Homosexual Bill of Rights on it. They walked within five inches of our bodies saying horrible things like, "I never used to believe in killing people, but now I understand why people do it." They were also saying "we are going to go home and sodomize, sodomize all night long." They would ask us ridiculous questions, but were not interested in our answers. They were so close that I feared for our lives. I kept wondering why no teachers or guards came to our rescue. They must have been outside; I wondered if they were ignoring us and had been warned of us coming, or were they just not outside and ignoring their responsibilities to their post? I could feel the student's hot breath down my back and I thought how easy for one of them to draw a knife or just punch us. They were ugly with rage. We just kept walking back and forth down the block and across the street. Chris and I decided to seek help in the office, but in asking other students its location, the jeering students would not let them answer us. We controlled our fear the best we could, knowing something had to stop this abusiveness. Eventually one of our friends joined us, and Martha Peralta could not believe what happened, for she too had experienced harassment. The aggressive intimidation began to lighten up, but they would not stop following us. At one point the female homosexual leader came out and tried to stop the others, but they would not listen to her. With time they all soon disappeared; with a few lingering in the shadows watching us walk to our cars. We were very upset and shaking physically, but eventually made it back to our friend's house. Thelma LaMotte, our other friend, told us her tale of how they would not allow her access to her car. They surrounded her also and ridiculed her.

No one should be treated in this manner when handing out information. It was an outright display of injustice toward our American way of life and our 1st Amendment Rights. I will forever remember the rage of this group. I remembered Scott's tales of harassment by homosexual activists. I also will remember, forever, what they did to my friends, good honest women who have given their life to the values of our land. The intimidation did not stop them for they continue to soar high as Eagles to be respected for their courage on this day.

The students passed out a Homosexual Bill of Rights saying that the "teachers and staff at Laguna Creek High School believe society's stigmatization of Lesbian, Gay, Bisexual and Transgender individuals is unjust." It proceeds to say what they think their responsibilities are as teachers and staff. Some of these are listed below.

1. Information about sexual orientation in books and materials.
2. Historical information in all books about art, literature, science, sports, and history.
3. Positive role models, in person and curriculum, accurate information about themselves, free of negative judgment, delivered by trained adults, who do not only inform but also affirm.
4. No verbal or physical harassment. (I guess this only goes one way)
5. Be a part of all support programs that talk about problems of adolescence.
6. The right to hate free heritage. (But they can hate)
7. Advocacy by staff and faculty.
8. Inclusiveness in programs, curriculum, activities and teacher training that address issues of diversity. (Really means homosexuality)

The other side of the yellow sheet is "The Truth about Sexual Orientation." Some of the supposed truths are listed below.

1. The majority of child molesters are heterosexual men. (The majority of men are heterosexual)

201

2. Homosexuality is not a type of mental illness and cannot be cured by psychotherapy. (Untrue. See Chapter 19)

3. No one knows what causes sexual orientation. The claim is that some as young as 6, know they are attracted to the same sex. (Many children have these fantasies. They are not homosexual. See Chapter 19)

4. Therapy has failed to change sexual orientation in cases attempted. (Untrue. See Chapter 19)

5. Some people might like to think that a normal adult lifestyle is a heterosexual marriage with children but... (But what? It is.)

The other statements were worded in such a way as to give positive reinforcement to the lifestyle. The information was on bright yellow sheets. Many students and parents received this flyer. That evening I emailed the principal of Laguna Creek High School about what happened. I questioned this document and if the school supported these facts and the responsibilities of teachers and staff. I also requested a school assembly addressing the inappropriate behavior of the Homosexual Club members. Many students saw this behavior and we knew it was important for them to understand this behavior was not appropriate. The principal emailed me the next day and said he felt badly about the behavior and he would check it out. The student's behavior was never addressed. They denied everything. The yellow sheet was never addressed and if it was, we were never informed. We wrote letters to the school board and still nothing was done. My school board friend told me that probably the school did not support the Bill of Rights, but was not aware of any disciplinary action toward the students who produced it. Supposedly school officials were outside during the encounter; they denied that anything happened to us. They insisted that everything seemed normal and all interactions were calm and respectful. The school officials wrote a letter, published on the front page of our newspaper, saying that Eagle Forum had been mistaken in what had happened. The language of the article led people to believe that we lied and actually made up this story. It was our word against their word; we had no camera or tape recorder. My husband advised us to bring one. I used denial in believing this could happen and chose not to bring one.

I was saddened on the day I read the article on the front page of my hometown newspaper. I have lived in this town since its population was 7,000 and now it's over 100,000. It was a town of principle, but now deception and lies are corroding it. How far had our school officials compromised! I had a chill, for I knew anything was possible, and I felt the tears in my eyes for our children. How could we expect our children to act differently when their leaders have turned their backs?

Other events took place restoring my faith in humanity. Eagle Forum and Capitol Resource sponsored a Lobby Day. Our speakers alleviated any doubts that others are battling issues of homosexuality in the schools. We lobbied in the afternoon and met some wonderful Senators. It was during this Lobby Day that I met Mary. She is from Vacaville and her enthusiasm is contagious. She returned to her town and discovered that Silent Day was taking place in a high school without the principal's authority. She was able to get it stopped. Mary was open to Eagle Forum and she is now an active member leading others in Vacaville toward a "neutral" agenda in the schools. Lynn St. Denis, who I met through Scott Lively, was at Lobby Day. She became a member of Eagle Forum and called not only her schools in Rocklin, but also radio talk shows to help stop Silent day. She now teaches a course through Abiding Truth Ministries on "The Natural Family" to middle and high school students who not only enjoy it, but also encourage it to fellow students. The Lobby Day was beneficial. It elevated our spirits in preparation of our unforeseen event involving Scott Lively.

Our Eagle Forum meeting took place on April 3, six days before Silent Day. Scott Lively would talk on The Natural Family v Homosexuality. The room was filling with people when it happened. One of the High School's Principals and at least five other high ranked position leaders came through the door; the expressions were tense. I was tense. Scott's talk is intense. We had not told them our location, but it was Mary McIntyre, the Newspaper reporter who revealed the location when they called the paper to find information. I was thankful for her input, but unsure as to the outcome. After a brief prayer and introduction, I gave a history of our organization and what our goals were in reference to Silent Day. I proceeded to introduce Scott Lively, but before he had a chance to begin the Chief of Staff of the School District rushed forward. He gave the Districts view on the day and miscellaneous bits of information as to their decision to hold it. Scott thanked him for his "commercial" and continued with his presentation. Scott was magnificent, the best I have ever seen him. All of the officials left with their heads a little lower than upon entrance. Scott was powerful in bringing out what a man knows already; homosexuality is not the natural order of life. Indeed, the only school district official that ever apologized to us about being harassed took place that night by the Principal of Elk Grove High School. I am thankful and appreciative of his acknowledgement. Though I saw a change of attitude that evening in the school officials, I knew it was short lived, for they were already in *Stage 4* of *mind control* and they would not stop the Day of Silence. Mary McIntyre, our wonderful reporter, saw the importance of this story. Her article in the *Elk Grove Citizen* was good, as usual. It was a memorable evening, the way it was meant to be.

A few days before Silent day Scott Lively and Brad Dacus wrote letters to all the high schools in the Sacramento and Elk Grove School District and to the Superintendent of Schools. It was clearly written that if Silent Day proceeded in the classroom, it might lead to litigation. The letters were strong and made their point; the youth could not be held captive in a classroom for a narrow interest agenda.

All had been done. The night before Silent Day, the District sponsored Wayne Jacobsen, a speaker on "Compromise" for parents, students and interested citizens. He talked for two hours on compromise and how important it is to come to some middle of the road opinion on issues such as Silent Day. At the end of the night, the Superintendent of Schools spoke to the group. He apologized to the homosexual students in the audience for this last minute decision. He could not allow the Day of Silence in the classroom. It could happen before, after and during lunch hour, but not in the classroom. I knew it to be the right one. I was happy, but sad as I saw this man continuing to patronize these students so unaware of the dangers of this lifestyle. What are even sadder are the parents who support the lifestyle because their child is involved. I thought of my Father-in-law who died years ago. I thought of my Dad. This generation encouraged men of solid principles; they would never support a child in this lifestyle. I know there are others like them. Why did we have to resort to other means, such as litigation, to accomplish this goal rather than on our men of virtue? In the end, the certainty of litigation is what probably influenced the decision. I looked around the room; some men were in suits, some in work clothes. It did not matter for all barriers had come down. The men lost my respect that evening and I felt sorrow for them. They compromised their position as fathers, grandfathers, educators and protectors of children. I applaud the men in our country who stand in principle and are not afraid of saying it, for as we have seen they are battling many by doing so. The Superintendent announced they would be forming a committee, and this group would work on guidelines for school clubs. The purpose was to avoid the confusion of next years Silent Day.

We celebrated our victory! It was also a victory for the other side, but they did not see it this way. Having the silent day outside of the classroom was not enough for them and I realized why. The enclosed atmosphere of the room held importance in carrying out the stages of *mind control*. The day will not be as successful for they will not have the captive audience on which to use their tactic of silence. Their annoyance was apparent through the continuing of letters to the newspaper and general attitudes of anger toward our group. We continued in our joy for we had saved the children, at least in the classroom (on that one day).

The most "fun" was our "Teach Out" Day. Eric Hogue and Karen England planned to do this at the Secretary of State Office building in downtown Sacramento. It took place on Silent Day. It was a celebration. Children and parents in the Sacramento area were welcome to come. They learned about our government and constitution, in place of silent day. Tim Le Fever, Brad Dacus, Scott Lively, Karen England, and I spoke on related topics. Assemblymen Tim Leslie and Ray Haynes spoke about how to handle legislative discouragement in government when their conservative proposals are consistently shot down. Their uplifting spirits elevated ours and students and adults learned that the principles of our country must be worked for, even if at times we are defeated. I was proud to be an American on this day!

In May, Teri, who wrote many letters protesting Silent Day, and I were invited to be on a planning committee for school clubs in the District. We were happy to be a part of the planning committee. What happened on Silent Day was a thorn in the activist's side. Our name continued to be mentioned throughout the country in GLSEN articles, even in news coverage in England in regards to Silent Day. As for the price paid, some of us lost friendships. A few acquaintances, we knew for years, had family members that either were homosexual or supported homosexual lifestyles. This automatically made us the bad guys. There are, however, stories of our activities giving people hope. The strengths of Eagle Forum are encouraging the public to open their eyes to the District's liberal homosexual policies thus beginning to expose the "real agenda." In May, I was shocked into the reality of the behind "closed" door *mind control* when I finally met a male teacher who was a traditional thinker before going through the SEED program. In his words, "I was absolutely transformed and realized that homosexuals are people like you and me. SEED was the best thing for me and I back Silent Day all the way." He was in *Stage 4* and there was no changing his mind. I was elated that we pursued freedom for all students and parents that believe sex does not belong in the classroom.

Dedicated people worked together to rid the classroom of objectionable subject matter. Grammar, middle and high school's responsibility is to protect the students with a primary goal of teaching Math, Reading, History and other subject matter, not sexual content. The tolerance and diversity programs are taking time, money and the very soul of our American spirit! I know that we can take back our schools. We just have to elevate "our" *cause* and move forward in belief of traditional values. If we speak together in numbers then parents and citizens across America can reclaim our schools.

The school year is ending and with summer almost here, the SEED Program weighs heavily on my mind. The trainings this summer will introduce more adults and students to concepts behind "closed" doors, entwining them in a web of deception, under the guise of love. My comfortable blue chair will only be a dream; this summer will see me in a new chair for my husband bought me a high backed, adjustable burgundy chair. It sits appropriately in front of the computer, waiting for me daily. It offers support of my body giving me the endurance needed to finish my book. I find words flowing too quickly for my fingers to keep up, but my enthusiastic nature accepts the drawbacks being happy I have the ability to type on my friendly computer. My life has taken on new force and I will not stop in my pursuit of revealing programs that are deceptive and destructive to our young. The loss of youth's innocence is not to be taken lightly. My heart saddened, I elevate my spirit through writing in hope of recovering our lost little ones abandoned by our world of indifference!

30

SEED SURPRISE

Surprises can be happy or sad, dependent on the nature of the *cause*. A mini-miracle, for me, is not of supernatural *cause* but of extraordinary circumstance. It was a mini-miracle one early morning when I listened to my voice mail. I can only relate to the voice by "he/she" or the "voice." He/she wants to remain anonymous. Whatever the reason, I will honor it. The individual will remain a hero in my eyes. The voice was sincere in delivery, offering information about the SEED program. I returned the call with eagerness. Our conversation was meaningful; the words flowed naturally as it does when two people are honestly pursuing the truth. It was an uplifting experience, the best since beginning my adventure. I held my emotions intact. Clarity was important; this moment may never come again. He/she was courageous in revealing information carried a long time. The burden needed release. I was receptive to the words being thankful for the honesty I felt. I wrote everything down so to be accurate.

The SEED program, in the Elk Grove District, was initiated at least 4-5 years ago. He/she followed articles and letters in the newspaper and called me to lend credence and support to our exposure of the SEED program. The order seemed important and my fingers worked furiously to keep up with the Expose'. It appears that it evolved into the district by a "few" people who had the power to make it happen. It had been rejected once, as it was thought not to have proper classroom specifications to lend itself as an accredited class for teachers. The decision was fought and it was allowed into the District. It was kept under very close supervision by a very "few" people in authority. Workers were uncomfortable with it, but could do nothing; jobs and reputations were on the line. During these years, it is reported that the rules pertaining to all workshops were bent to meet the demands of the SEED Program. Some of the concerns were as follows:

1. Signing in procedures necessary for attendance were lax and often done on recollections.
2. Repeat of SEED Program for repeat credits happened often.
3. Standard policy for District was "no" repeats of classes in order to get salary credit; it was not followed with SEED.
4. SEED was not district-approved curriculum and rules relating to other district workshops were ignored for SEED workshops.
5. Co-coordinators felt allegiance to the SEED Director's issues and not the districts issues.
6. Time spent in SEED workshops apparently took time from curriculum activities necessary to the traditional model of education.
7. Personnel working with this subject matter had to go along with this program even though they were uncomfortable bending the rules.
8. There is no clear content to the SEED Program. Generalities of the philosophy of Seed were interpreted by this person and included the following:
   a. Journey into the individual's life.
   b. Understand your background to change your ideas.
   c. Acceptance of others based on reevaluation of your own values.
   d. Trained facilitators to guide group.
   e. Understand the who and why of others and be the windows and mirrors of each other's soul.
9. No one can visit the class. It is behind "closed" doors.
10. Teachers using SEED philosophy and circle in the

classroom, as reported by the students, are replacing traditional subject matter pertinent to the class. Students reported activity to this person and their parents.

11. Money spent is not all grant money. The concern for the workers was how much was spent and where was it coming from? Was it at the expense of other educational programs?

The voice struggled with words for it is difficult subject matter. I continued to listen attentively as this individual poured out how uncomfortable it was for him/her and others to work with this program in knowing it was dangerous to participants. I never forgot the voice's words, "there was evil and deception that seemed to permeate the program." Personal information is revealed behind "closed" doors and the person reporting said they heard of one teacher who was ostracized because of remarks they made offending another teacher during one of the "closed" door sessions. The district leaves itself wide open to litigation under these circumstances.

In fact as I Listened, I wondered why no one sees the philosophy behind SEED as a Religion. If we define religion, as in The American College Dictionary, to mean a particular system in which the quest for the ideal life has been embodied[1], then we may well call SEED a religion. The Hegelian Dialectic is used in a systematic way to educate the participants in humanist "religious" education.

I kept wondering why this new "system" of education got approval from the board. All of our concerns were written in my letters to the Board and Superintendent, to which they never responded. This individual heard that the people who actually worked with this program, and were upset with it, had sent a letter to the Superintendent and yet nothing was ever done about it. Apparently the Superintendent never responded to this information either. I included a letter to him in regards to the SEED program also. The Chief of Staff heard my concerns during our meeting so he knew about it. I know for certain the Board knew, for I had placed the information right in front of them at the Board meeting in January. My thoughts were racing; my future steps seemed uncertain since letters did not seem to work. As for now, I wanted to treasure this special person who called.

At this moment, I wanted to show my appreciation and wished I could jump through the telephone and say thank you face to face. Knowing this wasn't possible; I offered my sincere verbal thanks for the courage of this act. I knew this to be a tough decision, but one based on good basic principles of right and wrong. The voice estimated hundreds of teachers had been trained in this philosophy already. I wondered how many students and parents are *brainwashed* because of it? The injustice of this program was never more felt than in this moment. The voice's intensity sent me the message that people must be informed of this program. I knew my book was the only way. I also knew that the district was never going to reverse itself, for it had gone too far in its indoctrination of the teachers. There is always hope for the uncompromising parents who can remove their children through opt outs or private schools. He/she said many others were silently cheering us on, our work vital to the exposure of this program and similar ones throughout our country. Joy filled my heart. The mini miracle gave me support and I assured this hero that his/her identity would be held in confidence. The voice gave me one more surprise, direction to a particular website giving me further information about one of the Social Justice Programs.

One of the SEED program facilitators is involved in a curriculum called "Tools For Building Justice." The ten "isms" of this program are: Racism, Classicism, Sexism, Heterosexism, Sizeism, Anti-Semitism, Linguicism, Ableism, Adultism and Ageism. The idea of this curriculum is to initiate campaigns to resist these "isms' and resist institutional "oppression." The curriculum utilizes many of the same tools used in SEED, photos, video clips, music, cartoons and readings.[2] The site represents many *causes*; indeed, it was instituted by one of the facilitators of the SEED program.

We are teaching children "ism" education which is not only accusatory in nature, but also Marxist and Socialist in theory of oppression. It brings on chaos and thus changes.

My fingers found new freedom. They typed quickly for I knew the importance of delivering this information to others. People still exist that believe in Godly principles, some may not follow a religion or go to church, but they are wise in the knowledge that

211

without our Godly based principles and God fearing leaders, we will collapse. Our liberty will be gone. Underlying my writing was the happiness I experienced while talking to my caller. It enriched my body with the reality of good people who still care.

My burgundy chair, with its high back and cushiony support, gives me what I need in this moment, comfort in knowing I can go forth with this book. Reality tells me some will read it and despise me. Active homosexuals and compromised people (*Stage 4*) will not change, though I keep hoping they will see the light on the other side. Undecided individuals will most likely take a stand after reading this material. Uncompromising individuals will pick up new information to aid them in their battle of good and evil. I don't know the real outcome, nor will I ever of my writing, but this caller has been affected by Eagle Forum's action and he/she chose, wisely, to call.

I accepted my surprise of the day. It returned me to childhood memories when summer was a special time of anticipation. Now I awaited my next surprise with the eagerness of days gone by.

31

TESTIMONY

The weeks passed quickly and my writing was a priority. Discipline became my reality, but as I wrote I kept thinking about my conversation with the hero. During one of those moments, I remembered the hero mentioning another person who had attended SEED functions. Perhaps I could talk with this individual. The person in question was not listed, but I investigated the information line, found the number and left a message. Considerable time passed; there was no response. One evening, quite unexpectedly, I had another surprise. There were three messages on my voice mail. The messages were strong, anger poured out about the horrors of the SEED program and its danger to our education system and youth. The new voice encouraged me to return the call. The strength of their conviction echoed over the telephone; I was drawn to return the call immediately!

The individual had experienced the SEED Program both in Elk Grove and in a college environment. It was a force that was growing, no one seemed to know about it, but it was spreading like oozing decay. The tactic was the same in both schools, a direct encounter with people from the SEED Program. In Elk Grove there was a scheduled Saturday seminar. The new caller thought the woman visitor was Peggy McIntosh, but could not remember for certain the name. The individual speaking to me was disturbed by the "new age" rhetoric used by this speaker in her presentation. I can understand for after reading the SEED material, I had to sift through my thinking just to begin to unravel the clarity of their position in education. I then had to do it over again. This caller apparently felt the same way and attended the break out session, which was to explain the SEED Program further. The caller still could not understand it for there was no clear content. The content became clear to this person when two women walked boldly in front of the room and held hands. Homosexuality was then portrayed as gentle, not intending to hurt anyone. The two women were presented to be just like everyone else. The message was to return to the classroom and inform the students that there is no danger in this lifestyle. I was absolutely stunned. The individual proceeded to say the almost identical words of the first caller, "The Program is filled with evil and deception. We must stop it." My mind was swirling with the image of two women standing in front of this audience, presenting this lifestyle as being normal and healthy. I was sick inside, not homophobic, as some would accuse me. Fear was not an issue, but aversion to the lifestyle is a reality and thus we would more accurately be classified as homo-aversive. In other words, we still love the person, but have an aversion to the behavior and activist homosexuals who want our children and our family units. The boldness has gone far enough! How many knew about this display of homosexuality in front of the classroom and what's worse, how many would have the courage to complain about it? How many people feared loss of their jobs if they complained? I was limp with disbelief! The men and women of yesteryear are disappearing and with them go generations of beliefs that have kept us together as a Nation. The brave caller had the same experience in attending a college class in Sacramento. The couple walked hand in hand in front of the classroom and did the same routine. The message was the same. What harm could this loving couple do to anyone? The strategy is, once again, love everyone, accept the behavior no matter how they live and let's get used to this lifestyle for there is absolutely nothing unusual or abnormal about it.

The caller then proceeded to verbalize reasons for his/her distaste of the program and its *brainwashing*. The caller feared for children and the lowering of age for sexually explicit material to be taught. The open policy that everything is of equal merit was a big concern. The blatant assault on our Judeo-Christian values bothered the caller, along with promotion of the secular humanist "religion." Other attendees had similar concerns. They were afraid to say or do anything against the program for their jobs and reputations were at risk. The caller was very upset by this experience in Elk Grove. The individual felt evil permeated the SEED Program. It sent shivers down my spine. The individual's excitement about our group shook me out of the terror I felt inside and I continued to focus on the words. The caller encouraged us in continuing our endeavors to rid the schools of programs that seek to destroy the innocence of youth. I believe that our minds and hearts were totally connected on the night I spoke with this caller. I felt the individual's desperation and I knew mine. The call was a blessing, another mini miracle and a great second surprise. If I never speak to this person again, I know this conversation will last me a lifetime. The sincerity reached through the telephone, into my heart, mind and spirit with a message enlightening the core of my reality. It was real, these callers stamped the approval of my convictions by two that were present, two who boldly decided it was time to come forth with the truth. I will be forever thankful to the unexpected callers, the heroes of today!

The interaction with this courageous person motivated me to write even more. I wished for endless hours of mental clarity and research visibility that would take me to new heights with my book. I wanted to run down the streets shouting at the top of my lungs, "Don't you see what is happening to our children." I wanted to run into every corner of the world shouting at the top of my lungs, "Stop hurting our little ones." However, knowing I would be arrested for insanity, I chose not to. I decided, instead, to escape into research, which took me into educational programs for teens that dealt with homosexuality. The information I found moved me beyond anything I thought possible. If anything would prove the importance of putting a stop to these programs, this subject matter convinced me, for I knew it was possible to happen right here in Elk Grove. I was glad for my high backed burgundy chair for it offered me support as my friendly computer released the sickening information. I knew unless we stop it now, it will branch out into every educational facility across our country. The event took place on March 25, 2000 in Massachusetts.

32

MASSACHUSETTS SCANDAL

Dedicated to my book and the passage of information to others, I asked myself how much more can a human spirit take before losing total faith in humanity? My surprise callers heightened my mood and I thought about their request to not reveal their names. Good people are afraid to speak out and I realized how intimidation has taken its toll. Our country is taking away our freedoms. Everywhere there is chaos and we are making it happen. If we stayed in the truth of our traditional principles, there would not be this mess. I can't think of a political agenda that is not in grave danger of falling into lawlessness. It stems from the highest courts, black robed judges, all the way through Congress to our state representatives and filters into our communities, businesses, educational systems, churches and homes. I know Elk Grove does not stand-alone. It was precisely on this evening that I found this to be true. I found out what can happen if we don't heed the warnings.

I resisted the interjection of explicit sexual material in this book because I wanted it free of "smut" language. However after reading about this day of education, I gave in to a small amount of verbal usage necessary for exposure of this program. I also gave in to being physically nauseated, once again, at the subject matter of what is following. The content is truly vile, the worst one can imagine being inflicted on our youth by homosexual activists.

Since 1992, the State of Massachusetts has actively pursued "safe schools" in order to encourage GSA programs on campuses throughout the State. They have over 180 schools that house these clubs. Governor Celluci always allocated $1.5 million yearly in his budget for these programs. If and when parents or citizens would complain, they were accused of being homophobic. The Governors Commission for Gay and Lesbian Youth does much of its work through the Educational Network. On March 25, 2000, the Massachusetts Department of Education, the Governor's Commission and GLSEN co-sponsored a "Teach-Out" Day at Tuft's University. It was to be a "gay" friendly seminar in order to encourage more clubs and appreciate differences in order to insure safety of homosexual students on campuses. Children as young as 12 came and schools throughout the state and nation-wide were encouraged to attend. Children were bussed in and homosexual activists from around the country attended.[1] The rest of the tale is a nightmare!

The Massachusetts News told of one teacher who had nightmares and could not sleep for days following the conference. Three overtly homosexual teachers taught classes. One seminar was called, "What They Didn't Tell You About Queer Sex and Sexuality In Health Class." The ages were 14-21and some say there were children as young as 12 in the classrooms. The training was also for adults to prepare them for running the clubs on campus. The youth were encouraged to be openly blunt about their sexual feelings and graphic about homosexual sex. It became so open that I read the material in disbelief.

Interactions took place between teachers and young students. Concerned parents taped the interactions for it was the only way they could prove the "truth" of perverted sexual teaching. Anatomical terms were used for bodily orifices that were disgusting. Detailed descriptions of items inserted into orifices were varied, with discussion on types of dildos and encouragement of "fisting" by the following documented statement:

> "Fisting, forcing one's entire hand into another person's rectum or vagina, often gets a bad rap....It's an experience of letting somebody into your body that you want to be that close and intimate with...and to put you into an exploratory mode."[2]

I cringed thinking of children hearing about sex for the first time. Fisting was described as being a highly respected way of showing how much you want someone close to you. All forms of sexual behavior, including oral sex, were vividly described as to how to do it, what certain body fluids looked and smelled like and how climaxing could be attained by rubbing bodies together with the clothes on. Discussion of tongue jewelry and how it was useful in oral sex was also included.[3]

Another workshop involved AIDS/HIV prevention. It was reported the class was in session for almost an hour before the word prevention was used. They were then told they should make "informed decisions" as to whether to use condoms or not. The emphasis was not on abstinence. Another topic discussed was "Tired of Denying It." It was apparent teachers felt sex was central to life and even to teenagers. They encouraged teens to make their own decisions about sex. Campaigns such as "No sex, no problem" only makes those having sex feel badly. The messages of each seminar were crude, rude and beyond levels of tolerance. One teacher showed movies of homosexual activity in Greek society, portraying older men having sex with younger boys as normal. The teacher encouraged this behavior. Disturbing material was handed out after the sessions that included condoms and packages that were to be used for "rough" sex. The Sidney Borum Community Health Center and Planned Parenthood participated in distribution of sexual packages.[4]

The Parents Rights Coalition taped the event, certain that some people would not believe what was said. Many parents and citizens heard the message. The proof was on the tape. Concerned citizens had complained repeatedly that inappropriate sexual material was in the schools but to no avail, thus they decided to tape it. Thirty parents presented this information before the Board of Education in Pittsfield and they were dismissed without any discussion. It was after this encounter that they decided to go public with the information. The Parent's Coalition, however, was brought to court with an estimated $200,000 in legal fees; The Gay and Lesbian Advocates and Defenders (GLAAD) sued for violation of privacy. Lawyers took the case of parents who had recorded the "teach out" day. The following is a brief outline of what happened in the case. It is clearly indicative of the power our judges hold to reverse our constitutional law.

1. Judge van Gestel used the law intended for crime surveillance and wire tapping to justify the parents recording as not lawful. This was a public education meeting for all were invited. People tape all the time at public and town meetings.
2. The judge's classic statement is the following. " I feel very strongly about someone secretly taping my daughter and selling it on the State House steps. (He has a 17-year-old daughter) (The Voices were altered, not to be recognized. It was not possible to recognize the voices.)
3. An Emergency Restraining Order was put in effect. No one was allowed to discuss the graphic sex on the tapes, not even the State Senate, which is unthinkable.
4. The state refused to discontinue funding the homosexual programs in the state, which apparently comes under the heading of "suicide prevention money."
5. The Boston Globe misinformed the public as to the accuracy of the incident and totally ignored the unconstitutional event.[5]

It took three months before two of the teachers were fired. The organizers were never fired and the tapes were not allowed to be distributed. The Education Board finally apologized for the incident and Governor Celluci never acknowledged the horrors of the day. He continued to defend the programs and the money spent on them. It appears homosexuals are very powerful in this state as they helped the previous administration win the governorship. Of an estimated 700 GSA clubs throughout America, 180 are located in Massachusetts. According to some sources, Celluci carried on the traditions of Bill Weld in continuing to give homosexual activists money and access to the schools. Celluci's actions seem to support this theory, in that he never once spoke with parents and never addressed the "Teach-Out" day. He supposedly would not talk to Alan Keyes, who attempted to reach him by scheduled appointment, when the Governor's candidacy for Ambassador to Canada was in doubt due to the scandal. Governor

Celluci, however, did receive his appointment as Ambassador to Canada, though repeated letters were sent to officials in Washington in regards to his behavior.

The above story represents the abuse of our justice system. It bent the law to meet an evil need of perverted members of society. What happened in Massachusetts is outrageous. This wickedness is not just in Massachusetts, but spreading everywhere through diversity programs. Purposeful inaccuracy of news reporting also took place. This speaks loudly about our news media and their "spinning" of the facts to meet the homosexual agenda. I feel regret for the parents that fought this battle. I give respect to Brian Camenker, President of the Parents Rights Coalition and everyone working with him for their courageous effort to bring dignity to our teenagers.

The "teach-out" not only took place in 2000 but also in 2001. The Massachusetts News estimates 400 students and 250 teachers and administrators attended. Public funds helped the private sponsor, GLSEN, pay for the event, plus the Massachusetts Senate continued to authorize money be given for homosexual programs. It is thought that the money from the homosexual suicide prevention programs went into this 2001 Education Day. I knew GLSEN sponsored these programs, but never realized the depravity of the content. Phyllis Schlafly's Education Reporter, in June 2001, gives some classes taught and events of the day.[7]

1. "A Look At Last Year's Setbacks in Massachusetts, What we Have Learned and How We Can Move Forward."

Phyllis went on to explain one of the descriptions given under this class.

"Over the past year, one of the nation's most successful safe schools programs for GLBT (gay, lesbian, bisexual and trans-gender) youth has been beset by attacks from reactionary forces both inside and outside the public education bureaucracy."[8]

220

Parents and Citizens are now considered "Reactionary forces: to be looked upon as "challenges." I do not see parents upheld as authority figures in any of these sessions. They are not given respect nor addressed as wise people sought after for guidance. The workshop was to be used to explore responses to the challenges.

2. "Addressing GLBT Issues in Preschools, Daycare and Kindergarten: A Networking Summit and a Chance to Share Experiences" was another class.[10]

I flashed on noted authorities and friends insisting it would never reach our grammar schools. It is now in the grammar schools.

3. Other workshops were the following: "Gay Rights 101, Incorporating the Basics of the Gay Rights Movement Into Your U.S. History Curriculum," "From Lesbos to Stonewall: Including the History of GLBT Individuals in HS or Middle School World History Curriculum," "Incorporating GLBT Inclusive Literature in the High School English Curriculum," "Using the Arts to Express and Explore GLBT Issues in Your School," and "Homophobia in School Athletics.," "What They Didn't Tell You About Queer Sex and Sexuality in Health Class: A Workshop for Youth Only, Ages 14-21," "Putting the Sex Back Into Sexual Orientation: Classroom Strategies for Health and Sexuality Educators." Teens were advised to see their "really hip" advisors for advice on how to "come on" to potential sex partners. [11]

4. Tufts University police "prevented parents and journalists from observing events at the conference." The press was allowed a pre preview of display tables, to attend lunch and see the final event, a play that was cleaned up from crude jokes and content of the past year.[9] The entire day was behind "closed" doors. It all falls in place with the

agenda. *Mind control* is best done behind "closed"
doors. Deception and lies thrive in this
environment of "secrecy." How can teachers and
administrators not understand when something is
done in secrecy, there "is" a reason why!

In summer of 2003, the National Education Association
(NEA) met and passed resolutions. Interesting that they believe in
early public school education programs from birth through age eight.
They believe that the Sex Education Program should facilitate the
realization of human potential, and it is the right of every individual to
live in an environment of freely available information and knowledge
about sexuality. Diversity of sexual orientation, gender identification,
sexual harassment and homophobia must be included in the program.
They believe that the program should be an "appropriately established
program." [12] Is the above GLSEN program appropriate? What is and
is not appropriate? Who determines this? Nowhere are the parent's
rights given priority under the GLSEN programs.

Information given out, at the Teach Out, by the Political
Research Associates is called The Ex-Files. It is about the ex gay
movement, which they say, is a "new threat to democracy and
diversity." The information teaches how to challenge those who have
turned away from homosexuality by choice or by spiritual
intervention. [13]

Once again, this ties in with the NEA's Convention
philosophy in July of 2003. A 2nd Grade teacher attempted to speak
in support of a bill that would necessitate teaching, along with
homosexual material, the current research on reparative therapies and
sexual reorientation. She wanted the term ex-gay to be used in all
sexual orientation material and to offer unbiased material for sexually
confused youth. She felt that discrimination is used against those with
unwanted same sex attractions by withholding available information.
She was "booed and jeered during her two minute presentation by
people in a group of 9,400 people. "They did not want to consider the
issue," she told the Agape Press. [14] Following the convention, Dr.
Warren Throckmorton, Associate Professor of Psychology and
director of College Counseling at Grove City College, described this
policy as "common sense" and "balanced." He said that nearly "26%

of teens were uncertain about their sexuality, but that only 3-4% of adults identify as homosexuals. There is much room for self labeling." He also stated that the NEA refused to sell booth space to ex-gay group PFOX, stating they had run out of room but continued to sell to other groups.[15] Supposedly they have granted them space this year but continue to ignore the message.

The intent is clear, bold and dangerous. GLSEN wants our children. Immigrants come to our country to find a new life; instead they have their freedom taken away. They cannot raise their own children by a solid moral code. Randy Thomasson, Executive Director of Campaign for California Families, says the Russian community in Sacramento is concerned about queer agenda bills passed by the legislation. I myself have talked with them at gatherings at the Capitol. They came as legal immigrants and now face issues they never anticipated. I hear similar stories from Ed Hernandez, who volunteers his time to work with activist groups to help better the world for his wife and children. He comes in contact with many people who have the same concerns. Our freedom to raise our children is slowly eroding due to the homosexual *cause*. All cultures share the "deception of diversity" as their common bond, for it is meant to teach homosexuality.

The Land of Freedom rang in my mind as I sat in my Burgundy chair grasping for the appropriate way to describe the horrors of this program. I could not describe all of what I read, but I did my best. I did not want to ruin the integrity of my words with the disgust of what was taught in Massachusetts 2000 and 2001.

33

HOMOSEXUAL FRIENDSHIPS

The Massachusetts scandal was not easily erased from my mind. After days attempting it, I decided it best to accept its reality. Schools everywhere have changed and it's a fact. Because of the impact of diversity programs, the homosexual armies are on the rise. I thought of the young today for they do not hear messages so clearly given to my generation. "Beware of playmates and pick ones of good character." The schools, instead, teach children that everyone and everything holds equal merit. Parents must be strong in their discernment and recognize dangers of homosexual friendships. Children proclaim to be angry when parents say "No" to them. In truth they want discipline; this depicts genuine care for their well being. Linda Harvey of Mission America experiences tearful parents who did not say "No." They relate stories of their children changing after associations with homosexual friends. Bonding is important in *mind control*. Friendships can change your child's sexual orientation. Her powerful information, along with my own past experiences, was important for me to be able to relate to you some major points to remember when raising teen-agers.

1. Teenagers will try and protect a friend if she or he "comes out." They want to help them to avoid bigotry amongst peers.[1] They may even join GLSEN or homosexual clubs on campus with their friend. The interactions draw them close and soon a homosexual relationship begins. I have heard people say that homosexuals do not "go" for heterosexuals. Reading material and experience

224

prove this statement false. Books are available with subject matter on how to seduce a straight man. I used to market health products. One year my girlfriend and I decided to have a booth at a homosexual event at the Capitol. I made numerous contacts and met with one woman a week later to discuss the products. She was flirtatious and made attempts to push the meeting further than health products. Once again I lived it. I also knew a man who grew up in San Francisco. Indeed he had older men soliciting him when he was the tender age of 12, for this is the age when pedophiles seek our little boys. Associating with children who may be involved with this lifestyle can introduce pedophiles to your children also.

2. Parents may feel secure in knowing their daughter has male homosexual friendships. This is not safe. Men with gender identity issues are drawn to women. They are capable of having sex with both. Many ex-gays say they had sex with both. It can be to avoid loneliness or test their masculinity. Straight girls will have sexual encounters to "save" their homosexual friends. Alcohol can induce feelings to promote sexual activity. A woman can develop fantasies of the man changing and being hers completely.[2] It is the same syndrome of women actively pursuing married men when they know they cannot have them. As a nurse, I remember a girl at the hospital who consistently became involved with married men. She lived her life thinking each one would change and leave his wife. It is unrealistic to think we can change others, but the quest can cause severe mental problems to the individual who becomes involved in such situations.

3. If sexual relations begin, the problem of transmitting diseases enters. Now we are dealing with life and death. Men who are homosexual will

225

usually have sex by the time they leave high school. It will be in casual bars, bathrooms and even parks. This involves a high risk of HIV contact that may infect your child. Homosexual women who are bisexual can carry disease to your son or daughter.[3] Your child can die from a one-night stand with a friend. Choose wisely when it comes to saying "no."

4. If there is no sexual contact, the influence comes in other ways. Ideas regarding homosexuality change as their friends relate that heredity caused the condition. If not heredity then they angle the argument of what harm can we do our society. Female homosexuals are many times feminists, their philosophy radical and non-traditional. Influences of how to be feminine and masculine enter discussions and soon dating patterns may change. This happens to both the boy and girl. Role models become neutral gender people. Even marriage becomes neutral.

5. Children must be kept from relatives or mentors who are homosexual.[5] The dangers are grave and last a lifetime. Adults can alter the course of a child's life by their role modeling.

The responsibility of parents today is heavy; they must take it seriously and not shrug their shoulders. Children are to be protected, cherished and guided for their better interests, not that of the homosexual agenda. Keep close watch on your children's playmates and friends. Saying "No" can demonstrate loving strength to your child. If done with respect, it may encourage the friends of your child to seek proper guidance in returning to heterosexual orientation. We do not have to leave our place of absolute moral conviction to compromise. The compromise can be deadly for your child and others.

34

PEDOPHILIA

We had acquaintances that were active in boy and girl scouting. I asked the man, one day, his thoughts on homosexual scout leaders. He indeed shrugged his shoulders. "What harm can they do" was his response. I have never forgotten his reply and the casualness of his attitude. Indeed, pedophilia is a very intense subject matter and it was a good time to examine it. I hope never to read the subject matter again. It took me three days to begin this chapter. I struggled with emotions of varying degrees, caused by scenes of innocent children being mutilated by disgusting adults feeding on their bodies. The casual attitude of the Boy Scout leader is beginning to penetrate society. Though I began to accept the depravity of man's intellectual status chapters ago, I know there are still some genuinely intelligent people left in our world. I will struggle through this perverted material putting it in words so others will understand the ugliness of it's content.

The Pedophilia movement is a repeat of the 70's with the American Psychiatric Association once again moving in directions of change, but this time it is for Pedophiles. In 1994, behind "closed" doors they changed the Diagnostic and Statistical Manual IV (DSM-IV) by redefining definitions of sexual perversions, including pedophilia. The behavior must do the following, "cause clinically significant distress or impairment of social, occupational or other important areas of functioning" to be diagnosed as having a paraphilia condition or perversion. [1] In 1998, the American Psychological Association stated that sex between adults and children may be less harmful than thought, with the "willing" gaining positive benefit from it. The article also addressed vocabulary. Words such as abuse, molestation and victim were judgmental. Instead adult child sex was more appropriate. In July of 1998, the National Association for the Research and Therapy of Homosexuality came out in strong opposition to the above. Eventually both organizations conceded to the fault of their wording and revised again their stand on pedophilia. The American Psychological Association pledged to develop legal briefs that would not allow any organization to misuse the article. They promised to disassociate with any organization or publication advocating sex between child and adult.[2] The American Psychiatric Association wrote a letter to the Family Research Council saying they "strongly hold the position that sex between adult and child can never be condoned or considered normal behavior…"[3]

Already the great men in white coats caved to the agenda of perversion. I am sure many members were once again not aware of what happened, but it shows clear intent of some to make changes necessary for pedophilia acceptance. A well thought out manifesto and power to push the homosexual agenda, gave homosexuals their *cause* of normality. It will happen in the same way with pedophilia. The homosexuals led the way and we caved in. Our moral code is gone and we have no standard by which to judge any longer. We allowed seeds of deception to grow into unthinkable food. Having been digested by so many, it cannot help but spread into pedophilia. Books are sold in stores and on line promoting this lifestyle. Literature introduced to our children encourages them to take charge of their own lives, including sex with adults. Universities are true to their reputation of indoctrination. James Kincaid, tenured English professor at University of Southern California (USC) in Los Angeles, provides justification for perversion. He speaks at conferences sponsored by the Human Rights Campaign, Americas largest homosexual activist group. His writings are beginning to appear in gender and queer studies at Cornell University. He says the following:

> "It is possible that the pedophile's marginal position
> alerts him not only to self-interest, but the pains
> suffered by all the outcast. This is not a necessary
> consequence of loving boys, of course, any more than
> virtue is of poverty. Still, that passion for "helping"

228

the child is so strong in relations between men and boys that even the police acknowledge it."[4]

English professor Ellis Hanson has taught a class at Cornell University called "The Sexual Child." Professor Hanson told *Campus Report* that the course was designed to "undermine preconceived notions about what a child is, what sexuality is and what it means to love a child."[5] He denies his class is pro-pedophilia, but it does debate whether it is evil. According to the meaning of evil, as that which is contrary to the moral law, then it is evil! It really seems simple to me. The course was listed in Accuracy in Academia's *Campus Report*. It included the writings of a number of pedophile scholars. Frank York and Robert Knight in "Homosexual Behavior and Pedophilia" list some of the authors included in the *Campus Report*. Mr. York and Mr. Knight's research was beneficial and contributed to my research on the beginnings of pedophile teaching in the university setting.

1. Theo Sandfort, a former member of Paidika (Journal of Pedophilia published in Holland), has written many books dealing with pedophilia. They are sold in stores such as Wal-Mart and on line shopping. Pedophilia books are sold routinely in many stores. Sandfort is famous in certain circles for his 1981 study in the Netherlands on man-boy relationships. He studied 25 boys, ages 10-16, who were involved in ongoing pederastic relationships with men. He concluded that for most boys, the experiences were positive. [6] Of course there are the usual evaluations and criticisms of his work, which draws attention to the subject matter. The intellectually gifted take notice and either give or not give approval. If enough give approval, in time it will be elevated to the *cause* of normality by the intellectual elites.

2. The second name in the Campus Report is Daniel Tsang, editor of *The Age Taboo*, published by homosexual Boston-based Alyson Publishers. He

was editor of *Gay Insurgent: A Gay Left Journal.*
He has been a reporter for the *Michigan Free Press*
and ex-correspondent for *Gaysweek.* The book
deals with homosexual intergenerational sexual
activity.[7] The articles and essays are intended to
stimulate thought about the subject matter,
introducing another tool to be used by pedophiles
to promote acceptance as normal. In the 1970's,
Mr. Tsang realized his two identities, homosexual
and Asian American came together and he said "at
the time many of us remained active in progressive
causes because we sought a radical restructuring of
America." [8] His *cause* of normality is part of the
chaos we live today.

3. The third name jetted out at me. I was reading her
    material the other evening shuttering at her
    vulgarity. The excerpt was from her book called
    "Public Sex" written by Pat Califia. It was called
    "Forty –two Things that You Can Do to Make the
    Future Safe for Sex." They included the following:
    write a sex ad, defend an abortion clinic, shut down
    the Justice Department's antiporn campaign, give
    away some pleasure, write a letter to mayor or
    officials opposing sex offenders having to register
    with the cops, make art about how sex feels,
    crossdress, hand out clean needles and condoms, if
    city cracks down on bathhouses or sex clubs, write
    them and let them know you have a right to have
    such places clean in order to have sex.[9] If that is
    not enough, she says in Daniel Tsang's *Age Taboo*
    that women are a big part of pedophilia since they
    have more access to children. She believes this
    fact will become known in the future. She believes
    children should be freed from sexual "oppression"
    and writes extensively on the subject matter. The
    cause for yet another oppressed group appears to
    be for children. She feels children are robbed of

> sexual pleasure with adults and believes all age
> laws should be eliminated to ensure freedom for
> children to decide for themselves. She has worked
> for the homosexual magazine *The Advocate*.[10]

The books and classes are in Universities. Let there be no mistake it
is coming into high schools. Across the country we have a program
called Project 10, mentioned earlier, begun by Virginia Uribe, a
homosexual high school teacher from Los Angeles. It is a program
that offers support to teenagers suspect of being homosexual. They
offer counseling and adult homosexuals serve as mentors. They
purchase books for high school libraries. One of them is entitled *One
Teenager in Ten: Testimony of Gay and Lesbian Youth*. It teaches
teens that they can choose whatever sexual orientation they want and
go back and forth. It contains an essay that describes the seduction of
a teenage girl by her homosexual dance teacher.[11] The seeds of
deception are now coming into the high schools and they will destroy
our children.

I tried to find homosexual quotes or articles condemning
pedophilia but could not. I consistently found homosexuals writing in
favor of pedophilia. Perhaps it is split as in Hitler's regime. An
element of homosexuals favored pederasty but some did not. I found
one GLSEN activist from Packer Collegiate School in New York
defending the education process at kindergarten age. She says
kindergarteners are "developing their superego and that's when the
saturation process needs to begin."[12] It is evident that the saturation
will include pedophilia also. It will not stop, as so clearly indicated
by David Thorstad, spokesman for homosexual rights movement,
pedophile and founding member of NAMBLA.

> "The ultimate goal of the gay liberation movement is
> the achievement of sexual freedom for all-not just
> equal rights for 'lesbians and gay men', but also
> freedom of sexual expression for young people and
> children."[13]

For those who think it has not come to mainstream America, it
is now in deceptive form through the productions in high schools of

the "Vagina Monologue." It is a play that involves gyrations, graphic descriptions of sexual pleasure scenes and words to describe the vagina such as cunt. I use this word with horror for it is so disrespectful of women and yet in 2004, mothers were interviewed who actually felt liberation for their high school daughters and themselves in using it. The interviews were on Bill O'Reilly's *No Spin Factor* following a high school production of this play given in (ironically) Amherst Massachusetts, the State that beats California in perverted behavior. Another mother said she saw no wrong in a 24-year-old woman seducing a 16-year-old girl. Most who attended gave permission for their high school daughters to be in it and to view it. Very few town folk protested its production. I deeply respect the gentleman interviewed on *Fox News* for he was one of seven who stood for decency in a town gone mad with immorality. He described the show and how the scenes led to sudden outbursts of applause from middle aged men and women when the young girls, age 16, would show themselves to be climaxing on the stage.[14] It is truly perverted and is without a doubt pedophilia in its highest form of voyeurism, disguised as education and art. It is awful and the town should not only be embarrassed beyond any doubt, but also know that they all gave their approval to pedophilia.

I collapsed in my big blue chair. My body seemed to mold itself into its comfort and was drained of all ability to move. It was done, but I also found myself with a burning desire to stop the horrors of pedophilia. The John Jay study, commissioned by the Catholic Church to study the priest abuse of children from 1950-2002, found that of the 10,667 cases of child sexual abuse it was more than 80% homosexual in nature. [15] We must be concerned with the adult homosexual and his or her impact on our children emotionally and physically. I admire the church for moving forward with this study and making the facts known to us. On this night I thanked God again for the strength to write this chapter. It was extra thanks, in and above the usual. It had to be for the material was out of line with sanity. Within minutes my eyes were heavy with anticipation of sleep. I moved my body into the mode of getting ready for bed, doing the usual bedtime rituals. Soon I climbed into bed closing my mind to the horrors of the night. My eyes closed thinking happy thoughts.

35

GLSEN BOOKS

The colors of autumn, along with the cool night air, make Fall a special time of year. People begin preparing their homes for winter and hibernation becomes a comfortable thought. I remember making leaf houses in our front yard when I was a child. Our neighborhood playmates knew intuitively when the leaves were right for our designs. We met in our front or backyards; which ever had the most colorful leaves. Raking the leaves into the formation of rooms, we eventually produced a house in which we played. Watching leaves fall from trees makes me remember those happy times. I want them again, but they will never be. Those carefree times are gone.

I didn't want to do it, but I knew it had to be done. I struggled from my chair, wanting instead to rake leaves. GLSEN books had to be viewed by the public, for citizens have a right to know how future citizens are being raised in our schools. I began the task of looking up GLSEN suggested reading material for K-12 grades. I also decided to review information about the group and others connected to it.

GLSEN began in Boston as a small volunteer group. In 1993, they led the fight in Massachusetts to ban anti-gay discrimination in public schools. Kevin Jennings, Executive Director of GLSEN, gave this speech at a Human Rights Campaign in 1995 to explain the success of their campaign.

> "We immediately seized upon the opponents' calling card — safety — and explained how homophobia represents a threat to students' safety by creating a climate where violence, name-calling, health problems

and suicide are common. We knew that, confronted
with real-life stories of youth who had suffered from
homophobia, our opponents would automatically be on
the defensive: they would have to attack people who
had already been victimized once, which put them in a
bully position from which it would be hard to emerge
looking good. In Massachusetts, no one could speak
up against our frame [of the debate] and say, 'Why,
yes, I do think students should kill themselves.' This
allowed us to set the terms of the debate."[1]

He used the lie of "common" incidence of suicide, violence
and name calling to win the diversity programs in Massachusetts.
Many of these have already been disputed and proved false. I
flashed on "lie" once again and its use to win public support. The
hypocrisy of their movement staggers my imagination. The
homosexual activists are quick to accuse others of violence toward
them, but deny any allegations of their violence toward others.
Activists have sabotaged *Pink Swastika* at Amazon for they don't
want to be seen as perpetuators of violence during the Holocaust.
They believe it's their place to be seen as "victims" and not
"victimizer." The facts remain that homosexuals as well as
heterosexuals were brutal aggressors during the Nazi regime. Many
serial killers are homosexual. Dr. Brian Clowes shows the statistics
of the top eight of ten serial killers in the United States were
homosexuals, and 68% of all mass murderers as being homosexual. [2]
It's substantiated by factual information, but we're considered hateful
if we talk about it. We are, however, to believe lies as truth, even
with no evidence, when it meets their needs for normalcy. The claims
of Abraham Lincoln being homosexual are ridiculous, or perhaps St.
Augustine, as stated by, homosexual, Vassar English Professor Paul
Russell in "The Gay 100: A Ranking of the Most Influential Gay Men
and Lesbians." He states the following:

"What I am claiming here is that Augustine appears to
have indulged, in his early life, in pleasures of the
flesh, both with males and females." [3]

234

The Federal National Endowment for the Arts funded the studies for the book. Russell readily admits he has no facts to corroborate his evidence. Interesting that Professor Shively, the pro-pedophilia individual responsible for Lincoln's story of alleged homosexuality, and Professor Russell have no facts to back up their claims, yet we are to believe them.[4] Scott Lively has incredible evidence of homosexual predominance in Hitler's regime, but they discount his book as a lie. This is the climate of GLSEN and the other Organizations involved in the movement.

GLSEN became a national organization in 1994 and has over 85 chapters with a national office in New York and San Francisco. Their income is in the millions and their mission statement is clear, "...fight the homophobia and heterosexism that undermine healthy school climates."[5] Even in their mission statement they discriminate against us, the vocabulary is evidence of it. They also promote a class called Homophobia 101 and 102.[6] GLSEN boasts of training over 400 staff in their programs. They work to educate everyone about the "ism's," especially sexism. Massachusetts built their safe program for schools around the GLSEN model. We already saw the model of their work in the sex classes given. I still can't find any words from the homosexual hierarchy about the horrors of that day.

The group works closely with the Human Rights Campaign based in Washington D.C. It is the largest homosexual organization in the Nation with a reported income of over $16 million. The membership is over 400,000.[7] They work steadily to educate Congress as to all the homosexual issues. Groups supporting homosexuality work together, and through GLAAD they have access to media change. The Gay and Lesbian Alliance Against Defamation (GLAAD) is the lobbying group for the movement. In 1992, the Entertainment Weekly said they were perhaps the most successful organization influencing the media. In 1987, they were able to change the New York Times policy to using "gay" instead of "homosexual." They pride themselves on influencing newspapers, magazines, television, motion pictures and even the successful campaign against Dr. Laura.[8] The GLAAD website is bold in announcing that particular conservative activist groups are "paid staff to defame and dehumanize lesbian, gay, bisexual and transgender people and families while to deny them fundamental civil rights protections locally and nationally." The groups mentioned are the following: the American Family Association, the Traditional Values Coalition, Focus on the Family, Family Research Council, The Christian Coalition, Citizens for Community Values, Concerned Women for America, Coral Ridge Ministries, the Free Congress Foundation, Eagle Forum and others.[9] Their intimidation tactic becomes clear as they recommend individuals respond to President Bush's "Marriage Protection Week" by calling newspapers and questioning the discrimination of their families and civil rights. They ask them to scrutinize the "hateful" intolerance of the group's involved.[10] It is really humorous to watch, as these citizens do not seem to grasp that no rights have been taken from them. They have every right to marry, but as said earlier it must be someone of the opposite sex. Where is their right taken away? The power stays with the majority and the majority is against homosexual marriage. GLAAD, however, continues to use intimidation, for they suggest homosexuals write editorials to newspapers with ideas that their families are oppressed because they are not protected in the same way as heterosexual families. Let's examine this premise. Who made the choice to be homosexual and to have a family outside of marriage? It was not our choice, but theirs, and now they expect us to make it right for them because they deem it above majority rule. Where is the logic in this erroneous judgment, but does it matter? GLAAD will sway public opinion by intimidating the media and they will successfully represent us as hateful people and homophobic mongrels. In actuality we have no fear of homosexuality, just an aversion to it. Just as homosexuals are guaranteed the right to persuade us otherwise, we have the right to discern this behavior for the protection of our civilization.

Of course, PFLAG works with the groups to justify the behavior of their children and rid themselves of any personal lingering guilt. They are in *Stage 4* of *mind control* and most likely will never come out of it. With over 76,000 members and over 425 local groups, they teach that ignorance is what has made life unbearable for their children. [11] Once again they blame someone else for their children's behavior, instead of their child. They do not accept ex-homosexuals who profoundly preach that recovery is possible, but continue to promote homosexuality as normal and natural for their children.

Perhaps my wait to start researching books was for a good reason. I received an incredible email from Linda Harvey at Mission America, the subject matter exactly what I needed, the reading material from GLSEN. With my own review of their site and this information, it's evident the reading list is degenerate; most adhere to principles of NAMBLA. GLSEN has its reading list separated into K-6 and 7-12 grade levels. The majority of the books for young children K-6 deal with family structure. They use catchy titles that encompass the alphabet or use ducks and cats as an allure.

1. *Daddy's Roommate*, by Michael Willhoite. The subject matter is about a boys father who is divorced and living with another man. It tells about their daily life together and how they engage in normal activities just like everyone else.
2. *Asha's Mums*, by Rosamund Elwin and Michele Paulse. An African Canadian girl becomes the subject of curiosity to her classmates because she has two lesbian mums. This book clarifies that it is nothing unusual, just the ordinary.
3. *All Families Are Different* by Sol Gordon. This makes light of different families of color, adoption and foster care in order to show that the same sex heads of families are no different than anyone else. All family structures are okay. The illustrations are utilized to promote acceptance.
4. *1 2 3 A Family Counting Book*, by Bobbie Combs. This book celebrates alternative families and teaches children to count to twenty.
5. *Heather Has Two Mommies*, by Leslea Newman. This book caused controversy when it was published in 1989. It was the book that opened the way for other homosexual books to be marketed.
6. *King and King* by Linda de Haan and Stern Nigland. This is a fairy tale about same–sex relationships.

7. *Lucy Goes to the Country*, by Joseph Kennedy and John Canemaker. This is a about a cat that takes a trip into the County for the weekend. It is the tale of a cat's-eye view of her adventure. It gives valuable lessons about different kinds of families.[12]

This reading material is sexual in content, but it is recommended for young children to read. Following a short break, in order to gain my composure, I continued. The books for age level grade 7-12 shows the horrors of deception by a group that insists they are here only to prevent harassment. Do these books sound like a group recommendation to prevent harassment? The last I've heard, statutory rape is a crime! We must get rid of these books based on the laws of this land. We must say "no" to pedophilia.

1. The book called *Growing Up Gay/ Growing Up Lesbian* tells about two ten year olds graphic exploration in sexual play together.[13] .
2. The book called *Queering Elementary Education*, with the forward by the President of GLSEN, gives a story about a couple who raised their daughter to be"queerly." By the time the girl is eight years old she has attended many homosexual parades. She also has experienced older men, a man she met on the bus that she has sex with in a restroom.[14]
3. *Rainbow Boys* tells about three boys who explore their homosexual attractions. The themes include sexual magazines, videos and graphic descriptions of male sexual encounters.[15] It also features several explicit heterosexual scenes, but the worst one is the description of sodomy between the boy and a 29-year-old man who he met via the Internet.[16] This subject matter is against the law and yet the GLSEN has it on it's website as recommended reading for our children.
4. Author Mary L Gray writes "Young people are just as capable of exploring or asserting their sexual identity as adults." Her book called *In Your*

Face: Stories From the Lives of Queer Youth is
recommended. A young man, 15 years old, talks
about seducing his friend's dad, who is 29 or 30
years old. It is described as a "Wild night. We did
everything."[17] Another story tells of a 12-year-old
boy having sex with his cousin who was 16.[18] The
next story tells of a youth who says he identified
himself when he was 6 or 7 as being homosexual.[19]
How remarkable children this age grasping the
permanence of their sexual orientation. Their
misguided experiences and normal fantasy are led
by such books to believe they are homosexual.
There was one more from this book. It was about a
16 year old boy who picked up a boyfriend from a
youth group called Positive Images. It is a Sonoma
County Gay, Lesbian, Bisexual Youth group. The
man he met was 25; he was 16. [20]

Mission America and Eagle Forum of Sacramento share a
common goal to protect our young from reading material such as the
above. How can educators possibly overlook the reading material of
GLSEN? It is after all a great way to judge an organization's values
and ethics. I would not want my child reading or associating with
people who thought the above good literature, and yet schools nation-
wide continue to allow programs in their schools sponsored by
GLSEN. The content made me sick and I knew it was time to leave
this subject matter. However, if there are still doubters as to our
children being attacked, let me introduce one more scenario to you.

The Executive Director of Traditional Value Coalition,
Andrea Lafferty, took copies of a coloring book to every freshman
Senator on Capitol Hill. She found them as part of the James Hormel
Gay and Lesbian Reading Center at the San Francisco Public Library.
The coloring books contained pages of female genitalia for the
children to color. James Hormel was U. S. Ambassador to
Luxembourg, and Attorney Ashcroft had concerns as to his
appointment because of his ideas on homosexual activism. Public
officials denounced Ashcroft; including Senator Diane Feinstein who
continued to denounce Ashcroft for his concern about Hormel.[21] Now

I can see why Ashcroft was concerned! I never heard or read about this grotesque situation from anyone, but discovered it while doing research for the Book. Benjamin Lopez, Lobbyist for Traditional Values Coalition, said the story was true and I can't help but wonder what the freshman Senators did with this information. Are they living a "lie" also? We're not protecting our young, for we've sold their bodies, minds and souls to a dark side only to avoid the rebuke of a miniscule narrow interest group and a few votes. I'm ashamed of politicians that ignore this subject matter. It is one thing to respect another as a human being, but it is another to teach and encourage our children to live an unnatural lifestyle. Twenty years from now adults will pay psychiatrists for help in sorting out their sexual confusion. In 20 years it will not only be homosexuals, bisexuals or transvestites seeking reparative therapy, but also normal individuals who were educated to be homosexuals. I find this rather amusing. Justice will find its reward, for the parents of children today will wish they had listened.

36

HEROES

I thought about the word "ashamed," how I felt toward many people in our land. It's not about judgment, but mortification at the attitude of its people. I know in my heart some people still care and that is why I wrote this book. My motivation for writing has been to educate people about the *causes* of change, the repercussions of the changes and positive actions we can take to stop the mania in order to protect our children, family, and future generations. Endless hours of research in areas of darkness have not been easy. It was most difficult saying "No" to fun activities, isolating myself in order to write. Typing wasn't my best subject in high school, now I'm thankful I had the class. It helped me to work with my friend computer in a more efficient manner, but my daily contact was still with an inanimate "object." I missed human contact! My husband, however, took care of me. His encouraging words got me through each day and he always made sure I ate my dinner. Many nights he ungrudgingly cooked when he came home from work. He is a great chef (he excels in all he does); better still, my special friend and I love him deeply. My rewards have been many since I began the adventure of writing a book and I am happy with my decision. My goal to understand the process of change in our country has been accomplished and it is helping me cope with the chaos.

Twentieth Century influences fostered a climate of change in America. Multiple groups with *cause* using bigger *causes* of love, brotherhood, normalcy and equal merit, effectively manipulate power for this change. It continues with the use of tools of manipulation such as vocabulary, rituals, learning materials, intimidation, humor and intellectual status. Our schools, communities, churches and governments incorporate their *cause* into every area of learning. Change isn't coming; it's here and continues to foster more change. *Mind control*, through dialectic thinking is doing its job. The pace is fast and people can't keep up, so instead they give up, allowing "secular humanism" to take over as our "religion" of life. Maybe one-day lawyers will take on Secular Humanism as a religion in our institutions across America. The Humanists have their own Manifestos I, II and III, which can be found on their website. I have included the Manifesto II in the back of this book. [1] Already our Courts have given them religions status in cases such as United States v. Kauten (2d Cir. 1943), Fellowship of Humanity v. County of Alameda (1957) and in the Supreme Court decision of Torcaso v. Watkins in 1961. [2] If Christianity is not allowed in the classrooms, businesses, or government then the Humanist religion and SEED should not be allowed. No wonder I have become totally bewildered by my research, for these deceptive programs are against the law and yet no justice is served against them. It shows moral decay out of control and it will not stop, continuing instead to throw our children into dungeons of destruction. I long to escape thoughts of it; Eagle Forum Conference was right around the corner. I would be there for I welcomed the camaraderie of fellow traditional citizens striving to maintain a sane world.

The attendance was good, especially from California. I was happy that our son's girlfriend, Josilyn, decided to attend. She is a beautiful woman who has achieved many of her life dreams through discipline, hard work, and outstanding moral character. Her enthusiasm for politics is uplifting, for even with a full time school and work schedule, she manages to stay positive and attend meetings and conferences. Our Secretary and Legislative Director, Angela Azevedo, attended and is a joy to work with. Angela has an amazing way of making legislation look easy and I see a great future in politics for her. She works hard for our local and state Chapters of Eagle Forum and is a great role model for her children and grandchildren. In general, conferences are packed with activity. Eagle Forum 2003 proved to be the same, and one of the most inspiring conferences I ever attended. While listening to one of our speakers, I was suddenly overcome with the reality of how many heroes were present in the room. I began to make mental lists of individuals and groups that were dedicated to the values of our country and active in their demonstration of them. Some of these people do receive attention, but many go unnoticed. I had a strange thought that perhaps, in some way, I might be the one to bring some light on them. Now writing this Book, I am able to do so. Everyone has people in their life that are heroes, and perhaps the individuals I write about will remind you of them and their above average dedication to being active in traditional beliefs.

Erin, who gave an unforgettable presentation on Illegal Immigration, deserves recognition for her bravery to speak out about this subject matter. Erin's story is one of untold sorrow. It is the horror of illegal aliens crossing borders on privately owned land, 1,000 daily, destroying everything in their path. They leave garbage, plastic bottles and diapers behind as they struggle to survive. It is not unusual to find animals with plastic bottles hanging from their mouths following death from eating them. Not only animals, but also people suffer from the violence. The once peaceful families must ride their ranges with a gun, a two-way radio and a telephone. If they do not have all three, there is a great chance of not making it back alive. Owners can't sell the land, for no one wants it now. They must live daily with lawlessness and the fear that the next 9/11 terrorists may very well enter through their property. The families who courageously face this intrusion each day are heroes.

The topic of Immigration passed to our brave congressman, Representative Tom Tancredo and John Hostettler, who tirelessly fight the political battle in Washington over illegal immigration. John Fund, author and speaker, educated us to the realities of voter fraud and the many dangers that surround it. William Federer and David Barton gave a positive perspective on our country's heritage. Their factual books are an inspiration to us to learn more about the history of our Nation. We need all the inspiration we can get for after listening to David Limbaugh, author of *Persecution*, we knew that our liberties connected to our faith and religion were in serious trouble. Virginia Armstrong, Founder and President of the Blackstone Institute, is a lawyer who confronts issues of constitutional law. Her online courses are educational, but to hear her speak inspired us to learn even more about our great legal system.

Quality of education at the conference is accompanied by the excitement of meeting the speakers. Joe Scarborough, MSNBC *Scarborough Country* and once Congressman, is a man who stands tall, not only in physical stature, but also in his moral values that predominate his news program. It was obvious he lived a strong family ethic from his two boys who accompanied him during dinner and dressed in suits.

Judge Roy Moore, defender of the Ten Commandments in Alabama, is not easily forgotten. His command of words is like watching a sunset. The image of what he says is lasting and beautiful. His humbleness when speaking with him is apparent. His wife received the "Mother of the Year" award. I could feel her strength as I watched husband and wife interact. Everyone left his presentation in awe of his family, his life and his commitment to law and its foundation in Judeo-Christian principle.

I suddenly found myself aware of how many young people were in the room. Their eyes seemed glued to the speakers for they were not just listening, but truly interested in the subject matter. I thought of other young people and how they inspire us through their actions and decisions in life. Our Daughter Michelle began a group called Traditional Ladies Coalition (TLC) at U.C. Davis to make known the conservative women on campus. She is also active in the Davis College Republicans and when they held a "Coming Out Conservative" day she spoke on feminism, as did other members on "politically correct" issues. Though they are jeered at such events, the members continue to speak and write on conservative policies. Michelle's testimony to belief comes in how she lives, for discipline shows in her dedication to dance, gardening, and high academic achievement. Her special girlfriends, and the wonderful man she is now dating, Steve, share her traditional values.

Other young people such as Tim Buehler show incredible courage in the face of danger. He is a senior high school student unafraid to voice his opinions about multiculturalism and political correctness in his high school newspaper. He even began a conservative club on campus. Peers who disagree with his philosophy stalk him daily, and he receives death threats and aggressive emails everyday. His school, Rancho Cotate High School in Santa Rosa CA., refused to help him until the media stepped in with the story. The school received thousands of emails in his support. Tim now has police protection while at school. His grandfather, a Pearl Harbor survivor, taught him about the glory of our country. Tim feels we must stand and protect what has been given us by the brave and courageous effort of those before us.

Families that home school are bringing children into the light of truth that shines when their children proudly demonstrate the principles of our land through oratory debate and speeches. Chris and Aimay Krive do just this with two of their children, David and Jonathan, excelling as national debate champions. They both graduated high school before 16 and now have finished paralegal courses. Jonathan, the head of Teen Eagles in California, is hopeful to begin chapters throughout California. Attending conferences with your teenager, like Steve and Lori Nelson and their daughter Kirsten from our Chapter, is an ideal way to promote learning and love of country.

I thought of the importance of the family unit. We have lots of friends who have been married over 25 years. Many of them are from the neighborhood in which we raised our children. These individuals, who refuse to walk away when the times get rough, carry on the family unit. This is where strong values can be taught to children, young and old. I still know of parents that have not accepted their children or partners into their homes when living the homosexual lifestyle. It may seem harsh but it seems to work, for in some cases the strong family ethic wins over the unnatural behavior and they seek therapy. Some special friends have divorced, due to circumstances beyond their control, and it takes great stamina to move on with life and continue being a dedicated parent. Positive attitude is crucial in teaching our children that a strong family is achievable through dedication and hard work whether you have been through a divorce or not.

Successful grand parenting is important. Craig and Mary Ann truly represent loving grandparents. With a family history in Ranching, they enjoy teaching the grandchildren about their past and the traditional lifestyles and values that many parents today have forgotten or deny. Bill and Carol are a stabilizing force for their grandchildren because they teach them the Judeo-Christian values in a fun, but meaningful way. Elizabeth teaches her grandchildren how to save money and be creative through the art of sewing. Joe and Dee Madruga are Eagle Forum parents and grandparents who offer their services to pro-life organizations, the Republican Party, and their church. Bunny Collins is a senior citizen who also understands the importance of civic duty. They give freely of time and effort for organizations that preserve our freedoms. They are proud to be Americans and say it to their grandchildren. I thank senior citizens who speak out against behavior that is destructive of their grandchildren's future.

Of course hero status is "clearly" indicated for families that lose children and loved ones in unexpected daily accidents (my friend Claudia's husband was killed in his airplane. She had 5 children) or world tragedies such as war, 9/11, Columbine or the Oklahoma Bombing. I look to them with great admiration for their courage. The brave soldiers who give life for our freedom are high on my list of heroes. I still wonder why at parades everyone is not cheering each time a military unit walks by? Or how about our Boy Scouts who need our support, for the ACLU has truly been discriminatory towards their traditional beliefs. All the above individuals deserve our utmost respect, for their incredible courage helps us survive the turmoil of our times!

Traditional marriage and family is an important unit and one of the few unchanged forces in our land today. We must preserve one-man and one-woman marriage, for it will sustain us as a nation. I looked around the room and hoped that the young men and women present would take seriously the message of this weekend and make good decisions in regards to family values such as my friend Maggie, who decided to leave the workforce and stay at home with the children. Her husband Dan supports this decision that will not only affect their family unit, but also the cohesiveness of our country. We must take back our Patriarchal Family and be proud of being male and female. I admire dads and moms willing to give up certain riches to find others!

It was wonderful to share the day with people of high moral character! The joy in each moment gave me comfort, almost like being in my comfortable blue chair. The first day was a good one!

The days that followed were filled with uplifting speakers that continued to bring my thoughts to everyday heroes and their positive influence in my life. Sometimes we don't see the hero, but only the special person we have known for so long.

Our son Michael and my brother Walter are such people for they share an eye condition called Retinoschesis. It is a sex linked hereditary disease, which leaves them with limited vision; the retina literally shreds leaving them holes to see around or not to see at all. They must work twice as hard to accomplish what we take for granted. Both of them are extremely successful individuals. My brother's incredible management skills, innovative ideas, and outgoing personality working at Bell Telephone Company, brought him many honors. Our son graduated from College this summer Summa Cum Laude (Highest Honor) for he sets high standards for himself in all he does. His discipline has aided him in carpentry, bodybuilding, sports activities and his personal held belief system, by which he lives his daily life. Walter and Michael move forward in life with an ease that makes their vision defect unnoticeable to people. They are a constant source of inspiration to others.

My mother died 11 years ago. During her 3year battle with cancer, her courage was apparent to us through her words and actions. Her vibrant smile and sense of humor welcomed us, and she never complained even though she suffered terribly. My friend Carol lives with a life threatening disease. She acquired HIV due to her husband who died of AIDS years ago. She lives through forgiveness by speaking to groups about the disease, the lifestyles that encourage it and the ability to change through acceptance of Jesus into your life. Debbie, a good friend, lost her vision in her 30"s. I love to visit with her, for she truly is a fun lady that has remained positive through all her ups and downs in life dealing with her Diabetes. She contributes to the family income by crocheting beautiful dolls that marvel all people who look upon them. Many people do not dwell on the negatives, but on the successes of life. It is not the affliction that makes one a hero, but the individual's attitude toward it.

Caregivers need to be commended. My girlfriend Barbara drove to Modesto, California from San Francisco every weekend for three years to take care of her mom and dad suffering from debilitating illnesses. One family member, Jean, continually takes care of sick family members in her home, even though she herself has been through numerous cancers and surgeries. Nancy Reagan and the people above are examples of truly loving individuals who genuinely give of themselves.

I looked around the conference and realized that no one is free of pain or struggle. It is in our attitude that we survive, and one of our strongest American attributes is to never give up. Setting goals and achieving them through the tradition of hard work for family survival is important. I thought of the patriarchal leaders in our family: my dad Walter, father-in-law Mike, brothers-in-law Tony and Mike and my husband. They have worked very hard to make a comfortable life for their families. Their parents or grandparents came to this country as immigrants and knew the true meaning of "working" for what you get. There were no "hand outs" when they arrived in America! They passed the work ethic to their children. The injustice of activist group's accusations that they gained it because of "white privilege" is outrageous. My mother, Margaret, and mother-in-law, Ruth, worked long hours as children and knew the toil of backbreaking labor. They moved forward in life with a positive attitude. They were survivors teaching their own children the value of American tradition and strong family unity.

My three sisters-in-law Chris, Kathy and Joanne, who are like my sisters, demonstrate commitment to family by contributing, for 30 years, to monthly-organized holiday and birthday dinners. We planned yearly camping trips that included extended family members LeRoy and Sharon and children. Bonding activites such as fishing, hunting, swimming, cooking, playing, and eating together are "glue" to a family unit; they bind and leave everyone with special family memories. Our children, plus nephews and nieces Steve, Josh, Amy, Gina, Laura and friend Zach, and Jennifer and her husband Dave participate in the family gatherings. I am confident they will pass on the traditions that are important for the survival of our country. Family is important! I am grateful to my parents who showed me the benefits of hard work and principled living, for it led me to an understanding of family unity as being a solid base for future stability. I still call my Dad for His wonderful words of wisdom and to tell him I love him. Of course, to hear him say how much he loves me truly makes my day! I can still hear my mom whispering how much she loves me.

Churches are like family units and the spiritual leaders, who boldly stand in truth, must work courageously to influence the world. I thought of last year, 2003, when Bishop Wiegand told California Governor Davis he was no longer welcome at the Holy Communion Rail due to his position on abortion. Maybe, one day, more traditional religious leaders will stand strong on homosexuality, bisexuality, transgender identity, and pedophilia in the same way. These are acts against the very sanctity of our human bodies that God made in His image and likeness. Francis Cardinal Arinze spoke out against homosexuality and its mockery of the family. He came under severe fire following his words at Georgetown University's graduating class. This took tremendous courage, for there are only a few that do speak these words. Our Pope came out with a strong message to the world; abortion is wrong and homosexuality is not in line with God's word. Reverend Michael J. Sheridan, the Bishop of the Diocese of Colorado Springs, has clearly outlined the Duties of Catholic politicians and voters. There is little doubt as to our duties after reading this Pastoral Letter. These are faithful followers of God's law; not afraid to differentiate between good and evil and then deliver it to the people. They could have easily been silenced due to the homosexual climate of pedophilia that was discovered in the Catholic Church. A courageous Pastor Jay of Harvest Worship Center in Vacaville CA., has initiated a special day called "Americans for America" in order to celebrate the Declaration of Independence and the signing of our Constitution. He understands how church and state can work mutually together for the benefit of America. Other churches are coming aboard. With a new pastor at First Baptist Church in Elk Grove, it appears that the congregation may become more involved in programs that will educate them as to current affairs and their role as active Christians in the changing world of today's declining moral values. Other courageous churches in the Sacramento area are Capitol Christian Center, Arcade Baptist Church, and the Church of Latter Day Saints. They are not afraid to speak out against the evil in our country.

Matthew Kelly, a remarkable speaker and author from Australia, began delivering the message of a balanced life through God when he was in college. A brilliant student, with any career possible, he chose to leave home and speak in high schools, universities, conferences and retreats unafraid to share his words of hope. The youth are receptive to this message and tell him they are thankful for a path to follow for righteous living. His staff included dedicated young people such as Julie Gomez who found meaning in life through the Matthew Kelley Foundation. Her family supported her endeavors as she faithfully ran complicated retreats and trips as if she was born with this gift.

Dr. Dobson and his wife Shirley have committed themselves, for 30 years, to Focus on the Family, a nation-wide Organization that is pro-life and pro-family. He is well known for his courageous stand on morality issues affecting the family and is bold in his television appearances and radio interviews.

I thought of other organizations and their contributions. Countless hours on the computer have brought me to sites such as: Abiding Truth Ministries, American Center for Law and Justice, American Family Association, American Policy Center, California Pro-Life, California Republican Assembly, California Rifle and Pistol Association, Campaign for California Families, Christian Coalition, Concerned Women for America, Coral Ridge Ministries, Culture of Life Foundation, Eagle Forum, Exodus, Family Research Council, FrontPage, Gun Owners of America, Heritage Foundation, Jews for the Preservation of Firearms Ownership, Liberty Counsel, NARTH, National Rifle Association, Northern California Coalition for Limited Government, Mission America, News Max, Pacific Justice, Political Vanguard, Preserve Liberty, Reclaim America, Religious Freedom Coalition, Right to Life, Traditional Values Coalition, and World Net Daily. These are but a few of the groups that dedicate time and effort to truth and action to support it. People need to be aware of these groups. Become active in them and give financially to their *cause*, for it is only with your help that they can survive to protect our precious freedoms. These organizations and volunteers need our recognition and thanks!

The radio talk show hosts Rush Limbaugh, Dr. Laura Schlessinger, Roger Hedgecock, Michael Medved, Michael Savage, Sean Hannity, Bill O'Reilly, Glenn Beck, Joe Pursch, Eric Hogue, Mark Williams, Michael Reagan, Dennis Prager, Hugh Hewitt, Michael Gallagher, Tom Sullivan, Phyllis Schlafly, Barbara Simpson, Janet Folger, Melanie Morgan, Sharon Hughes, and many others educate us to fact and give us great alternatives to the horrors of gangster rap and politically correct TV shows. Women such as Phyllis Schlafly, Ann Coulter, Michelle Malkin, Condolezza Rice and Laura Ingraham represent women who are intelligent, active politically and proud to be feminine. They are frequently on radio and television, as are men such as Jessie Petersen, Alan Keyes, J.C. Watts and Colin Powell. Whenever interviewed, they always uphold our Constitution accurately to stand for individual rights, not global rights. The uniqueness and individuality of man is central to their beliefs, not classification by group status or global classification. Michael Medved is a man who believes this principle. He is an example of a truly genuine man that I respect not only for his writings and radio program, but for the intense honesty I felt when I had the joy of meeting him when he spoke in Sacramento. I also felt this genuineness when I met Laura Ingraham. Courageous people, such as the above individuals, show conviction through their words and actions and it helps us survive the turmoil of our time.

How about the men and women who run for office? A good man's character will shine if he wins, but when loss occurs it may be different. There is a big difference between an Al Gore attitude and the attitudes of two men I had the joy to work with this year, Senator Rico Oller and Craig DeLuz. Though they lost a hard and long battle for Congress and City Council Representative, they continue to serve the people and portray an optimistic attitude. A letter of humble thankfulness came from Rico Oller, who encouraged us to support Dan Lungren, a man of integrity, in his campaign for Congress. We are now working with Gary Podesto, Mayor of Stockton, who is running for State Senate; his platform involves protection of our children. He is a good man who is not afraid to speak out against the hidden agenda of those who would prey upon our young.

Why would we vote in people like Barbara Boxer, Dianne Feinstein, Ted Kennedy, Hillary Clinton, Howard Dean, Sheila Kuehl, Hannah-Beth Jackson, Mark Leno, Christine Kehoe, John Laird and many more who support programs to harm our children, instead of people who can return us to the solid principles that will keep our children and teens safe? In California we see dedicated people like Senators' Tom McClintock, Pete Knight, Richard Mountjoy, Bill Marrow and Assemblymen Ray Haynes and Tim Leslie working diligently to protect marriage and our children. Nation-wide we look to Senators such as Rick Santorum (R-PA), Jeff Sessions (R-Al), Sam Brownback (R-KS), Jim Gerlach (R-PA) and other dedicated Congressmen for strong moral leadership. Find out about your candidates and make sure you understand their platform before you vote for them. Vote in quality people or you too will have legislation that I have listed in the back of the Book (Appendix E). Take a look at the California top ten legislative bills of 2004. You will see how far a small number of homosexual legislators have taken us from traditional family values that protect our family and country to social construct issues that are destroying our youth. Because of our radical homosexuals, we pay our legislators for spending time and effort on issues that will destroy America. We already have in place all the necessary legislation to protect everyone from unjust discrimination (prejudice), but the bills keep pouring in to force us to give in to lifestyles that are against our natural order. Good politicians will stand for your values, so find them and support them. Traditional men are examples of what made our country great!

Our young boys need examples of real American Men and honest politicians that do not push homosexuality on our children. We need to keep at the forefront good men, who run websites, such as Thomas Del Beccaro of Political Vanguard, David Horowitz of FrontPage, or Joseph Farrah and David Kupelian of World Net Daily and Whistleblower magazine. With the increasing number of people becoming Anti-American, the written words of traditional men are crucial to producing future heroes. Our young will learn solid values through their writings. It takes hard work to do what is required, above the ordinary, to make a difference.

We must continue our pioneering spirit to renew our American dreams. I thought about the everyday lives of my diverse friends and their unique individuality. My friend Connie is a successful businesswoman. She is black, but I don't dwell on color, only our friendship. She has a wonderful family and we share many of the same values; we do not need to be forced, through tolerance and diversity programs, to like each other. Our friend Juan owns a Mexican restaurant and catering service; he works long hours to support his family and teach them the American way. A Palestinian man just opened two Network Communications stores in the Elk

Grove area. His father worked hard selling rugs door to door to save money to buy his own grocery store, which supported his children attending college. He believed in the American dream for his children. Grimaneza's family is Portuguese and she is my friend. Her family came to America for a better life. It was a struggle, but with hard work and determination they have managed to assimilate into the American culture. They maintain their former identity by continuing Portuguese traditions within their families. My associate and friend Chris came from Germany when she was 11 years old. She was determined to learn the English language in 3 months. Chris wanted so much to be a part of this great country and be called an American. Her parents encouraged this spirit, and she did learn the language in 3 months. These individuals not only give us example of the American dream becoming a reality, but also an awareness that one must take responsibility for achieving it. In today's world, accepting responsibility takes on special significance for many people have lost the desire to do so.

My mind was racing with images of people I admired including the mothers who were about to speak on sex education. I knew their plight and admired their courage as Pam Thomason and Kathy Stohr proceeded to the podium. Pam fought PTA and school officials in Hunstville, Alabama to rid the health programs of a nation-wide program known as "Girls INC." It is a liberal organization that fights gender stereotyping, homophobia, and discrimination against teens that want sexual freedom, including the right to abortion. Most parents in the school district were not aware that the facilitator of the program encouraged lewd material, discussion, and the carrying of condoms in every girl's purse. Pam's persistence to stop it, worked eventually and the district was forced to call "Girls INC" and cancel the program. Kathy Stohr was informed of a survey on suicide and drugs that was to be given teens in Fairfax, Virginia and most troubling were 9 questions of sexual content. The questions were invasive and suggestive of sexual conduct being normal. It was a hard battle but with support of legal action and other dedicated individuals, the surveys were not given. These committed individuals made a difference and are heroes.

We have a hero in Elk Grove by the name of Teri. Her voice is heard repeatedly in the school district as she stands courageously before many to defend our moral code in raising our children. She represents many parents who are afraid to be bold due to "fear" of community rejection and of retribution against their children if they speak out. I am continually amazed at her strength in confronting authority figures in the school district and in holding them accountable for their actions. Years ago we had assurance of parent's common moral values in sending our children to a public school. Authority figures, such as our past Principal of Kerr Junior High School, shared our values. I miss him and the teachers that were role models for our children. There are a few left who fight against the immorality of this time, but most remain silent. It was reported to me that one of our children's grammar school teachers knew of the SEED program. She didn't like it, but chose to remain silent. Many of the good teachers just leave the profession and leave the mess to those who caused it (the followers of the NEA). Teachers who buck the system are true heroes and we must give them credit for their courage and example to our young.

The conference sped by and soon I was boarding the plane for home, but the vision of heroes lingered as I thought of Phyllis Schlafly who has been a hero all of her life, and her wonderful assistants Lori Waters and Julia Algya who have successfully put together the conferences. I have enjoyed not only their company and knowledge, but also their amazing commitment to Eagle Forum. On the trip home, I thought about all the brave heroes of our time. They give us courage to never give up, but to push forward in truth. I thank them for they give our country support in its timeless principles of the American Way. Thoughts of Eagle Forum's future in the protection of our children entered my mind. I flashed on the SEED program. Eagle Forum can find no further information on it and no one in the school district will address it or reveal its status. We know it still exists for the district has refused to remove it as requested by parents involved with litigation. This motivates me even more to finish my book so others will be exposed to its content. Upon exposure of the book there will be discussion, but I am realistic enough to know SEED will not be easily stopped. Once people are in transformation and *Stage 4* of *mind control*, they usually do not reverse their stand. With an estimate of over 500 teachers involved, it is evident it has taken its toll in the once quiet town of Elk Grove, California.

37

WEAVE

T he phone rang within minutes of my return from conference. Even though I was exhausted from the trip, something prompted me to pick up the receiver. Teri called about yet another program being squeezed into the system. The WEAVE Program, being introduced into middle and high schools in the Elk Grove area and greater Sacramento area is a typical example of another organization that has been usurped by a narrow interest group to promote their agendas.

WEAVE, Women Escaping a Violent Environment, began in the 1970's by abused Hispanic women. The Resource Center and Board of Directors was formed in 1981; management has changed since its original formation. WEAVE now includes a shelter, legal department, children's and adult counseling, teen education and sexual assault cases. It is a non-profit organization that provides holistic services to victims of domestic violence. The information on the web site appears neutral, not promoting any particular narrow interest group agenda. An education department does offer programs in the schools to help prevent violence and has been in existence for a number of years. An incredible message is delivered to children via this program and unfortunately it is abusive. This is rather ironic since they are advocating against abuse! I wonder if the narrow interest group makes known the below material to parents and the community.

The curriculum being taught to the children is far from neutral. There are seven chapters; one chapter is discriminatory against the white, male, middle-aged, healthy, rich and heterosexual. It is in violation of California Education code #51501 which prohibits schools from using any material that adversely reflects upon persons because of their sex or color. The students are introduced to this material by reviewing a two-sided chart at the beginning of the education series. It is as follows:

	Power	Non-Power
1.	white	non-white
2.	rich	poor
3.	middle-aged	young, elderly
4.	able-bodied	disabled
5.	male	female
6.	heterosexual	homosexual

Power has many definitions. It depends on how one defines it, for the definition can be manipulated to make "power" sound good or bad. Power ultimately is the ability or capability to do, act or affect something or someone. The above chart "sets" up the power structure as particular groups who "possess" the authority over others. It "sets" up oppressor and victim statuses before it happens, that are neither true nor relevant for teaching violence prevention to our youth. For every study indicating whites are the perpetrators of violence, there is a study showing blacks are the perpetrators towards whites. It is a no win situation and only introduces more racial material, which separates, not unites. Violence does not exist because of groups, but individuals within "all" groups. This chart "sets" up fear and discrimination against the supposed power groups and power itself.

At the bottom of one of the pages, the curriculum talks of the "power" wheel. It then said the following:

> "Be sure to emphasize that being on the power side does not make you an oppressor. What it means is that you have sometimes been given more "privilege" in our society. When people on the non-power side tell you that their experience of the world has been different, it is your responsibility to believe them and make sure you are not contributing to oppression or negative stereotyping."

This statement is out of line with the purpose of this program. It is setting up, again, the oppressor and victim *cause* status, and the students are receiving this message. This statement introduces a philosophy of "unearned privilege" which is discriminatory.

The next topic is gender teaching. The youth are given pictures of two boxes, one labeled male and one labeled female. The activity is "Act like a man-Act like a woman." The students discuss male and female in regards to appearances, manner, emotions, jobs and sexuality. It goes on to determine, once again, where the power lies in the boxes. The idea is that it is very difficult for men and women to have peaceful relationships if there are expectations of their gender. An example in the teaching curriculum is that our society puts pink on girls and blue on boys when they are born, with certain expectations of them due to their gender. It appears that gender is being redefined in the classroom to bring a unisex message to our youth. Redefining gender is inappropriate and goes against, once again, Code 51501 and Code 49091.12 which prohibits material or teachings that would promote students to disavow or affirm any personally held world view, religious doctrine or political opinion.

Parents have the right to teach their children male and female characteristics and to look at the world in terms of male and female. Teaching unisex or beliefs contrary to parental knowledge is inappropriate and not acceptable. Teaching this type of material carries a very serious message to our youth. It undermines the uniqueness of male and female and the pride one feels in representing their gender. It is discriminating against the worldview of traditional values for it is okay to put pink on a girl and blue on a boy and raise them as such. It is the authority of the parents to decide this issue.

Sexual topics are included in the above activity and this is a sensitive issue among families today. It is the parent's right to teach their own children the appropriateness of sexual lifestyles. The program states, to those passing out the handouts to the students, "also remind them that they can always go to their parents for help." I would think it should be a consistent theme in the program, but instead I found another statement, "The Philosophy of the Teen Education Program is that the students are the "experts" about what is happening in their own lives." This is also the SEED program philosophy.

The first few chapters of this program introduce philosophies that are against traditional family values. It is discriminatory, deceptive in its facts, and is being used to promote a narrow interest agenda that is not related to original intent. The rest of this program is neutral and would be beneficial to the youth.

I called the Sacramento WEAVE association and the Director of the program said it could be altered to meet the community needs. Pacific Justice Institute supported our theory that the above information was against education codes and discriminatory in nature. We did not want to stop the program, but only eliminate the objectionable material. Eagle Forum and Teri wrote letters to the School Board and Department Heads asking them to remove the particulars mentioned above. We knew that originally the parent board gave its approval, apparently the school board also, for it has been included in the curriculum. I do not know the reasons why the parents or board approved it, perhaps the way it was presented or perhaps the composition of the parent's advisory board. I do know the majority of families we talked with were against this presentation. A number of concerned parents and families were willing to pursue further action if this was allowed in the district schools.

Within a few weeks we received a letter from the District, the two chapters that we found discriminatory would be removed. Naturally Eagle Forum was pleased with the results, but we still know that WEAVE will be presenting this to other schools in the same format. If the "real" purpose is to prevent violence then the program can be taught without the oppression chart and gender nonsense. We hope they will remove this material from the other programs.

It's disheartening to know this message has been delivered to teens and even adults for the past ten years. Not only does this false information stir up racial tension, but also it's demeaning and antagonistic toward white, male, hard working, heterosexual men. It also eliminates the education of youth as to up to date surveys that show all groups own violence! It is the "individual" in the group that must take responsibility for his or her actions.

Of course we get rid of one injustice and right around the corner there is always another. We wondered what would be next in the saga of the Elk Grove School District.

258

38

THE LAST SAMURAI

Michael encouraged me to see the movie, *The Last Samurai*, with Tom Cruz. It appeared to be yet another politically correct movie. I wanted to forget all political agendas on our date night, for I was tired of them and the people perpetuating them. Forgetting didn't help; the programs kept coming.

Following the WEAVE incident, another occurred in Santa Rosa. Our Eagle Forum State President had called to inform me the Santa Rosa School District was holding a meeting, subject matter was Tolerance Education in the Schools. The organization introducing it was GLSEN. I thought of Massachusetts. In searching for someone from GLSEN to condemn what happened in the schools, I found words of a representative from GLSEN who backed the teachers who were fired in the Massachusetts scandal. "We absolutely do not think this was the appropriate response. These women are getting reprimanded for doing work that needs to be done, but that no one else wants to do." [1] It was apparent GLSEN had no remorse for the perversion of the Tufts University Education Conference. The second "Teach-Out" in Massachusetts was behind "closed" doors. How will they teach it in Santa Rosa? Other organizations, a County Supervisor and five churches have backed the GLSEN Tolerance Program. The cost to teach educators was enormous and coming from funds better used in other areas. Cost does not seem to matter for I eventually found out the Skits in Elk Grove cost over $30,000. The decision of the Santa Board School District will depend on the meeting. I thought of the coincidence of GLSEN influence in states where the SEED Program exists. California and Massachusetts have well developed SEED Programs. The saga begins again, only now it is hitting hard with hard-core programs like in Massachusetts.

Michael continued to encourage our movie night and something reversed my thinking. *The Last Samurai* is about how "horrible" our country is, and this time it dealt with our infringement on Japan and our desire to westernize them in the 1870's. Though I was determined not to see this movie, I allowed myself to go, for I wanted to see how they handled the subject matter. I found out, but was pleasantly surprised.

I realized as I watched this movie that the subject matter was appropriate not only for the movie makers decision to make America look "bad" again, but for our own situation in America today. Not even knowing it, the producers were delivering a powerful message about courageous people in our country. The Samurai were fighting their last stand in a civilization being taken over by "other" values and morals far different than the previous 900 years of their culture. I shivered as I thought of America. You and I are The "Last Samurai." We are indeed fighting to save the very moral fiber of our country. I was not down on America throughout or following the movie, for the producers had accomplished just the opposite with me. I was pumped with the adrenaline of positive action and more motivated, than ever, to continue in our *cause* to preserve the Judeo-Christian Principles upon which America was founded. Even though we are being shot down everyday, just as the Last Samurai were in the movie, we will continue to stand and fight for our *cause*.

Marge Griffin, a dear friend, took a stand in November of 2003 when she saw that Nordstrom's did not have gift cards with the Christian message for Christmas, but did have Hanukah, Kwanzaa and plain gift cards. She spoke out at the store and then notified us. We went to work notifying the business office in Seattle that we would not tolerate this and would do something about it, unless they did something about it first. Friends called from Bible study, Christian Woman's Club, Eagle Forum and other organizations to protest the discrimination of our faith. The executive offices had a meeting and decided to pull the cards from stores nation-wide since there was not time to make Christian ones for this season. We thanked them and are appreciative of their concern for the traditions of Christmas. Next year we will work with other groups to boycott any store that does not include our Christian heritage by mentioning "Christmas." It is, after all, centuries of history that we now are fighting to preserve. The power of standing for what is right can make a difference. We took a stand.

The Sacramento Community Center has a number of sculptures outside its building. When children go to the Nutcracker Ballet or adults attend community theater, they see a naked Poseidon Sculpture, a Buddha sculpture and a sculpture with separated heads, arms and legs with water running over them to indicate that we must stop hating others and stand for diversity. With the idea of our daughter Michelle, Eagle Forum of Sacramento decided to petition the Arts commission allowing us to build a Moses with the Ten Commandments outside of the community center. We believe it the perfect setting for introducing the law that allowed freedom for our diversity. In fact the Texas 5th Circuit Court of Appeals declared that the Ten Commandments are historical in nature and provide a foundation for Western law. Teri was able to find a professional Disney artist, Matthew Bates, who sketched the drawing and Bruce Carty, a professional sculptor who may sculpt and erect it. We are taking a stand and we hope others will petition their cities to erect a sculpture of "The First Law."

We took a stand when we saw the statistics of 1,000,000 new teen pregnancies yearly and an ever-increasing number of STD's, HIV and AIDS cases. Teen Sex Programs aren't working; abstinence is the only sure way to combat this issue. With two teens acquiring HIV every hour in every 24-hour day, is it any wonder that we want not only Alcohol-Free and Drug-Free Schools, but also Sex-Free Schools? Surveys indicate that sex ED doubles the sexual participation by teens and has little effect on stopping active sex lives. Are parents so naïve as to honestly believe that educational classes about sex is going to diminish interest in having it? Are parents so deep in denial that they think putting condoms on a cucumber is going to squelch sexual desire in a normal 15-year-old male? Do parents honestly think that their child is not vulnerable to these devastating diseases that KILL! We must get sex out of the schools! Congressman Duncan Hunter (R-CA), Chairman of the House Armed Services Committee is introducing a bill called the "Parents Empowerment Act." It will provide civil action for a minor damaged by someone who introduces material such as pornography and inappropriate entertainment products. It allows the parents or guardian to sue anyone who fosters these actions. We must push for this legislation for minors that are damaged because of sex Ed in the schools that introduced them to harmful lifestyles and actions. What are we thinking when we allow these programs to dominate our children and their lives? Our stand is simply stated:

Alcohol-Free, Drug-Free, now Sex-Free Schools!

We're going nation-wide with this idea and encouraging other organizations, parents, and citizens to join us in protecting our youth from serious physical and mental disease. I am confident that people of all races want this deceitful sex Ed out of their schools. Routinely I hear not only the Russian community, but also Asians, Chinese, and Hispanics complaining about the tolerance and diversity programs and the destruction that awaits our youth. Let's get rid of sex-focused education and bring back "real" education to the classroom. We want girls to be proud in saying "No" to sex and our boys respectful of the ones that do. We can reduce the number of teen pregnancies. Let's give the youth of America another chance to get focused on learning, and not about sex, but subject matter pertinent to their future. This is American tradition and Real Americans do not push teens into sex!

I understood the Samurai fighting for survival of their traditions. Identification was at the forefront of my thinking as I happily thanked my husband for taking me to the movie. It was a simple camaraderie that I shared with these men of great courage. Eagle Forum and others like us are, after all, taking a stand that may very well be our last.

39

ADVOCACY

Christmas is the most beautiful time of year. This year it held incredible importance in my life for I was blessed with an overwhelming sense of peace. My answers were found and now I needed to deliver them to others. Memories of the last two years flooded through my mind. The burden of my unknowns is now an identity of a country and its people as they travel to destruction. It sounds terrible, but there is a comfort in coming to its reality and what we can do to slow the process. I handle objectionable situations with assurance of experience and knowledge gained along the way. I have never been stronger in my convictions or my ability to stand behind them without leaving my absolute position of truth. My success comes in living the moment and being the best that I can be when confronted with the chaos of today. I've never been happier for my sense of balance has been restored. Christmas passed quickly. The usual lows associated with taking down decorations was absent. I was excited to begin the New Year with finishing my book being my 2004 resolution.

January began with the realization that I had a lot to finish on the Book. A combination of two factors contributed to this dilemma. I was a novice at writing a first book and I am a spontaneous person. Last year when I wrote, I didn't put my footnotes in the computer, but on paper. Oh yes there is one more factor, my handwriting and printing is indistinguishable. Needless to say I left the house three times in January and worked long hours sorting through what was obviously my fault, a lack of ability to read my notes. I forgave myself and learned to appreciate again my endurance levels and my discipline. It was a nightmare, but I thought of the last Samurai, and I knew I could do it.

Numerous things helped me keep my sanity. In December Joe Pursch offered me the opportunity to tell my tale on his radio show. He gave me a two-hour live show devoted to the Book and the allowance of Eagle Forum members to talk about their areas of concern. I thank him from the bottom of my heart. Because of this show, in January, I've had numerous calls in regards to Eagle Forum and the subject matter of this book. Joe and his wife Tina are dedicated to the Judeo-Christian principles of our country and are not afraid to say it. This opportunity encouraged me to push forward with my book.

Karen England and CRI are battling school boards about students signing off campus without parental consent. Their battle over parent's rights encouraged me to move forward with my book so people will be aware of this horrible issue. Teenagers in grades 7-12 can sign out from school for drug and suicide counseling, or an abortion without parental consent. Schools believe they have the right to elevate teenager's rights over parental authority. Brave parents are realizing the power of their ultimate authority over school districts and are taking a stand against this horrific policy. Unfortunately school board members, such as in Folsom-Cordova District CA., will not listen to parents who pleaded with them to change the law. They voted against the family in favor of children's rights. Parents left the meeting devastated, but determined to get the four who voted against them out of office. It is up to the individual district as to how they structure the laws and they could have easily changed them. I hope that these parents will be examples of how important it is to know your school board members before voting them in. It could save your family. I give thanks to the parents, Karen, and Mary in Vacaville who work hard for our most precious unit the family. Their courage gives me the strength to move on.

Our 2004 California State Eagle Forum Conference, in February, proved valuable in offering me support to finalize my book. Our state president, state board members, and state chapter leaders encouraged me everyday through their newsletters, emails, positive activism, and now a well-planned conference. To share this conference with them was uplifting in giving me the final push to make my book a reality. Phyllis Schlafly, being our featured speaker, honored the state conference. She continues to inspire audiences with her command of meaningful presentations. I was elated to be a guest speaker at this conference and humbled to share important information from my book with attendees.

One of the enthusiastic men, Kevin, came forward and boldly announced at the microphone that he intended to become an activist. He offered his help, in any meaningful way, in order to educate the public about Immigration and Border control. His courage gave me optimism that there are still good people wanting to serve America and perhaps my book may encourage them to come forward.

Courageous young women traveled distances, such as Justine Kyker and Heidi Swanson, who come from Nebraska to tell their devastating physical and mental effects of abortion. They tell of coercion by Planned Parenthood to entice teens and women to have abortions. Is it any wonder that they would do this for evidence of their moral code lies in the following report put out by Life Dynamics?

> The firm, Life Dynamics, Inc., based in Denton, Texas, said in an eight-page summary of its data that "among girls 15 and younger who become pregnant, between 60 percent and 80 percent of them are impregnated by adult men." Some girls are even as young as 10 years old, said the summary. [1]

Planned Parenthood encourages these teens and children to have abortions but tells them to keep quiet the fact of the father being an adult man, for if they tell Planned Parenthood then they are required by law to report the case to the police. These interactions have been caught on tape and are on line for your listening. [2] Planned Parenthood covers up pedophilia, rape, and abortion side effects. They are responsible for many women's suffering such as the above ladies and Jennifer O'Neil, a movie star who had an abortion and now speaks out after years of suffering mental anguish. Women find refuge in organizations such as "Silent No More" that encourages truth be told about the devastating effects of abortion. Our liberal legislators at the Sacramento Capitol refuse to pass legislation that would require girls to sign a paper that they were not coerced into the abortion. Once again, to vote in leaders that will stand for good moral principles is crucial for our country's survival and our Children's survival.

The conference helped me to focus even more on changes that may occur because of my book. I am positive that it will make a difference in the education of children. If parents and citizens become informed, they may want to remove their children from public education and favor vouchers that would allow them this option. If voucher programs are controlled adequately, they have a positive effect on a child's education and life.[3] The immediate success of reversing "social engineering" education to "real" education is questionable and; therefore, encourages parents to support legislation for vouchers. Parent's concern for quality education and safety must come first and the only way they will get it is to pick a school of choice that meets their criteria for their child. Why should parents have to worry about what their children are taught in school for it should be a given right of children and families to be taught traditional academics in a good moral climate.

Parents have the right to know what is occurring in the schools and Teri decided to initiate a group that would help deliver information to them. Teri's adventures keep me positive as I write the last part of my book. Teri is writing a column in the town newspaper called "Parent Patrol" that alerts parents to what is happening within the schools in Elk Grove. Eagle Forum wishes to thank the paper for their contribution to education; however, the paper, so as not to offend the school district, has already carefully scrutinized her work. In reality her first article was done very tastefully, but rejected because it told the truth. The second article was never printed. The Editor made it known to Teri that he will not print conservative ideas that may be controversial about the school district. The paper obviously has changed through the years and perhaps it has to do with the new editor. The word is that the new editor has been discriminatory toward some members of the staff for their religious views. This would make sense because the recent articles being printed never would have been in the paper years ago, for the immoral content

266

would dictate otherwise. The parent patrol will continue even if the *Elk Grove Citizen* rejects the truth, as they did to us at Laguna Creek High School. We are encouraging all concerned parents in schools nation-wide to begin this program and attempt to find a media outlet that will supply the information to the public. Teri called me numerous times the last month filling me in on information of shock value. One program reminded me of SEED and once again, the School District deemed it necessary.

Advocacy is the name of a social engineering program in Elk Grove middle and high schools. They can be one hour a week or 20 minutes daily. How nice if this time was allotted for Math or Reading but instead it is used to teach "life skills." The reason for the program is stated below as taken from the Sixth Grade Teacher's Guide:

> "...life skills are usually not taught at school; they are **not** usually taught to us at home, college or on the job." [4]

The schools are now the parents and have indicated this by assuming the family no longer teaches life skills. This sounded familiar to me for SEED says teachers no longer teach what is necessary. Both programs promote transformational change through *cause*. I can just imagine how many *causes* teens will think up while gaining power through the collective whole. The Sixth Grade Teacher's Guide states that "facts" no longer work, so they will now work with *causes* in the curriculum for Advocacy sessions. This program discusses many topics such as cultural and religious differences and stresses in family, school and social situations. Questionnaires are used with Yes and No responses, Agree or Disagree or Fill in the Blanks. Some of the questions follow that require the students to answer with Agree or Disagree:

1. "Often cultures promote a belief in their own superiority to other cultures."
2. The more important your religion is to you, the more intolerant of other religions you will be.

3. Being a teenager is a subculture that all young people share.
4. My family's subculture values often come in conflict with the values of the larger culture.
5. It's normal for people to be "afraid" of people who are different from them.
6. Tolerance of other religions is important.
7. What is disrespectful in some cultures may be perfectly normal in others.[5]

As a Sociology Major, I know that questions are introduced to put ideas in people's minds. The questions above certainly do that and are loaded with issues that are not school concerns. These questions can lead to revealing personal issues that are confidential to children's home lives. This section goes on with fill in blanks on naming as many religions as you can think of and similarities and differences.

Next we go to stress. This was broken into many departments, each with a specific questionnaire. For family stress they ask the following questions with Yes and No required.

1. My parent(s) guardians and I fight a lot about what's important.
2. My parents(s) guardians criticize the way I dress.
3. My parents(s) guardians yell at me in front of my friends.
4. My parents(s) guardians I argue about my curfew.
5. My parents (s) don't treat me as well as they do the other children in my Family.
6. My brother(s) or sister(s) and I have trouble getting along.
7. My parent(s) guardian won't let me make my own decisions.
8. My parent(s) guardian load me down with responsibilities.[6]

I could not go on. The intrusion on privacy amazed me. It appears the schools have stepped over the boundaries of their authority. This is none of their business. They offer suggestions for taking care of your stress. At the bottom of the sheet is the suggestion to ask a parent, teacher or school counselor for help. It is at the bottom of the sheet, not at the top where it belongs.[7]

Teri found out the sessions start in a circle. They learn relaxing techniques in the classroom, *Stage 2* of *mind control* and the bonding begins. Relaxation encourages an altered state of mind by freeing it of prior thoughts or ideas and then the activity follows. The questionnaires used following circle are geared to present paradoxes as talked about earlier, *Stage 3*. Discussion follows and the teens begin their transition. They are easily transformed under group allegiance, *Stage 4*. The sessions end in confidentiality and the students informed not to tell anyone the content. They are not to share the information with anyone. This is SEED philosophy and I am sure if a parent wanted to sit in routinely on the classes they would be refused based on confidentiality of the other children. This is extremely dangerous and indicative of secrecy. It is inappropriate and wrong and must be stopped. The questionnaires are collected by the teachers and not allowed out of the room. This is a behind "closed" door technique and does not belong in the schools. This is but a sampling of what the program promotes. There are questionnaires in regard to community duty that deal with the good of community over the individual. It is the perfect setting for *mind control* and implantation of secular humanist ideology.

Teri has confronted the school about these issues. Once again she was given the run around as to books used and her being able to view them without a "babysitter." Teri is an educated woman and questioned why she needed someone sitting with her while she read the books. They said the woman could answer any questions she may have and they tied up personnel to sit with Teri while she read books. The answers were flimsy and she was told "no" to reading them at home even though there were two sets of books. Other questions we have are the cost. As mentioned earlier, the cost of the Michael Fowlin skits were well over $30,000. The SEED program cost to the district is still not clear for there are grants, but the school must pay a certain percentage for people attending and for materials the facilitators bring back. The cost for books, printing, paper and education of teachers for Advocacy is yet another expense. While

California is hurting for school funding, we are squandering what we do have on Tolerance Programs!

Teri continues to question, but the educators in Elk Grove say they believe in the program, and that parents want it based on surveys. How many parents put their okay on the survey and how was it presented to them? Every parent needs to see the questions asked, how the class is conducted and give their permission before the school allows intrusion into the privacy of the child and family. Another side of the controversial program needs to be heard by the parents before such programs are introduced.

The programs will not end. New names, new angles, they will keep coming, but we will also not go away. Eagle Forum will continue to uphold the natural family and the rights of our children to be raised by their parents and not the schools. I thought of my last weeks of writing and how the many people in my life have influenced me. My women's prayer group faithfully prays for success in our Eagle endeavors. The women in my weekly Bible study give me strength to move forward through their smiles, encouraging words, and prayer. My blessings are many for I am surrounded by people I am proud to call my friends.

40

ONE LAST CHAPTER

S ighs of relief were apparent as I finished my book, but above the joy of completion is the overwhelming peace I experience in knowing this information will be available for public view. J.R. Harris, from AuthorHouse, has been patient and supportive throughout the final stages of publishing. He was so right when he said, "One does not finish a book, but only abandons it." It has taken two months beyond when I guaranteed him I would be done, but I have finally reached the stage of being able to "let go." For anyone contemplating the idea of writing a book, take the chance and do it for it is truly an enriching experience. I now can reap the rewards, and I look forward to happy hours of promoting my book with him and through his company. I am continually encouraged by organizations and people who have asked me to speak and have placed orders for my book.

I listened to Mel Gibson tell his tale of writing and directing the movie on Christ's Passion and Death. Though he knew he would receive insults and abuse because of content, it didn't matter for he had to tell the truth. It was an amazing movie in that you lived it with Jesus, not just watched it. In the courtyard scene when people decided freedom, for the murderer and thief Barabbas, over freedom for an innocent man Jesus, I thought of how our country does this daily as we pick humanist ideals over Judeo-Christian principles. It was a profound movie leaving an indelible mark of God's love for us, and it will go down as one of the greatest movies of all time. Mel Gibson's courageous example supports what each person must do to face their fears in order to stand for what they believe in.

I was confident in abandoning my book, for it was finally time for the readers to give it a conclusion and stand for their beliefs. It will have a different ending for each person; his or her actions will determine its outcome. Through education and political activism, I know we are still capable of saving some of our constitutional rights. However, time passes quickly and if inactivity continues to rule it, we will no longer exist as the faintest resemblance of the free Nation we once were. Our treasure is, indeed, the greatest civilization of free men to ever exist. If each person does something positive we may have a chance for survival, but if the lethargy continues we have none.

The ultimate last stand is the family. Through all the turmoil of the last century and all the *brainwashing*, our marriage unit is the only refuge we have that has not been altered in its definition. It is indeed the basis of our family unit and when run according to sound moral principles, is the backbone of our country. This is why we must fight hard to preserve it so there will still be parents saying no to indoctrination through programs such as SEED. With churches caving in to compromise, the only stable unit we have left is the family. [1] If this is destroyed we have nothing to leave our future generations and we leave them with chaos. I dwelled on some of the chaos as I finished my book, but also on positive action taken that can make a difference.

I was very surprised to read about the Black Ministerial Alliance, the Boston Ten Point Coalition and the Cambridge Black Pastors Conference issuing a joint statement that they opposed the chaos of homosexual marriage. They believe their allegiance lies in the voice of God through Scripture. Courageous leaders such as Rev. Wesley A. Roberts, president of the Black Ministerial Alliance representing 80 churches and some 20-30,000 members, said, "it was an easy decision because our faith forces us to recognize something that is biblical and that history has affirmed." [2] He is not alone in his conviction for another brave leader stands with him by the name of Bishop Gilbert A. Thompson, Sr. pastor of New Covenant Christian Church in Mattapan. He heads the largest Protestant congregation in Massachusetts and states that there are many reasons for black ministers to speak out. His statements are bold and extremely courageous.

"We're weighing in on this because we're concerned
with the epidemic rate of fatherlessness in America
and in our community and we don't think gay marriage
helps that cause."[3]

He proceeds to say the following in reference to
homosexuality:

"To say there is such a thing as a gay Christian is
saying there's an honest thief."[4]

He continues with commenting on what former presidential
candidate Carol Moseley Braun said in reference to her belief that
there is no difference between same-sex marriage and interracial
marriage:

"We believe the difference is enormous. Today we
look back with scorn at those who twisted the law to
make marriage serve a racist agenda and I believe our
descendants will look back the same way at us if we
yield to the same kind of pressure a radical sexual
agenda is placing on us today. Just as it's distorting
the equation of marriage if you press race into it, it's
also distorting if you subtract gender." [5]

The Rev. Imani-Sheila Newsome-Camara, a United Methodist
minister who is an assistant professor of theology at Boston
University supports marriage between only a man and woman. [6]
These brave black leaders will face much harassment in the future
because of their stand and their comments on homosexuality. Their
courageous stand needs to be shared, for it gives us faith that the
black community is finally realizing how the homosexual activists
have used them. Perhaps this may encourage other churches and
communities to follow their example. Chaos of homosexual marriage
was planted when the Supreme Court redefined our Constitutional
laws by using Global laws to base their decision of Lawrence v.
Texas. It was a defiance of their pledge to uphold the U.S.

Constitution. They made a mockery of this case and we see its outcome in San Francisco where Mayor Newsom allowed over 3000 homosexual illegal marriages to take place with other states following his lead. The California Health and Human Services Agency has issued a statement they are not acceptable for issuance of licenses. They will not be accepted because the name of bride and groom had been altered to "Groom 1" and Groom 2"[7] I wonder if the Agency will honor the above statement? One thing I do know is that same sex marriage will never be accepted by God or by the majority of Americans. What is sad is to see these people so hopeful of attaining normalcy by breaking the law. We feed into their fantasies by continuing with this injustice.

Imagine that it took almost a week for Governor Schwarzenegger to tell Attorney General Bill Lockyer to initiate proceedings to stop this nonsense. The Attorney General eventually went to the Supreme Court. The Court refused to take action and allowed the flagrant breaking of our State laws. The out of control legislators in California planned to promote yet another bill allowing same-sex marriage that will override the will of the people who voted for proposition 22. The citizens clearly stating marriage is reserved for a man and woman have been totally ignored. Lawlessness was seen throughout our country in Minneapolis (Mayor R.T.Rybak), in Salt Lake City (Mayor Ross C. Andersen), in Plattsburgh, N.Y. (Mayor Daniel Stewart), and in Chicago (Mayor Daley) when they gave their approval to same sex marriage.

If anyone has any doubt about the homosexual *cause* being used to destroy our country, then you need to seriously evaluate this situation in our land and what the results will be if we continue down this path. The most recent study, by Stanley Kurtz, a research fellow at Hoover Institution, shows Scandinavia's social structure in complete upheaval after homosexual marriages became legal and it is not for the better. In Norway, though the churches and people were against it, the judges, lawmakers, and media forced it upon them. Mr. Kurtz sites two homosexuals who readily admitted the push for marriage was only to gain " social approval for homosexuality."[8] It's obvious the same thing is happening in our country, for if a Mayor issued assault gun permits, he would be arrested but it seems the law changes for homosexual activists. It appears we are being "told" what to do even if it's against the law.

No one has been arrested, nor has the conspiracy of certain elected officials supposedly involved in this lawlessness, ever been investigated. Instead Rosie O'Donnell's wedding picture, kissing her girlfriend, was on the front page of every liberal paper across America. Only 9 brave men and women during the first week pushed through the crowd in town hall and demanded that the marriages be stopped. They were the ones arrested, but the lawlessness of illegal marriage continued. [9] I thank these dedicated individuals for their time and devotion to our country's values, as I do organizations that filed lawsuits and are battling this issue. I don't know the outcome, but I believe this issue will divide our country and people will be forced to make a decision between good and evil. It will also make people realize that we must clean up our courts if we want our laws upheld according to our Constitution.

Other states know that to defend our family unit they must pass legislation to protect marriage, and Ohio has taken steps to guarantee the preservation of marriage by being the 38th state to pass a Defense of Marriage Act (DOMA). Governor Taft signed it in on February 4, 2004. His words are profound on this topic:

> "Marriage is an essential building block of our society,
> an institution we must reaffirm. At a time when
> parents and families are under constant attack within
> our social culture, it is important to confirm and
> protect those environments that offer our children and
> ultimately our society, the best opportunity to
> survive."[10]

It was uplifting to see the accurate statistics of other state DOMA bills and the high numbers of those against same-sex marriages. In Nebraska it was 70.1% to a 29.9 % margin, in Nevada it was 69.6% to 30.4%, in California it was a 62% to 39 % margin.[11] Virginia and Arizona are working on legislative action. Many of the 38 DOMA states include, in the Acts, that marriage entered into in another jurisdiction will have no reciprocity or recognition in their state, and civil unions will not guarantee partner benefits. Del. Robert

F. McDonnel (R-Virginia Beach) won passage of a resolution that calls for the constitutional amendment to protect marriage and to also eliminate civil unions in all 50 states.[12] It is reassuring to hear our courageous President Bush and Senate Majority Leader Bill Frist say, with certainty, that marriage is between a man and a woman and that activist judges have no right to redefine marriage. Hopefully they will encourage a Constitutional amendment to keep marriage a protected unit. [13]

There is hope that still prevails for our moral survival through legislative changes. Recently I read about the U.S. Court of Appeals for the Eleventh Circuit who upheld Florida's anti-gay adoption law. Apparently the author of this article was not happy with the decision, for her theme was that Anita Bryant lives again and her comments were not favorable. We, however, are happy with this decision, for all testing shows children are better off in traditional homes of one man and one woman.[14] It ultimately protects our children. I am especially happy for Anita Bryant's campaign to "Save Our Children" in the 70's, for it is resurfacing in this anti-gay adoption law. Indeed Anita has returned!

Not only was I happy in the above, but also days later I found that the South Dakota legislature plans to challenge Roe v. Wade. As of February 25, the Senate has passed H.B. 1191 that would ban nearly all abortions in the state. The 5th U.S. Circuit Court of Appeals has agreed to hear Norma McCorvey in the Roe v. Wade case. For 10 years this woman has tried to overturn this decision and for 30 years she has seen the disastrous effects of her testimony that swayed the court in Roe v. Wade. Finally she will have a chance to state what really happened during the court proceedings so long ago. Cases such as this spring up across America, but the news media in most cases keeps it secretive with little mention.

Senator Zell Miller delivered an incredible speech called "Deficit of Decency" to the Congress following the Super Bowl Game that outraged America.[15] It was a powerful statement about just what it says, the lack of decency in our country compared to our past history of morality. It is included in the back of this book (Appendix C), an example of a man who portrays leadership qualities absent from many Congressmen today. We want men and women who legislate with their minds and not their hearts, as taught them by our feminists. The above are incredible wins in our battle of good and evil.

This battle does exist, as was apparent in the Super Bowl horror of 2004. The entire half time show was pagan in its allure, and the commercials were totally immoral for a family football show. People were outraged because it took their families off guard, but in reality it reminded them of what our country now stands for, which is immorality and paganism. In fact the big outcry really came because of humanities guilt for being silent for decades. The American people do not want to accept responsibility for their part in this atrocious display of depravity. Research now shows according to National Coalition for the Protection of Children and Families, 73% of boys and 78% of girls 12-19 years old watch more than six hours a week of *MTV*.[16] I wonder how many outraged parents that emailed or wrote letters, let their children watch *MTV*, *Will and Grace*, *Sex and The City* or attend movies with vivid sexual images or homosexual content. Was the outcry truly sincere, or a way to ease their own guilt for a halftime truly representing what we have become?

It is similar to an incident at Laguna Creek High School in Elk Grove that just occurred in February of 2004, that involved two young boys planning a Columbine type attack on this school. It was stopped because one of the boy's mothers reported her son acting strangely, which led to the discovery. She is a true hero. The town was upset and outraged by this incident, but why? It is the same high school where we were accosted by homosexual activists and then called liars on the front page of our town newspaper. It was thought some students had inkling about the planned attack, but were afraid to say anything. Would any student come forth with the apparent climate of the campus? After all, the students saw aggressive abuse of us by homosexual activists with no retribution, by any authority, for their actions. We continue to spend money on tolerance and diversity programs, but it does not help the violence, climate of discontent, and downplay of authority by our teens across America. This is well stated by a young girl who wrote an article in our paper called "Some Parents are too blind to realize the disturbance in their own kids." It is a perfect example of our authority figures disintegrating in the eyes of our young.

"It's difficult for the "average" teenager to talk to their parents about things happening in their lives that the parents would understand or even like, without judging their teens or choices. Some can't tell their parents that they denied drugs at a party or didn't shop lift with some buddies. They're afraid their parents would turn their friends in to the police or they wouldn't let them see them again."[17]

This article shocked me for not only the indifference toward the parent's right to judge, but also at the end she does not recommend students go to parents; but instead, she suggests that if you find someone outside the family then stick with it because this is a sure way of getting out of depression. She emphasized the confidentiality of the contract being important. This is the bond that exists in behind "closed" door school programs such as SEED and Advocacy. Of course outside of these programs are your counselors who now encourage teens and children to try homosexuality if they have flirtations with it. School nurses call for the ride for underage teens to leave school and have abortions without parental consent. They are no longer interested in preserving life, but destroying it.

Patriarchal authority is disappearing rapidly from our society. In fact, the present generation is the first generation ever taught that they do not "need" parents or grandparents. Never more apparent was this than when I heard our Superintendent's pathetic apology to the homosexual students for canceling an event in the classroom, never owed them, Silent Day. The cancellation was most likely due to the threat of litigation. I can't only blame him for his words, for he also represented the compromised adults present in the room who have given up their authority to the children, rather than being it. Parents and citizens have forsaken our heritage of owed protection to our children for the approval of teens. I no longer have to ask what happened to America, for it is clear that decades of people gave the okay to deceptive seeds planted for destruction of our nation. You can judge your nations downfall on its moral beliefs and acceptance of homosexuality. This statement speaks volumes for our once quiet town of Elk Grove.

Is it any wonder, within a week of our Laguna Creek High School incident, that Elk Grove High School had an actual fight between 30 students on campus that went out of control? There is now a debate as to whether it carried racial overtones. How could this be, for the town has spent money, time and effort training students, teachers and parents to love each other through SEED? The solution of course will be to implement more SEED programs or perhaps "mentor programs" that are being considered through a local church. Will they have to be trained first in diversity? What will be the criteria, and who will be the final authority in this decision? I hope that my friend, who is now the president of the school board, will choose future programs wisely, for how does the Superintendent and school board erase the *mind control* and destructive effect on our youth that has taken place the last 5 years, due to SEED and other similar tolerance programs? Forcing people to love each other through social construct education doesn't work!

What can work is a return to traditional learning and programs that would solve some problems? Orlean Koehle, California Eagle Forum President, is publishing an incredible book, *The Golden Rule School Program* that explains an effective education program based on the Golden Rule. It's simple, saves money and works in restoration of traditional values. Brad Dacus, and his wife Susanne, have written *Reclaim Your School,* which outlines 10 steps to make changes in your schools. Lynn St. Dennis teaches the Natural Family Course, mentioned earlier, and teens love it! They are eager for order and answers in their life as demonstrated by their many questions following her informative one-hour presentation. Jose Ochoa has successfully begun a Free Speech Club at American River College. The mission of the club is to give students the opportunity to speak upon key issues of our day such as abortion, evolution, human cloning, sexuality, religion, politics, humanism, education reform and any other issue that students find are important. Jose is the president of the club and a wonderful young man who truly works hard to preserve our American Way. Scott Lively has promoted these clubs as a way to preserve our "real" freedom to discuss controversial issues in a non-threatening atmosphere. We hope that more high schools and universities will organize Free Speech Clubs.

Lobby Days continue to be an educational tool for parents, citizens and students. If you are questioning what is really happening in the schools, come to one of these days with your teen and see how you can influence your legislators. Start one in your state if you don't have one. Become an educated parent in the happenings of your school district and start to make a difference. Imagine if once a month, hundreds of people lobbied their representatives holding them accountable for their narrow interest agendas. Legislators would begin to represent the true beliefs of the majority and not the lie. Amy Koons is a courageous young lawyer who represents CRI and routinely testifies for and against bills at the Capitol. Rodney Stanhope, Vice President of the Sacramento Republican Assembly, and Ken Payne, State of California Planning Division, allow time to actively support positive legislation as does Karen England and Angela Azevedo who routinely testify. Whether it is a planned Lobby Day, or you choose to go alone, it is an amazing learning experience in government policy. It also serves in teaching our Constitutional rights to some who have forgotten them. It's an effective way to teach our children the proper way to go about changing our law for the betterment of our schools and communities. We need more participation in these areas, but unfortunately many citizens and parents avoid seeking knowledge in areas where they are most needed.

Perhaps if Elk Grove parents knew more about their children's education they would better understand how there were, indeed, racial overtones that contributed to the High School fight preciously mentioned. Why the surprise? Children are being taught racial tension right in the classroom. Teri reports reading 3 required English books for a middle school in Elk Grove. The books were intensely focused on racial discrimination and she found them very offensive for all races to be reading. This type of material is a consistent theme in the district as new books of violence and morbid content continue to permeate the education system. Teri has chosen an alternative path for her son Bryce who reads other books of quality literature to meet his requirements.

Citizens of this community have all contributed to the violence by allowing tolerance and education programs that promote racial, sexual and every imaginable separation into group's rather than individual merit. Equal merit has no place in our education! Equal merit has students believing they can take the law into their own hands as the Mayor of San Francisco has shown can indeed be done. Yes, our authority is gone and now we have in Elk Grove an accepted belief that students are on equal status with our Superintendent, principals, teachers and their parents. The only way we will get authority back is by men and women of sound moral principle returning to their rightful position in our families and our society.

Three brave trustees, in an Orange County California school district, are assuming their rightful position. They will not revise their anti-discrimination policy to accommodate the social agenda of transsexuals, and others who are non-conforming to gender roles. All of the laws to prevent discrimination are in place already. They were threatened with a loss of federal and state funding anywhere from 12-40 million dollars, but this did not influence their decision. The President of the Westminster Teachers Association says, according to Joel Rubin of the *LA Times* "This decision is hurting the kids and sets a bad example for them." Can you imagine a representative from the teacher's association calling this a bad influence on the children, instead of supporting it? It is another example of a society turning "evil into good and good into evil." I hail these brave and courageous trustees! Their dedication paid off. In "Good News, Bad News," Bonnie O'Neil reported that State Superintendent of Education Jack O'Connell finally stated that the definition of gender, "person's biological sex," does comply with state law, and the state cannot demand that gender is "actual or perceived." This is a great victory, but California Senator Joe Dunn insisted that he would continue to legislate to have the district taken over by the state. However, if the Trustees continue in this direction, it could be the beginning of other school districts taking a stand on such issues. I am thrilled by their dedication to moral principles! They set the best example for our young to see that children are more important than money!

Although the chaos seems overwhelming, I continued to balance it with the positive actions I saw making a difference. I was surprisingly optimistic in finishing this chapter. I had another big surprise when very unexpectedly I came across startling information on the SEED program site, Emily Styles was no longer teaching the program in New Jersey. She had apparently returned to full time teaching. I found this odd, but eventually found an article about a school district fighting the SEED Program in New Jersey and it began to make sense. Not sure of the time sequence of events, I can't say with certainty that they are connected. I did find the article very interesting in that twenty vocal people fought the program in West Morris Regional High School with their concerns being similar to mine. The school board said it would make changes, but they apparently only changed the name of the program from SEED to Interdisciplinary Discussions of Education and Achievement in Schools and Society (IDEASS). Concerned parents and teachers say it is the same program in content. Officials in five other County Districts say most parents do not even know these programs exist.[18] I was thrilled knowing when people read my book they would have knowledge of the facts surrounding the SEED program. Another surprise came when I was reading the Humanist Manifesto II (Appendix D). I was interested in the content since it is central to tolerance and diversity programs. Under their ethics section I read the following statement.

> " We affirm that moral values derive their source from human experiences. Ethics is autonomous and "situational," needing no theological or ideological sanction. Ethics stems from human need and interest. To deny this distorts the whole basis of life. Human life has meaning because we create and develop our futures." [19]

The word *situational* is apparent in their philosophy and it seems clear that the word *Situationalism* is alive in secular humanism, which dictates that the moral choice of a teenager is dependant on his need of the moment, based on the situation. They clearly indicate in the Manifesto that the "varieties of naturalistic humanism include scientific, ethical, democratic, religious and Marxist humanism."[20] It is reassuring to read these words for they support the reality of the Marxist, deceptive programs being introduced by such programs as SEED, for the transformational purposes of changing our society. It is a battle between good and evil.

A sense of fulfillment filled my body and I sighed relief for I have found others like myself in New Jersey. In *Lord of the Rings*, it is said that people who hold rings of power are alone. Few will listen in Elk Grove; my discovery of SEED and other deceptive programs isolated me. I will call the brave 20, who dared to defy and soon hear their story. In the mean time, I am happy to know I may not be alone. These courageous parents and teachers are an important part of the Last Samurai. Perhaps, just perhaps, traditional America may win. The last stand will ultimately depend on God as stated so eloquently by Alabama State Supreme Court Chief Justice Roy Moore.

> "Anytime you deny the acknowledgement of God you are undermining the entire basis for which our country exists. Rights come from God, not from government. If government can give you rights, government can take them away from you. If God gives you rights, no man and no government can take them away from you. That was the premise of the organic law of this country, which is the Declaration of Independence. Because, if there is no God, then man's power is the controlling aspect and therefore power will be centralized."[21]

The book ends with you. If you work to preserve marriage and the family unit through our Constitutional law, then we will retain some element of the once great country that built its reputation on such qualities as protecting our young from seeds of deception and moral corruption. We can stop our destruction by giving credence to moral absolutes and principles on which our country was founded. Yes, it is hard work, but if we do not take a last stand, we will pay a heavy price for our indifference in the battle between good and evil. As for the present moment, I am sitting in my comfortable blue chair remembering when I began my journey. My identification with a little hobbit took hold, mesmerizing me with one of my favorite sayings in *Lord of The Rings* when Frodo looks out over the water and has these thoughts.

> "I wish the ring never came to me. I wish none of this ever happened." Gandalf answers him back and says,

"So do all those who live to see such times, but it is not for them to decide. What we must decide is what to do with the time that is given us."[22]

41

EPILOGUE

The absurdity continues as this book is going into publishing. One brave parent called to tell me that Sheldon High School sponsored an entire week of diversity education and celebration under the title of Unity and it dealt with, once again, student safety. Topics covered were bullying, alcohol, drugs, racism, stereotyping, and sexual orientation. There were assemblies with pre-writing and post-writing assignments in their classes. Scheduled activities included the sale of bracelets by the GSA Club. Skits played an important role in the week's scheduled events. Also included in the final assembly on Friday was a large poster contract for students to sign saying they pledge their support of tolerance and diversity. The weeklong celebration of unity took place after the national Day of Silence celebration. Wouldn't it be great if we could celebrate improved reading and math scores rather than sexually oriented subject matter?

All the above behaviors are discouraged during diversity trainings, except sex, and yet all statistics point to increasing pregnancies, disease, and death due to sex, especially in younger people under age 25. With this in mind, how can schools legally permit education that not only discusses, but also encourages sexual lifestyles that promote destruction? When drugs and alcohol are discussed, educators tell them to avoid the behavior. But students are encouraged to sign posters promoting acceptance of sexual lifestyles; the educators do not discourage it. Also if safety is a true concern of the schools then why are parents and students, who reject alternative lifestyles, being discriminated against with the schools offering no assistance to them? We obviously know the answer for tolerance only swings in one direction as seen by the email from Orlean, our Eagle

Forum State President. Tim Buehler (mentioned in Chapter 36), his conservative club, and some Eagle Forum members were protesting Silent Day at Rancho Cotati High School in Santa Rosa CA. Anger, aggression, and rudeness seem to dominate homosexual actions whenever anyone or group disagrees with their lifestyle. They actually told Tim they "wished a bus would run over him." Orlean's statement below brought reality to the forefront, for it was not just the students that participated but the teachers also.

> "We stood on the sidewalk across from the school holding our banners and posters saying such things as "Let's Silence the Day of Silence," "Support Academics Not Special-Interest Groups." The gay and lesbian students on the sidewalk across the street from us were very rude in the comments they were making and their actions. Two boys gave each other a passionate kiss, one boy mooned us, and several gave us "the finger." There was no discipline against these students by the principal or teachers with them. They were calling us "hateful," but what about their actions. Some of Tim's liberal friends tried to pass out the Conservative Club's newsletter among the students. Students were taking the newsletter, but teachers would yank it out of their hands and tear it in half and throw it into the street. So much for "free speech" rights. And what about littering especially by the teachers themselves? There were several police cars driving by and police on motorcycles. What a commotion over such a day! No wonder we are seeing less and less academics being taught, and less and less high scores on academic tests, when so much time is wasted on days like this."

Amazing that the one thing homosexuals accuse society of inflicting upon them, they freely and aggressively try to inflict on others. It's called silence! Silent Day also took place in Elk Grove. I was thankful that we were able to keep it out of the classrooms last year and this year, but the climate of homosexuality prevails the entire day through information on student's badges and the information circulating and available on tables. Joe Pursch, once again, gave us radio time to discuss this day and notify citizens of its existence. How appropriate for him to be involved this year, for he was a big factor in our success last year. The *Elk Grove Citizen* would not print our information about the day for they said it was controversial. The Paper did, however, write an extensive article about the Day of Silence when it was over. Guess they didn't think it was too controversial for everyone to read their positive input about a day that is indeed offensive to many people! The prior week they had extensive coverage and information about an acting group that would be performing at a local college. The play was titled *The Laramie Project*. It was about the homosexual martyr Matthew Shepard. Not only did they write a glowing article about the play, but they also promoted a "positive image" for the homosexual lifestyle. The town was informed of special attendees, like Assemblyman Mark Leno, who introduced the same-sex marriage bill at the Sacramento Capitol. They were encouraged to see the play and participate in the panel discussion following the performance; homosexual activists would be available to answer questions. The article presented the evening as almost a "night out" for the family; I thought again about the deceptive tactics that lure individuals into an acceptance of this lifestyle and *The Laramie Project* is one of them.

Teri called at the end of the week with one more "absurd" day in her son's middle school. It was called "Opposite Day." The students were encouraged to attend school dressed opposite of their normal attire. Some boys came to school dressed in skirts and dresses! Let there be no mistake, transvestites are walking hand in hand with homosexuals to take over our schools with unnatural lifestyles portrayed as normal. This is uncalled for and the district heard loudly from Teri on their voice mails and emails. My book will be published before we know the outcome of this scenario.

As I observe the rapid rise in the numbers of diversity and tolerance programs, I realized that legislative action to overturn the student directed homosexual agenda would take years. The impact on our children would be long since established before legislation would take effect. Therefore, I would encourage and support any boycott of our public school system. This is the only mechanism by which the average citizen can have a voice in this outrageous usurpation of the parent's right to socially educate his or her own child. The Southern Baptist Convention may well call for removal of their children from government schools. The resolution will be discussed soon. Dr. Dobson already has called on parents in California to remove their children from public schools. The social construct education will not end, but you can end it by taking back your rightful place in being the director of your child's moral upbringing. If enough parents take action, the schools will take notice.

As for one more surprise, today I received notice that the Sacramento City Unified School District passed, without opposition, a resolution to protect homosexual, bisexual and transgender people. The Task Forces have been working for a year on this resolution and are meeting on a regular basis to implement programs to teach even more diversity and tolerance throughout the Sacramento area. The press release made it very clear that it will be taught in "grammar schools." Any school that does not comply will be held liable. In fact the press release had a flavor of Nazi Germany and my skin turned cold. I could feel Hitler's presence that soon will be evident to everyone, for our opinions will be considered "hate crimes" and we will be silenced.

The article continued, but I found it hard to read further for I was stuck on the word SEED. Yes they talked about the great work of SEED in the Elk Grove Unified School District. We are now being used as an example, and I am sure this program will move quickly in Sacramento. Perhaps our Superintendent will be able to help them, for he is leaving our District to be the new Superintendent of Schools in Sacramento. Another reason I know it will move quickly is because the name at the top of the press release was the Contact man for GLSEN in the Greater Sacramento area.

How appropriate to open the *Citizen* last week and see a picture of the man who introduced the SEED program into Elk Grove actually receiving a national SEED award for doing so. He also received a special award from the Elk Grove Unified School District. This occasion caught the full attention of the *Elk Grove Citizen*. They had a half-page picture plus an extensive article about the recipient; he is the new principal of Franklin High School. Behind him, in the newspaper picture, were the school board representatives standing by their elevated chairs of distinction. I remembered standing before them over a year ago so naïve in believing that they would be interested in our information about this deceptive program. They knew all along about SEED. They did nothing.

When I looked again at the picture, I knew that many people across our country were deserving of this notorious award. It takes approving citizens to make these programs work and, for sure, the once sleepy town of Elk Grove has given its approval. I hope all who have accepted SEED and other similar programs are happy to know that because of them, we now have *Seeds of Deception Planting Destruction of America's Children*!

Hatch Letter

Goals 2000, Educate America Act— Sec. 1017.

PROTECTION OF PUPILS Section 439 of the General Education Provisions Act (20 U.S.C. 1232g) is amended to read as follows: "PROTECTION OF PUPIL RIGHTS "Sec. 439.

(a) All instructional materials, including teacher's manuals, films, tapes or other supplementary material, which will be used in connection with any survey, analysis or evaluation as part of any applicable program shall be available for inspection by the parents or guardians of the children.

(b) No student shall be required, as part of any applicable program, to submit to a survey, analysis or evaluation that reveals information concerning—

(1) political affiliations;

(2) mental and psychological problems potentially embarrassing to the student or his family; "

(3) sex behavior and attitudes;

(4) illegal, anti-social, self-incriminating and demeaning behavior;

(5) critical appraisals of other individuals with whom respondents have close family relationships;

(6) legally recognized privileged or analogous relationships, such as those of lawyers, physicians and ministers; or

(7) income (other than that required by law to determine eligibility for participation in a program or for receiving financial assistance under such program), without the prior consent of the student (if the student is an adult or emancipated minor) or in the case of an unemancipated minor, without the prior written consent of the parent.

(c) Educational agencies and institutions shall give parents and students effective notice of their rights under this section.

(d) Enforcement. —The Secretary shall take such action as the Secretary determines appropriate to enforce this section, except that action to terminate assistance provided under an applicable program shall be taken only if the Secretary determines that—

(1) There has been a failure to comply with such section; and

(2) compliance with such section cannot be secured by voluntary means.

(e) Office of Review Board.—The Secretary shall establish or designate an office and review board within the Department of Education to investigate, process, review and adjudicate violations of the rights established under this section.."

When does this act apply? When federal money is involved in the implementation and maintenance of a program. If a school district has a federal grant to write curriculum, this law applies. If the state has a federal grant for a particular program and in turn, provides grants to school districts for the same program, this law applies.

As the result of recent amendments to PPRA in the No Child Left Behind education law (Public Law 107-110, signed January 8, 2002), parents have additional rights to examine materials with regard to the surveying of minor students, even when the surveys are not Education Department-funded, and to opt their children out of surveys and certain non-emergency medical examinations.

Opt Out Form

From:_____

Address:

_____

To:_____Principal

of _____ School

_____, _____, USA

Dear _____:

I am the parent of_____ who
attends_____school. Under U.S. legislation and
federal court decisions, parents have the primary responsibility for
their children's education, and pupils have certain rights which the
school may not deny.

Parents have the right to be assured their children's beliefs and moral
values are not undermined by the schools. Pupils have the right to
have and to hold their values and moral standards without direct or
indirect manipulations by the schools through the curricula,
textbooks, audio-visual materials or supplementary assignments.

Under the Hatch Amendment, I hereby request that my child NOT be
involved in any school activities or materials listed unless I have first
reviewed all the relevant materials and have given my **written
consent** for their use:

Psychological and psychiatric treatment that is designed to affect the
behavioral, emotional, or attitudinal characteristics of an individual or
designed to elicit information about attitudes, habits, traits,
opinions, beliefs or feelings of an individual or group;

Values clarifications, use of moral dilemmas, discussion of religious or moral standards, role-playing or open-ended discussions of situations involving moral issues, and survival games including life/death decision exercises;

Contrived incidents for self-revelation; sensitivity training, group encounter sessions, talk-ins, magic-circle techniques, self-evaluation and auto-criticism; strategies designed for self-disclosure including the keeping of a diary or a journal or a log book;

Sociograms, sociodrama; psychodrama; blindfold walks; isolation techniques;

Death education, including abortion, euthanasia, suicide, use of violence, and discussions of death and dying;

Curricula pertaining to drugs and alcohol; Nuclear war, nuclear policy and nuclear classroom games; Globalism, one-world government or anti-nationalistic curricula; Discussion and testing on interpersonal relationships; discussions of attitudes toward parents and parenting;

Educating in human sexuality, including pre-marital sex, contraception, abortion, homosexuality, group sex and marriages, prostitution, incest, bestiality, masturbation, divorce, population control, and roles of males and females; sex behavior and attitudes of student and family;

Pornography and any materials containing profanity and/or sexual explicitness;

Guided-fantasy techniques; hypnotic techniques; imagery and suggestology;

Organic evolution, including Darwin's theory; Discussions of witchcraft, occultism, the supernatural, and mysticism; Political and/or religious affiliations of students or family; income of family; Non-academic personality tests; questionnaires of personal and family life attitudes.

The purpose of this letter is to preserve my child's rights under the Protection of Pupil Rights Amendment (The Hatch Amendment) to the General Education Provisions Act, and under its regulations as published in the Federal Register of September 6, 1984, which became effective November 12, 1984.

These regulations provide a procedure for filing complaints first at the local level, and then with the U.S. Department of Education. If a voluntary remedy fails, federal funds can be withdrawn from those in violation of the law. I respectfully ask you to send me a substantive response to this letter attaching a copy of your policy statement on procedures for parental permission requirements, to notify all my child's teachers, and to keep a copy of this letter in my child's permanent file.

Thank you for your cooperation.

Signed this _____ Day of _____,200__ .

Zell Miller, United States Senator from Georgia

Miller Delivers Floor Speech on
"Deficit of Decency" in America

WASHINGTON – U.S. Senator Zell Miller (D-GA) today delivered the following statement on the floor of the United States Senate addressing several social issues facing the country:

"The Old Testament prophet Amos was a sheep herder who lived back in the Judean hills, away from the larger cities of Bethlehem and Jerusalem. Compared to the intellectual urbanites like Isaiah and Jeremiah, he was just an unsophisticated country hick.

"But Amos had a unique grasp of political and social issues and his poetic literary skill was among the best of all the prophets. That familiar quote of Martin Luther King, Jr. about 'Justice will rush down like waters and righteousness like a mighty stream' are Amos's words.

"Amos was the first to propose the concept of a universal God and not just some tribal deity. He also wrote that God demanded moral purity, not rituals and sacrifices. This blunt speaking moral conscience of his time warns in Chapter 8, verse 11 of The Book of Amos, as if he were speaking to us today:

That 'the days will come, sayeth the Lord God, that I will send a famine in the land. Not a famine of bread, nor a thirst for water, but of hearing the word of the Lord. 'And they shall wander from sea to sea, and from the north even to the east. They shall run to and fro to seek the word of the Lord, and shall not find it.'

'A famine in the land'. Has anyone more accurately described the situation we face in America today? 'A famine of hearing the words of the Lord.'

"But some will say, Amos was just an Old Testament prophet – a minor one at that – who lived 700 years before Christ. That is true, so how about one of the most influential historians of modern times?

"Arnold Toynbee who wrote the acclaimed 12 volume A Study of History, once declared, 'Of the 22 civilizations that have appeared in history, 19 of them collapsed when they reached the moral state America is in today.'

"Toynbee died in 1975, before seeing the worst that was yet to come. Yes, Arnold Toynbee saw the famine. The 'famine of hearing the words of the Lord.' Whether it is removing a display of the Ten Commandments from a Courthouse or the Nativity Scene from a city square. Whether it is eliminating prayer in schools, or eliminating 'under God' in the Pledge of Allegiance. Whether it is making a mockery of the sacred institution of marriage between a man and woman or, yes, telecasting around the world made-in-the-USA filth masquerading as entertainment.

"The Culture of Far Left America was displayed in a startling way during the Super Bowl's now infamous half-time show. A show brought to us courtesy of Value-Les Moonves and the pagan temple of Viacom-Babylon.

"I asked the question yesterday, how many of you have ever run over a skunk with your car? I have many times and I can tell you, the stink stays around for a long time. You can take the car through the car wash and it's still there. So the scent of this event will long linger in the nostrils of America.

"I'm not talking just about an exposed mammary gland with a pull-tab attached to it. Really no one should have been too surprised at that. Wouldn't one expect a bumping, humping, trashy routine entitled 'I'm going to get you naked' to end that way?

"Does any responsible adult ever listen to the words of this rap-crap? I'd quote you some of it, but the Sergeant of Arms would throw me out of here, as well he should. And then there was that prancing, dancing, strutting, rutting guy evidently suffering from jock itch because he kept yelling and grabbing his crotch. But then, maybe there's a crotch grabbing culture I'm unaware of.

"But as bad as all this was, the thing that yanked my chain the hardest was seeing that ignoramus with his pointed head stuck up through a hole he had cut in the flag of the United States of America, screaming about having 'a bottle of scotch and watching lots of crotch.' Think about that.

"This is the same flag that we pledge allegiance to. This is the flag that is draped over coffins of dead young uniformed warriors killed while protecting Kid Crock's bony butt. He should be tarred and feathered, and ridden out of this country on a rail. Talk about a good reality show, there's one for you.

"The desire and will of this Congress to meaningfully do anything about any of these so-called social issues is non existent and embarrassingly disgraceful. The American people are waiting and growing impatient with us. They want something done.

"I am pleased to be a co-sponsor of S.J. Res. 26 along with Senator Allard and others, proposing an amendment to the Constitution of the United States relating to marriage. And S.1558, the Liberties Restoration Act, which declares religious liberty rights in several ways, including the Pledge of Allegiance and the display of the Ten Commandments. And today I join Senator Shelby and others with the Constitution Restoration Act of 2004 that limits the jurisdiction of federal court in certain ways.

"In doing so, I stand shoulder to shoulder not only with my Senate co-sponsors and Chief Justice Roy Moore of Alabama but, more importantly, with our Founding Fathers in the conception of religious liberty and the terribly wrong direction our modern judiciary has taken us in.

"Everyone today seems to think that the U.S. Constitution expressly provides for separation of church and state. Ask any ten people if that's not so. And I'll bet you most of them will say 'Well, sure.' And some will point out, 'it's in the First Amendment.'

"Wrong! Read it! It says, 'Congress shall make no law respecting an establishment of religion or prohibiting the free exercise thereof.' Where is the word 'separate'? Where are the words 'church' or 'state.'

"They are not there. Never have been. Never intended to be. Read the Congressional Records during that four-month period in 1789 when the amendment was being framed in Congress. Clearly their intent was to prohibit a single denomination in exclusion of all others, whether it was Anglican or Catholic or some other.

"I highly recommend a great book entitled Original Intent by David Barton. It really gets into how the actual members of Congress, who drafted the First Amendment, expected basic Biblical principles and values to be present throughout public life and society, not separate from it.

"It was Alexander Hamilton who pointed out that 'judges should be bound down by strict rules and precedents, which serve to define and point out their duty.' Bound down! That is exactly what is needed to be done. There was not a single precedent cited when school prayer was struck down in 1962.

"These judges who legislate instead of adjudicate, do it without being responsible to one single solitary voter for their actions. Among the signers of the Declaration of Independence was a brilliant young physician from Pennsylvania named Benjamin Rush.

"When Rush was elected to that First Continental Congress, his close friend Benjamin Franklin told him 'We need you . . . we have a great task before us, assigned to us by Providence.' Today, 228 years later there is still a great task before us assigned to us by Providence. Our Founding Fathers did not shirk their duty and we can do no less.

"By the way, Benjamin Rush was once asked a question that has long interested this Senator from Georgia in particular. Dr. Rush was asked, are you a democrat or an aristocrat? And the good doctor answered, 'I am neither'. 'I am a Christocrat. I believe He, alone, who created and redeemed man is qualified to govern him.' That reply of Benjamin Rush is just as true today in the year of our Lord 2004 as it was in the year of our Lord 1776.

"So, if I am asked why – with all the pressing problems this nation faces today – why am I pushing these social issues and taking the Senate's valuable time? I will answer: Because, it is of the highest importance. Yes, there's a deficit to be concerned about in this country, a deficit of decency.

"So, as the sand empties through my hourglass at warp speed – and with my time running out in this Senate and on this earth, I feel compelled to speak out. For I truly believe that at times like this, silence is not golden. It is yellow."

Humanist Manifesto II

-- Preface --

It is forty years since Humanist Manifesto I (1933) appeared. Events since then make that earlier statement seem far too optimistic. Nazism has shown the depths of brutality of which humanity is capable. Other totalitarian regimes have suppressed human rights without ending poverty. Science has sometimes brought evil as well as good. Recent decades have shown that inhuman wars can be made in the name of peace. The beginnings of police states, even in democratic societies, widespread government espionage and other abuses of power by military, political and industrial elites and the continuance of unyielding racism, all present a different and difficult social outlook. In various societies, the demands of women and minority groups for equal rights effectively challenge our generation.

As we approach the twenty-first century, however, an affirmative and hopeful vision is needed. Faith, commensurate with advancing knowledge, is also necessary. In the choice between despair and hope, humanists respond in this Humanist Manifesto II with a positive declaration for times of uncertainty.

As in 1933, humanists still believe that traditional theism, especially faith in the prayer-hearing God, assumed to live and care for persons, to hear and understand their prayers and to be able to do something about them, is an unproved and outmoded faith. Salvationism, based on mere affirmation, still appears as harmful, diverting people with false hopes of heaven hereafter. Reasonable minds look to other means for survival.

Those who sign Humanist Manifesto II disclaim that they are setting forth a binding credo; their individual views would be stated in widely varying ways. This statement is, however, reaching for vision in a time that needs direction. It is social analysis in an effort at consensus. New statements should be developed to supersede this but for today it is our conviction that humanism offers an alternative that can serve present-day needs and guide humankind toward the future.

Georgiana Preskar

-- Paul Kurtz and Edwin H. Wilson (1973)

The next century can be and should be the humanistic century. Dramatic scientific, technological and ever-accelerating social and political changes crowd our awareness. We have virtually conquered the planet, explored the moon, overcome the natural limits of travel and communication; we stand at the dawn of a new age, ready to move farther into space and perhaps inhabit other planets. Using technology wisely, we can control our environment, conquer poverty, markedly reduce disease, extend our life-span, significantly modify our behavior, alter the course of human evolution and cultural development, unlock vast new powers and provide humankind with unparalleled opportunity for achieving an abundant and meaningful life.

The future is, however, filled with dangers. In learning to apply the scientific method to nature and human life, we have opened the door to ecological damage, over-population, dehumanizing institutions, totalitarian repression and nuclear and bio- chemical disaster. Faced with apocalyptic prophesies and doomsday scenarios, many flee in despair from reason and embrace irrational cults and theologies of withdrawal and retreat.

Traditional moral codes and newer irrational cults both fail to meet the pressing needs of today and tomorrow. False "theologies of hope" and messianic ideologies, substituting new dogmas for old, cannot cope with existing world realities. They separate rather than unite peoples.

Humanity, to survive, requires bold and daring measures. We need to extend the uses of scientific method, not renounce them, to fuse reason with compassion in order to build constructive social and moral values. Confronted by many possible futures, we must decide which to pursue. The ultimate goal should be the fulfillment of the potential for growth in each human personality -- not for the favored few but for all of humankind. Only a shared world and global measures will suffice.

A humanist outlook will tap the creativity of each human being and provide the vision and courage for us to work together. This outlook emphasizes the role human beings can play in their own spheres of action. The decades ahead call for dedicated, clearminded men and women able to marshal the will, intelligence and cooperative skills for shaping a desirable future. Humanism can provide the purpose and inspiration that so many seek; it can give personal meaning and significance to human life.

Many kinds of humanism exist in the contemporary world. The varieties and emphases of naturalistic humanism include "scientific," "ethical," "democratic," "religious," and "Marxist" humanism. Free thought, atheism, agnosticism, skepticism, deism, rationalism, ethical culture and liberal religion all claim to be heir to the humanist tradition. Humanism traces its roots from ancient China, classical Greece and Rome, through the Renaissance and the Enlightenment, to the scientific revolution of the modern world. But views that merely reject theism are not equivalent to humanism. They lack commitment to the positive belief in the possibilities of human progress and to the values central to it. Many within religious groups, believing in the future of humanism, now claim humanist credentials. Humanism is an ethical process through which we all can move, above and beyond the divisive particulars, heroic personalities, dogmatic creeds and ritual customs of past religions or their mere negation.

We affirm a set of common principles that can serve as a basis for united action -- positive principles relevant to the present human condition. They are a design for a secular society on a planetary scale.

For these reasons, we submit this new Humanist Manifesto for the future of humankind; for us, it is a vision of hope, a direction for satisfying survival.

-- Religion --

FIRST: In the best sense, religion may inspire dedication to the highest ethical ideals. The cultivation of moral devotion

302

and creative imagination is an expression of genuine "spiritual" experience and aspiration.

We believe, however, that traditional dogmatic or authoritarian religions that place revelation, God, ritual or creed above human needs and experience do a disservice to the human species. Any account of nature should pass the tests of scientific evidence; in our judgment, the dogmas and myths of traditional religions do not do so. Even at this late date in human history, certain elementary facts based upon the critical use of scientific reason have to be restated. We find insufficient evidence for belief in the existence of a supernatural; it is either meaningless or irrelevant to the question of survival and fulfillment of the human race. As nontheists, we begin with humans not God, nature not deity. Nature may indeed be broader and deeper than we now know; any new discoveries, however, will but enlarge our knowledge of the natural.

Some humanists believe we should reinterpret traditional religions and reinvest them with meanings appropriate to the current situation. Such redefinitions, however, often perpetuate old dependencies and escapisms; they easily become obscurantist, impeding the free use of the intellect. We need, instead, radically new human purposes and goals.

We appreciate the need to preserve the best ethical teachings in the religious traditions of humankind, many of which we share in common. But we reject those features of traditional religious morality that deny humans a full appreciation of their own potentialities and responsibilities. Traditional religions often offer solace to humans but, as often, they inhibit humans from helping themselves or experiencing their full potentialities. Such institutions, creeds and rituals often impede the will to serve others. Too often traditional faiths encourage dependence rather than independence, obedience rather than affirmation, fear rather than courage. More recently they have generated concerned social action, with many signs of relevance appearing in the wake of the "God Is Dead" theologies. But we can discover no divine purpose or providence for the human species. While there is much that we do not know, humans are responsible for what we are or will become. No deity will save us; we must save ourselves.

SECOND: Promises of immortal salvation or fear of eternal damnation are both illusory and harmful. They distract humans from present concerns, from self-actualization and from rectifying social injustices. Modern science discredits such historic concepts as the "ghost in the machine" and the "separable soul." Rather, science affirms that the human species is an emergence from natural evolutionary forces. As far as we know, the total personality is a function of the biological organism transacting in a social and cultural context. There is no credible evidence that life survives the death of the body. We continue to exist in our progeny and in the way that our lives have influenced others in our culture.

Traditional religions are surely not the only obstacles to human progress. Other ideologies also impede human advance. Some forms of political doctrine, for instance, function religiously, reflecting the worst features of orthodoxy and authoritarianism, especially when they sacrifice individuals on the altar of Utopian promises. Purely economic and political viewpoints, whether capitalist or communist, often function as religious and ideological dogma. Although humans undoubtedly need economic and political goals, they also need creative values by which to live.

-- Ethics --

THIRD: We affirm that moral values derive their source from human experience. Ethics is autonomous and situational needing no theological or ideological sanction. Ethics stems from human need and interest. To deny this distorts the whole basis of life. Human life has meaning because we create and develop our futures. Happiness and the creative realization of

304

human needs and desires, individually and in shared enjoyment, are continuous themes of humanism. We strive for the good life, here and now. The goal is to pursue life's enrichment despite debasing forces of vulgarization, commercialization and dehumanization.

FOURTH: Reason and intelligence are the most effective instruments that humankind possesses. There is no substitute: neither faith nor passion suffices in itself. The controlled use of scientific methods, which have transformed the natural and social sciences since the Renaissance, must be extended further in the solution of human problems. But reason must be tempered by humility, since no group has a monopoly of wisdom or virtue. Nor is there any guarantee that all problems can be solved or all questions answered. Yet critical intelligence, infused by a sense of human caring, is the best method that humanity has for resolving problems. Reason should be balanced with compassion and empathy and the whole person fulfilled. Thus, we are not advocating the use of scientific intelligence independent of or in opposition to emotion, for we believe in the cultivation of feeling and love. As science pushes back the boundary of the known, humankind's sense of wonder is continually renewed and art, poetry and music find their places, along with religion and ethics.

-- The Individual --

FIFTH: The preciousness and dignity of the individual person is a central humanist value. Individuals should be encouraged to realize their own creative talents and desires. We reject all religious, ideological or moral codes that denigrate the individual, suppress freedom, dull intellect, dehumanize personality. We believe in maximum individual autonomy consonant with social responsibility. Although science can account for the causes of behavior, the possibilities of individual freedom of choice exist in human life and should be increased.

305

SIXTH: In the area of sexuality, we believe that intolerant attitudes, often cultivated by orthodox religions and puritanical cultures, unduly repress sexual conduct. The right to birth control, abortion and divorce should be recognized. While we do not approve of exploitive, denigrating forms of sexual expression, neither do we wish to prohibit, by law or social sanction, sexual behavior between consenting adults. The many varieties of sexual exploration should not in themselves be considered "evil." Without countenancing mindless permissiveness or unbridled promiscuity, a civilized society should be a tolerant one. Short of harming others or compelling them to do likewise, individuals should be permitted to express their sexual proclivities and pursue their life-styles as they desire. We wish to cultivate the development of a responsible attitude toward sexuality, in which humans are not exploited as sexual objects and in which intimacy, sensitivity, respect and honesty in interpersonal relations are encouraged. Moral education for children and adults is an important way of developing awareness and sexual maturity.

-- Democratic Society --

SEVENTH: To enhance freedom and dignity the individual must experience a full range of civil liberties in all societies. This includes freedom of speech and the press, political democracy, the legal right of opposition to governmental policies, fair judicial process, religious liberty, freedom of association and artistic, scientific and cultural freedom. It also includes a recognition of an individual's right to die with dignity, euthanasia and the right to suicide. We oppose the increasing invasion of privacy, by whatever means, in both totalitarian and democratic societies. We would safeguard, extend and implement the principles of human freedom evolved from the Magna Carta to the Bill of Rights, the Rights of Man and the Universal Declaration of Human Rights.

EIGHTH: We are committed to an open and democratic society. We must extend participatory democracy in its true sense to the economy, the school, the family, the workplace and voluntary associations. Decision-making must be decentralized to include widespread involvement of people at all levels -- social, political and economic. All persons should have a voice in developing the values and goals that determine their lives. Institutions should be responsive to expressed desires and needs. The conditions of work, education, devotion and play should be humanized. Alienating forces should be modified or eradicated and bureaucratic structures should be held to a minimum. People are more important than decalogues, rules, proscriptions or regulations.

NINTH: The separation of church and state and the separation of ideology and state are imperatives. The state should encourage maximum freedom for different moral, political, religious and social values in society. It should not favor any particular religious bodies through the use of public monies, nor espouse a single ideology and function thereby as an instrument of propaganda or oppression, particularly against dissenters.

TENTH: Humane societies should evaluate economic systems not by rhetoric or ideology but by whether or not they increase economic well-being for all individuals and groups, minimize poverty and hardship, increase the sum of human satisfaction and enhance the quality of life. Hence the door is open to alternative economic systems. We need to democratize the economy and judge it by its responsiveness to human needs, testing results in terms of the common good.

ELEVENTH: The principle of moral equality must be furthered through elimination of all discrimination based upon race, religion, sex, age or national origin. This means equality of opportunity and recognition of talent and merit. Individuals should be encouraged to contribute to their own betterment. If unable, then society should provide means to satisfy their basic economic, health and cultural needs, including, wherever resources make possible, a minimum guaranteed annual income. We are concerned for the welfare of the aged, the infirm, the disadvantaged and also for the outcasts -- the mentally retarded, abandoned or abused children, the handicapped, prisoners and addicts -- for all who are neglected or ignored by society. Practicing humanists should make it their vocation to humanize personal relations.

We believe in the right to universal education. Everyone has a right to the cultural opportunity to fulfill his or her unique capacities and talents. The schools should foster satisfying and productive living. They should be open at all levels to any and all; the achievement of excellence should be encouraged. Innovative and experimental forms of education are to be welcomed. The energy and idealism of the young deserve to be appreciated and channeled to constructive purposes.

We deplore racial, religious, ethnic or class antagonisms. Although we believe in cultural diversity and encourage racial and ethnic pride, we reject separations which promote alienation and set people and groups against each other; we envision an integrated community where people have a maximum opportunity for free and voluntary association.

We are critical of sexism or sexual chauvinism -- male or female. We believe in equal rights for both women and men to fulfill their unique careers and potentialities as they see fit, free of invidious discrimination.

-- World Community --

TWELFTH: We deplore the division of humankind on nationalistic grounds. We have reached a turning point in human history where the best option is to transcend the limits of national sovereignty and to move toward the building of a world community in which all sectors of the human family can participate. Thus we look to the development of a system of world law and a world order based upon transnational federal government. This would appreciate cultural pluralism and diversity. It would not exclude pride in national origins and accomplishments nor the handling of regional problems on a regional basis. Human progress, however, can no longer be achieved by focusing on one section of the world, Western or Eastern, developed or underdeveloped. For the first time in human history, no part of humankind can be isolated from any other. Each person's future is in some way linked to all. We thus reaffirm a commitment to the building of world community, at the same time recognizing that this commits us to some hard choices.

THIRTEENTH: This world community must renounce the resort to violence and force as a method of solving international disputes. We believe in the peaceful adjudication of differences by international courts and by the development of the arts of negotiation and compromise. War is obsolete. So is the use of nuclear, biological and chemical weapons. It is a planetary imperative to reduce the level of military expenditures and turn these savings to peaceful and people-oriented uses.

FOURTEENTH: The world community must engage in cooperative planning concerning the use of rapidly depleting resources. The planet earth must be considered a single ecosystem. Ecological damage, resource depletion and excessive population growth must be checked by international concord. The cultivation and conservation of nature is a moral value; we should perceive ourselves as integral to the sources of our being in nature. We must free our world from needless pollution and waste, responsibly guarding and creating wealth, both natural and human. Exploi- tation of natural resources, uncurbed by social conscience, must end.

FIFTEENTH: The problems of economic growth and development can no longer be resolved by one nation alone; they are worldwide in scope. It is the moral obligation of the developed nations to provide -- through an international authority that safeguards human rights -- massive technical, agricultural, medical and economic assistance, including birth control techniques, to the developing portions of the globe. World poverty must cease. Hence extreme disproportions in wealth, income and economic growth should be reduced on a worldwide basis.

SIXTEENTH: Technology is a vital key to human progress and development. We deplore any neo-romantic efforts to condemn indiscriminately all technology and science or to counsel retreat from its further extension and use for the good of humankind. We would resist any moves to censor basic scientific research on moral, political or social grounds. Technology must, however, be carefully judged by the consequences of its use; harmful and destructive changes should be avoided. We are particularly disturbed when technology and bureaucracy control, manipulate or modify human beings without their consent. Technological feasibility does not imply social or cultural desirability.

SEVENTEENTH: We must expand communication and transportation across frontiers. Travel restrictions must cease. The world must be open to diverse political, ideological and moral viewpoints and evolve a worldwide system of television and radio for information and education. We thus call for full international cooperation in culture, science, the arts and technology across ideological borders. We must learn to live openly together or we shall perish together.

-- Humanity As a Whole --

IN CLOSING: The world cannot wait for a reconciliation of competing political or economic systems to solve its problems. These are the times for men and women of goodwill to further the building of a peaceful and prosperous world. We urge that parochial loyalties and inflexible moral and religious ideologies be transcended. We urge recognition of the common humanity of all people. We further urge the use of reason and compassion to produce the kind of world we want -- a world in which peace, prosperity, freedom and happiness are widely shared. Let us not abandon that vision in despair or cowardice. We are responsible for what we are or will be. Let us work together for a humane world by means commensurate with humane ends. Destructive ideological differences among communism, capitalism, socialism, conservatism, liberalism and radicalism should be overcome. Let us call for an end to terror and hatred. We will survive and prosper only in a world of shared humane values. We can initiate new directions for humankind; ancient rivalries can be superseded by broad-based cooperative efforts. The commitment to tolerance, understanding and peaceful negotiation does not necessitate acquiescence to the status quo nor the damming up of dynamic and revolutionary forces. The true revolution is occurring and can continue in countless nonviolent adjustments. But this entails the willingness to step forward onto new and expanding plateaus. At the present juncture of history, commitment to all humankind is the highest commitment of which we are capable; it transcends the narrow allegiances of church, state, party, class or race in moving toward a wider vision of human potentiality. What more daring a goal for humankind than for each person to become, in ideal as well as practice, a citizen of a world community. It is a classical vision; we can now give it new vitality. Humanism thus interpreted is a moral force that has time on its side. We believe that humankind has the potential, intelligence, goodwill and cooperative skill to implement this commitment in the decades ahead.

We, the undersigned, while not necessarily endorsing every detail of the above, pledge our general support to Humanist Manifesto II for the future of humankind. These affirmations are not a final credo or dogma but an expression of a living and growing faith. We invite others in all lands to join us in further developing and working for these goals.

Top Ten Bills For 2004

Support

AB 1925 (Haynes) – Parental Consent for Sex Education

Although parents are given a general notice at the beginning of the school year that their children in public school are being taught sex education, existing law does *not* require that parents be notified if *outside consultants* (e.g., Planned Parenthood, the Gay, Lesbian, Straight Education Network, etc.) will be brought in to teach sex education. Some parents may be comfortable with their children's teacher discussing sex education, but would *not* be comfortable with liberal activists doing so. AB 1925 would require parental notification at least 14 days in advance of each incidence that sex education is taught by an *outside consultant* or when the instruction is given in *assembly*. AB 1925 helps to ensure that the moral and religious views of parents are respected. The subject of human sexuality is important, delicate and controversial. Parents have the right to know *who* is teaching sex education.

AB 2331 (Mountjoy) – Abortion: Fetal Pain

It has been well documented that pre-born babies experience pain, among other emotions, during the brutal and savage act of abortion. AB 2331 would, for an abortion performed in the third trimester, require the physician performing the abortion to offer to the pregnant woman information and counseling on fetal pain and offer to the pregnant woman anesthesia for the fetus. If the legislature will protect the lives of innocent unborn children, the least they can do is eliminate the pain felt by the child when it is killed. In this day and age, we spend a lot of time and effort debating the evils of "cat declawing" - because it is painful for cats. The least we can do is give the same compassionate consideration to unborn children.

Georgiana Preskar

SB 1221 (Morrow) – Parental Notification for Confidential Medical Services

Existing law allows school districts to permit minors, in grades 7-12, to leave campus for "confidential medical services" without parental permission or knowledge. Although a *general* notice is sent to parents at the beginning of the year alerting them to this fact, the notice is often buried with a host of other information and is never seen by the parent. SB 1221 would require that the above notice be on a *separate* page and typed on a minimum of 12 pt. font, thus helping to "flag" this notice for parents. SB 1221 will help to ensure that parents have *actual* knowledge that their children may be dismissed from campus for purposes of obtaining an abortion, being put on drugs like birth control, Ritalin, etc., receiving suicide counseling, etc. Parents will then be able to make informed decisions about their children's education and will also be able to challenge and change school board policies. CRI is sponsoring this bill.

SB 1283 (Morrow) – Banning Teachers with Child Porn Convictions

SB 1283 would prohibit the issuing or reissuing of a teaching credential to any person who has been convicted of, or who has entered a plea of "no contest" to, an offense relating to child pornography. (Existing law leaves this decision up to the discretion of local personnel.) Persons who have dappled in child pornography should *not* be allowed in the classroom to further exploit and harm children. Recent headlines have been filled with stories of teachers sexually abusing young children. We must keep our kids safe from these sexual predators at all times, at all cost.

Oppose

AB 1967 (Leno) – Gay Marriage

AB 1967 would amend the family code to legalize same-sex marriage in California. This bill has been introduced in flagrant disregard to the will of the people, as expressed in Prop. 22, that only marriage between a man and a woman is valid and recognized in California. Adults should not put their sexual desires ahead of the needs of children. Studies show us that children need a mom and a dad. Society should not gamble with the lives of children by permitting gay marriage. History has never before seen this kind of social experiment. If the definition of marriage is changed to permit same-sex marriage, this will open the floodgates for any two, three, or ten people who love each other to marry. When we don't define marriage as between one man and one woman, marriage loses all significance. It can become anything anybody wants it to be. To prove this point, we can look to Scandinavia as an example. Several years ago, Scandinavia legalized gay marriage. Since then, marriage has become practically non-existent because it doesn't mean anything anymore. If we re-define marriage, we *un*-define it.

AB 2208 (Kehoe) – Forcing Insurance of Domestic Partners

AB 2208 would require a health care service plan and health insurer to provide coverage to the domestic partner of an employee, subscriber, insured, or policyholder that is equal to the coverage it provides to the spouse of those persons. The state should not force private businesses to endorse or affirm relationships between same-sex couples to the same degree as marriage. This will violate many people's religious and moral convictions. Marriage is a covenant before God and a commitment for life. Studies show that homosexual partners view their "commitment" differently than married persons (even a "committed" same-sex couple still have an average of eight other sexual partners a year) and their relationships do not have the same longevity as married couples. This bill is simply an attempt by homosexual activists to get society to put their stamp of approval on their lifestyle and views on morality.

AB 2662 (Jackson) – CEDAW: Forcing Feminist Ideologies

AB 2662 would enact the principles of the Convention on the Elimination of All Forms of Discrimination Against Women (CEDAW) into California law. Although this bill has a nice sounding "ring" to it, it is an extremely dangerous bill that not only directly assaults traditional values, but also will gravely *harm* women. If this bill is passed, the state could assert that it has the power to eradicate discrimination in even *private* relationships. The main problem with CEDAW is that it defines "discrimination" as "any distinction made on the basis of gender." This is an extreme definition that will have far-reaching consequences on our everyday life. If there truly is no distinction between men and woman, this implies that women have nothing invaluable or unique to contribute to society! Other harmful items in CEDAW: It embraces the idea that women should be drafted into combat military. It requires the state to "modify the social and cultural patterns of conduct of men and women" and give assurances that it is following UN dictates about "family education." It would require revision of textbooks and teaching methods to eliminate any "stereotyped concept of the roles of men and women." This opens the door for biased feminist ideology to be taught in our textbooks and traditional roles of men and women to be ridiculed. It requires that wages be paid on the idea of "equal value" rather than objective standards of equal work. It also solidifies abortion rights, thus encouraging the continued destruction of human life. CEDAW would clearly diminish the rights and benefits California women now enjoy and give extraordinary powers to the state. Furthermore, this bill is unnecessary because existing law adequately deals with preventing discrimination against persons on the basis of gender. Many women in California enjoy the traditional roles of wife, mother, and homemaker. This bill is an insult to them and undermines their important role.

AB 2900 (Laird) – Forcing Agencies to Recruit Sexual Minorities

When introduced, the text of AB 2900 was *one sentence*. Recently it was amended and became 29 pages! Essentially, this bill expands the definition of "discrimination" in employment practices to include discrimination against someone's "sexual orientation" or their "actual or perceived gender." This broad-sweeping bill will amend the following codes: education, government, labor, military and veterans, public utilities, and welfare and institutions codes. Not only will state agencies be forced to keep records showing that they are hiring certain percentages of sexual minorities, state agencies will be forced to *actively seek out* transgender and homosexual persons for recruitment. Thus, persons will not be hired on the basis of their own qualifications and the quality of the workforce will continue to spiral downward. This bill will also force many businesses that do business with the state, or receive grants, to violate their consciences and their faith by hiring transgender and homosexual employees. State employees could also be charged with "discrimination" if they harass persons on the bases above. Harassment is a loosely defined term. Is voicing religious/biblical objections to homosexuality considered harassment? Only time will tell. This bill also promotes affirmative action for ALL categories of minorities. Persons should be hired on the basis of their qualifications and skills, not on the basis of the color of their skin or their gender, etc.

SB 1234 (Kuehl) – "Hate Crimes" Indoctrination and Civil Penalties

Crimes committed against persons because of their (actual or perceived) race, color, religion, ancestry, national origin, disability, gender, or sexual orientation are considered "hate crimes." Although current law provides for criminal penalties for "hate crimes," SB 1234 would authorize a victim of a "hate crime" to bring a *civil action* for damages. Hate crime legislation is a *bad* idea because it elevates certain specified victims above all others. ALL intentionally perpetrated crimes involve an element of "hate." Hate crimes legislation is simply a reaction to certain politically and emotionally charged issues (like promoting the homosexual agenda, for instance). SB 1234 would also require a course of instruction for police officer sensitivity training *every five years* to help prevent "discrimination." Curriculum for this sensitivity training would be developed by a panel comprised entirely of extreme liberal groups, such as NAACP, the ACLU, and NOW. Conservative groups like BOND, the ACLJ, and CWA, for instance, were *not* included as possibilities for the panel. (Did anyone mention *discrimination?*)

SB 1343 (Escutia) – Master Plan for Infant and Toddler Care

316

Georgiana Preskar

SB 1343 would require the State Department of Education to develop a master plan for infant and toddler care. This master plan is very dangerous because it will harm children, and potentially undermine parental rights and lead to compulsory attendance at younger ages. Liberals want to effectuate social change by grabbing hold of the hearts minds of young children at earlier ages. The most basic problem we have with SB 1343 is: the government should *not* be further intruding on the jurisdiction of the family by *plotting out the lives of our babies*! The main philosophy of SB 1343 is that young children belong in daycare and that strangers (i.e., daycare workers) are equal to parents when it comes to raising children. The state should not expand or promote day care for two reasons: 1) Many studies have shown negative affects of day care on children. Day care has been shown to have negative affects on a) the children's behavior; b) the children's social development; c) the children's cognitive development; d) mother-child interaction; and the children's health (greater risks of pneumonia, meningitis, ear infections, respiratory infections, asthma, diarrhea, etc.). 2) As much as day care workers may LOVE children, they will never love them the same as the child's parents. Policy should encourage young children to be nurtured in their loving homes by their caring parents, who know and love them best. If there is an issue with parents not being able to AFFORD day care, we should change our fiscal policy to enable one parent to be able to stay home with their young kids by giving them tax cuts, etc. Many parents would like to be able to care for their own children but are financially unable.

http://capitolresource.org/mailman/listinfo/capupdate_capitolresource.org

FOOTNOTES

Notes-9
MIND CONTROL
1. Edward Hunter, *Brainwashing*, (New York: Pyramid Gooks, 1956), pp. 185-186.
2. Mark Dunlop, "ex-FWBO," p.3. Found at http://www.ex-cult.org/fwbo/fwbosection2.htm
3. Ibid., p.4.
4. Ibid., p.6.
5. Ibid.
6. Ibid., p.8.
7. Ibid.
8. Ibid., p.10
9. Ibid., p.13

Notes-10
HITLER'S EVIL DECEPTION
1. Clarence L. Barnhart, *The American College Dictionary*, (Random House, New York, 1949), p.1131.
2. This section deals with interviews about Hitler seen on World History Documentaries in 2002.
3. Lothar Machtan, *The Hidden Hitler*, (Persues Press, 2001).
4. Scott Lively and Kevin Abrams, *The Pink Swastika*, (Veritas Aeterna Press, January 2002), pp. 105-106
5. David Pratt, H.P. Blavatsky and Theosophy, 'There is No Religion Higher than Truth', November 1997. Found at http://ourworld.compuserve.com/homepages/dp5/hpb.htm
6. Ibid.
7. Scott Lively and Kevin Abrams, *The Pink Swastika* (Veritas Aeterna Press, January 2002), p122.
8. Wulf Schwartzwaller, *The Unknown Hitler: His Private Life Fortune*, (National Press Inc. and Star Agency, 1989). "The Unknown Hitler: Nazi Roots in the Occult" by an unknown author published in above book and Found at http://www.stergods.org/Nazis_and_the_Occult.html
9. Trevor Ravenscroft, *The Spear of Destiny* (Ed Putnam's Sons, New York).

10. Ibid.
11. Gookrick-Clark, Nicholas, *The Occult Roots of Nazism: Secret Aryan Cults And their Influence on Nazi Ideology* (New York, New York University Press, 1992). Found in Scott Lively and Devin Abrams, *The Pink Swastika* (Veritas Aeterna Press, January 2002), pp.109-110.
12. World History Documentaries in 2002
13. H.F. Peters, *Zarathustra's Sister: The case of Elizabeth and Frederich Nietzsche.* (Crown Publishers, New York, 1977). P227. Found in *Pink Swastika*, page 138.
Dusty Skiar, *The Nazi and the Occult.* (New York Dorset Press, 1989).
14. Ibid., p35. Found in *Pink Swastika* page 139.
15. Ben McIntyre, *Forgotten Fatherland: The Search for Elisabeth Nietzsche* (NewYork, Farrar Straus Giroux, 1992) p187. Found in Pink Swastika page 134.
16. Helena Petrovna Bavatsky, *The Secret Doctrine* (The Theosophical Publishing House, 1893), p.446. Found in David Carrico, "Freemasonry and the 20th Century Occult Revival" Found at
http://www.saintsalive.com/freemasonry/fmoccult.htm
17. Ibid.
18. Aleister Crowley, *Ancient Wisdom and Secret Sects*, Time-Life Books, 1989, p.118 Found in David Carrico "Freemasonry and the 20th Century Occult Revival"
http://www.saintsalive.com/freemasonry/fmoccult.htm
19. "Carl Kellner" Found at
http://www.oto.de/hist_Kellner.html
20. Frater, U.D., Secrets of the German Sex Magicians, (Llewellyn Publications, 1991). Found at
http://www.saintsalive.com/freemasonry/fmoccult.htm
21. Jerry Johnston, *The Edge of Evil*, (Word Publishing, 1989), p.136
Found in Ibid.
22. Francis King, *The Rites of Modern Occult Magic* (The MacMillan Company,1970), p. 119.
Found in Ibid.

23. Anton Szandor La Vey, The Satanic Bible (Avon Books, 1969), p.139
Found in Ibid.
24. Aleister Crowley, *Magick In Theory and Practice* (Magickal childe Publishing Inc., 1990), pp.95-96.
Found in "Freemasonry and the 20th Century Occult Revival" http://www.saintsalive.com/freemasonry/fmoccult.htm
25. Trevor Ravenscroft, *The Spear of Destiny,* (Ed Putnam's Sons, New York).
26. Robert G.L.Waite, *The Psychopathic God Adolph Hitler.* (Signet Books, NewYork, 1977).

Notes-11
PAGANISM

1. Biblical Discernment Ministries, "New Age Movement," Found at
http://www.rapidnet.com/~jbeard/bdm/Cults/newage.htm
2. Ibid.
3. Douglas R. Groothuis, *Unmasking the New Age and Confronting the New Age*
Found at
http://www.rapidnet.com/~jbeard/bdm/Cults/newage.htm
4. Harold J. Berry, *What They Believe*, 1990, pp.117-138
5. "Who We Are" found on www.paganpride.org.
6. Ibid.
7. Ibid.
8. Vox Staff, "Popular Pagan Holidays" (Witches Voice, FL., January 31, 1997).
Found at Http://www.witchvox.com/xholidays.html
9. Ibid.
10. Ibid.
11. Linda P. Harvey, "Goddess Worship The Great Mother Goddess? It's All Baloney," Mission America 2003. Found at
http://www.missionamerica.com/feminist.php?articlenum=3& PHPSESSID=ef743f43439865e778912b063a6b95ac
12. Magick Shop Dictionary Found at http://www.themagickshop.com/Dictionary.html.

13. Ibid.
14. Ibid.
15. AzureGreen found at www.azuregreen.biz
16. Bob Trubshaw, "Fairies and their kin" At the Edge website Found at http://www.indigogroup.co.uk/edge/fairies.htm
17. Clare Nahmad, "Fairy Spells: Seeing and Communicating with the Fairies" Found at Http://www.sevenrays.com/books/_descriptions/n-z/n-o/nahmfair.htm
18. "What/Who/When are the Radical Faeries?!? Answers to Queries about Faeries," The Harry Hay Page, Found at http://www.geocities.com/WestHollywood/Heights/5347/radfae.html
19. "About the Fairies," at Who Are the Faeries? Found at http://www.nomenus.org/aboutrf.html
20. Ibid.
21. "Radical Fairies" Queries About Radical Faeries, Harry Hay Page, Found at http://www.geocities.com/WestHollywood/Heights/5347/radfae.html
22. Pat Califia, "Blood Mysteries: Are Cutting and Bloodsports a Women's Thing," *Cuir Underground* (Issue 2.2-October/November 1995). Found at http://www.waningmoon.com/darkpagan/lib/lib0040.shtml.
23. Amanda Silvers, "An Intimate Look at Ritual Pain," An Exploration of Dark Paganism. Found at http://www.waningmoon.com/darkpagan/lib/lib/0039.shtml
24. Ibid.
25. The College of The Sacred Mists: An Online Wiccan College. Found at www.workingwitches.com
26. Academy of Sorcery, "This Letter is for Magick Skeptics , Students and Beginners Only" Found at http://www.academyofsorcery.com/?OVRAW=magick&OVKEY=magick&OVMTC=stand

27. Sixth Annual Sacramento Pagan Pride Harvest Festival Found at http://www.sacpaganpride.org/index.htm

28. M. Macha NightMare, Biography found at http://sacpaganpride.org/authors.htm

29. Quill Enparchment, Biography found at http://www.sacpaganpride.org/classes.htm

30. Isina Schuler, Biography found at http://sacpaganpride.org/authors.htm.

31. Valerie Sim, Biography found at http://sacpaganpride.org/authors

32. Raven Grimassi and Ed Broneske information found at http://www.sacpaganpride.org/classes.htm

33. Clarence L. Barnhart, *The American College Dictionary* (Random House Inc., 1949), p.417.

34. The Light Party, "David Spangler on September 11th," (Mill Valley CA.), Found at http://www.lightparty.com/TruthBeKnown/DSpanger-9-11.html

Notes-12
NAZI HOMOSEXUAL CAUSE

1. Angelod di Berardino, O.S.A. Christian *Anthropology and Homosexuality –2* "Homosexuality in Classical Antiquity," Augustinianum Patristics Institute, Rome.
(Taken from L'Osservatore Romani , Weekly Edition in English, 19 March 1997), p.10.

2. Craig A. Williams. "Roman Homosexualtiy:Ideologies of Masculinity in Classical Antiquity," Oxford University Press.

3. Scott Lively and Kevin Abrams, *The Pink Swastika* (Veritas Aeterna Press, January 2002), p.43.

4. Eva Cantarella. *Bisexuality in the Ancient World* (New Haven Yale University Press, 1992), p. 7.

5. Angelo di Berardino, O.S.A. *Christian Anthropology and Homosexuality-2* "Homosexuality in Classical Antiquity," Augustinianum Patristics Institute, Rome.
(Taken from L'Osservatore Romani, Weekly Edition in English, 19 march 1997).

6. Scott Lively and Kevin Abrams, *The Pink Swastika* (Veritas Aeterna Press, January 2002), pp.44-45.
7. Ibid., p.106.
8. James D. Steakley. *The Homosexual Emancipation movement in Germany* (New York , Arno Press, 1975), p. 60.
9. Scott Lively and Kevin Abrams, *The Pink Swastika* (Veritas Aeterna Press, January 2002), p. 32.
10. Ibid., p75.
11. Frank Rector, *The Nazi Extermination of Homosexuals* (New York , Stein and Day, 1981), p 40. Found in *Pink Swastika*, p. 75
12. Scott Lively and Kevin Abrams, *The Pink Swastika* (Veritas Aeterna Press, January 2002), p. 74.
13. Ibid.
14. Chris Millegan, "The Order of Skull and Bones:The Secret Origins of Skull and Bones." http://www.bilderberg-mirror.org.uk/skulbone.htm#mill
15. Dr. Louis L. Snyder, *Encyclopedia of the Third Reich* (New York, Paragon House, 1989), p.55. Taken from Scott Lively *Pink Swastika*, p.89.
16. Konrad Heiden, *History of National Socialism* (New York, A. A. Knopf, 1935; Der Fuehrer,1944), p.371. Taken from Scott Lively *Pink Swastika*
17. H.R. Knickerbocker, *Is Tomorrow Hitler's?* (New York, Reynal and Hitchcock, 1941), P.55. Taken from Scott Lively *Pink Swastika.*
18. Walter Langer, *The Mind of Adolf Hitler:* The Secret Wartime Report, (Signet,1972), p175.
19. Frank Rector, *The Nazi Extermination of Homosexuals* (New York, Stein and Day, 1981), p.57. .
20. Scott Lively and Kevin Abrams, The Pink Swastika (Veritas Aeterna Press, January 2002).
21. Irwin J. Haeberle, "Swastika, Pink Triangle and Yellow Star: The Elite Rights Committtee,1992." Taken from Scott Lively *Pink Swastika.*
22. Dusty Sklar, *The Nazis and the Occult* (New York, Dorset Press, 1989), p.21.
Taken from Scott Lively *Pink Swastika.*

23. Scott Lively and Kevin Abrams, *The Pink Swastika* (Veritas Aeterna Press,January 2002), p.264.
24. Ibid., p.237.
25. "A Tale of Three Empires" Part 7 Found at http://www.geocities.com/bramlett2000/achp7.html

Notes-13
REVISION of AB 537
1. Johnny Esposito, *Temple of Darkness*, (Pacific Publications, Prestige Press, North Little Rock Arkansas, 2001), pp. 107-108.
2. Sharon S. Kientz, "Threat of Sexual Diversity Education in Public Schools," Guest Editorial, Published July 4, 2001, p.1.
3. Karen Holgate, Capitol Resource Institute, AB 537: A choice or a Mandate? www.capitolresource.org

Notes-14
TMD =PC
(Tolerance +Multiculturalism + Diversity = Political Correctness)
1. Joshua Claybourn, "Tolerating the definition of tolerance" (August 30, 2001). http://www.idsnews.com/story.php?id=5351 Found on The Indiana Digital Student website for Indiana University's student news site, by the Indiana Daily Student , Found at www.idsnews.com
2. Daniel J. Flynn, *Why the Left Hates America* (Prima Publishing, Roseville, CA. 2002), p.72.
3. Ibid., p.150.
4. Jessie Lee Peterson, *From Rage to Responsibility* (Paragon House, St. Paul, MN., 2000), p.29.
5. Gregory Koukl, "True Nature of Tolerance," April 1, 2002. Taken from Stand To Reason at www.str.org
6. Patrick J. Buchanan, *The Death of the West: How Dying Populations and Immigrant Invasions Imperil Our Country and Civilization* (New York,St. Martin's Press, 2002), pp.130-131.
7. Daniel J. Flynn, *Why the Left Hates America* (Prima Publishing, Roseville, Ca.2002), p.83.

8. Stanley Kurtz, "Diversity Questions," April 3, 2003 . Found at http://www.nationalreview.com/kurtz/kurtz040303.asp.
9. Stanley Kurtz, "Diversity Like You've Never Seen It," March 19, 2003.
Found at
http://www.nationalreview.com/kurtz/kurtz031903.asp

Notes-16
ACLU

1. George Grant, "Trial and Error" Found in "Revealing Facts on the ACLU" from its own writings, by Diane Dew.
Found at
http://www.dianedew.com/aclu.htm
2. William H. McIlhany, Betrayal at the Top: The Record of the American Civil
Liberties Union. Found at ACLU on Trial, Found at
http://www.geocities.com/CapitolHill/Senate/1777/aclu.htm
3. Dennis Pollock, "The ACLU Protector of our liberties or destroyer of our Heritage?" The Real Truth about the ACLU Found at http://www.utmost-way.com/truestoryofaclu.htm
4. George Grant, "Trial and Error" Found in "Revealing Facts on the ACLU" from its own writings, by Diane Dew.
Found at
http://www.dianedew.com/aclu.htm
5. Funding the ACLU under FreeRepublic section found at Capitolresearch org. This Information is Found at
http://www.freerepublic.com/focus/f-news/922358/posts
6. George Grant, "Trial and Error" Found in "Revealing Facts on the ACLU" fromIts own writings, by Diane Dew. Found at
http://www.dianedew.com/aclu.htm
7. Ted Lang, "Lawyers for Communism: From Moses To Marx," 2003. Found at
http://www.sierratimes.com/03/09/11/tedlang.htm
8. Richard Thompson, Thomas More Law Center, "ACLU Aiming to De-Christianize Nation"
http://www.ajc.com/opion/content/opinion/0703/24moore.html

Notes-17
THOUGHT REVOLUTION

1. Derek Freeman, *The Fateful Hoaxing of Margaret Mead: A Historical Analysis of Her Samoan Research* (Boulder, CO. Westview Press, 1999)
2. Sam Francis, "Franz Boas-Liberal Icon, Scientific Fraud" Found at http://www.vdare.com/francis/boas.htm.
3. Judith Reisman Ph.D, *Kinsey, Crimes and Consequences* (The Institute for Media Education, 1998), p. 311.
4. Ibid., p. 182.
5. Traditional values.org: "Exposed: The Myth That "10% Are Homosexual" Found at www.traditionalvalues.org/urban/two.php.
6. Newsweek "The Homosexual Numbers," March 22, 1993, p. 37.
7. Joseph Nicolosi, Ph.D. "The Six Fallacies Behind "Project Ten" Found at http://www.qrd.org/qrd/religion/anti/FRC/project.10-family.research.council.letter
8. Jeff Lindsay, "Homosexuality: Seeing Past the Propaganda" Found at www.jefflindsay.com/gays.html.
9. "Hatch Letter" Found at ACLJ (American Center for Law and Justice) at http://www.aclj.org/hatch.asp
10. Stanley K. Monteith , *HIV-Watch*, (Volume I, Winter, 1993), Found in *New York Times* Article, (April 1, 1993), p.1.
11. Department of Health and Human Services, *HIV AIDS Surveillance Report*, U.S. HIV and AIDS cases reported through December 2001, (Centers for Disease Control and Prevention, Atlanta Georgia 2001), Volume 13, no.2. p.14.
12. Ibid.
13. Robert E. Rector, Kirk A. Johnson, Ph.D. and Lauren R. Noyes, "Sexually Active Teenagers Are More Likely to Be Depressed and to Attempt Suicide," Center for Data Analysis Report #03-04, June 3, 2003. Found at http://www.heritage.org/Research/Family/cda0304.cfm

14. Judy McLemore, *The Aspen Institute and Marxist Praxis* (Institute for Authority Research, Herndon, Kansas, 2002) Volume I, p3.
15. Stanford Encyclopedia of Philosophy, "Friedrich Nietzsche" Found at http://plato.stanford.edu/entries/nietzsche
16. Johnny Esposito, *Temple of Darkness* (Pacific Publications, Prestige Press, North Little Rock Arkansas, 2001), p. 166.
17. Judy McLemore, *The Aspen Institute and Marxist Praxis*, (Institute for Authority Research, Herndon, Kansas, 2002), p.2.
18. Ibid., p.5
19. Johnny Esposito, *Temple of Darkness*, (Pacific Publications, Prestige Press, North Little Rock Arkansas, 2001), p. 155.
20. Scott Lively and Kevin Abrams, *The Pink Swastik* (Veritas Aiterna Press,January, 2002), pp. 302-303.
21. Will Roscoe, Mattachine: Radical Roots of Gay Liberation. Found at http://www.shapingsf.org/ezine/gay/files/gaymatta.html
. 22. Douglas Kellner, "Herbert Marcuse" http://www.gseis.ucla.edu/faculty/kellner/Illumina%20Folder/kell12.htm
23. Daniel J. Flynn, *Why the Left Hates America* (Prima Publishing, Roseville, CA., 2002), pp. 58-60.
24. Ibid., p.60
25. Read Mercer Schuchardt, "The Cultural Victory of Hugh Hefner," Found at God Spy Faith at the Edge Found at http://godspy.com/issues/The-Cultural-Victory-of-Hugh-Hefner.cfm
26. Ibid.
27. Elizabeth Wright, "In the Name of "Civil Rights" Homosexuals Remake Society" (Issues and Views, New York, NY 10025, December 31,2003). Taken from reprint from Spring 1996 Found at http://www.issues-views.com/index.php/sect/2004/article/2061

28. Dudley Clendinen, "Anita Bryant, b. 1940, Singer and crusader," St. Petersburg *Times*, published November 28, 1999.

Notes-18
INTIMIDATION
1. Paul E. Rondeau, "Selling Homosexuality To America," (Regent University Law Review, Volume 14, Number 2, Spring 2002), FULL TEXT: PDF MSWORD Found at http://www.regent.edu/acad/schlaw/lawreview/articles/14_2R ondeau.PDF pp.460-461. A second source is Found at http://www.boundless.org/2001/regulars/kaufman/a0000605.ht ml. .
2. Charles W. Socarides, M.D., "How America Went Gay" Found athttp://www.leaderu.com/jhs/socarides.html
3. Ibid.
4. Charles W. Socarides, M.D., "New Business: NARTH Los Angelos," National Association For Research And Therapy Of Homosexuality. Found at CA. http://www.leaderu.com/orgs/narth/1996papers/socarides.html
5. Jeffery Satinover, *Homosexuality and the Politics of Truth 32* (Grand Rapids, Michigan, 1996).
6. Ronald Alsop, "Cracking the Gay Market Code-But Brewers Empty In-Your-Mug Approach" *Wall Street Journal*. June 29, 1999.
7. Air Transp. Ass'n of Am. V. City of San Francisco, 1998 U.S. Dist. LEXUS2937 (N.D. Cal. 1998). United Airlines and the American Center for Law and Justice sued to invalidate the mandate. United lost in a 1998 federal court ruling. http://www.glaad.org/action/alerts_detail.php?id=1407&
8. Paul E. Rondeau, "Selling Homosexuality To America," (Regent UniversityLaw Review, Volume 14, number 2, Spring 2002), FULL TEST:PDFMSWORDp. 474 Found at http://www.regent.edu/acad/schlaw/lawreview/articles/14_2R ondeau.PDF
9. Patrick Poole, "Who's Afraid of Dr. Laura?" 2000 World Net Daily.com Found at http://w114.wnd.com/news/article.asp?ARTICLE_ID=20040

Georgiana Preskar

10. Gay and Lesbian Alliance Against Defamation, "GLAAD Applauds Cancellation of Dr. Laura," (March 30, 2001). Found at http://www.glaad.org/media/archive_detail.php?id=3186&
11. John Knoebel, "Nontraditional Affluent Consumers," Am. Demographics, (November 1992) Found in # 10 "GLAAD Applauds Cancellation of Dr. Laura"
12. Cynthia Grenier, "The Gay '00s," World Net Daily .com Found at http://wnd.com/news/article.asp?ARTICLE_ID=18305
13. Scott Lively and Kevin Abrams, *The Pink Swastika*, (Veritas Aiterna Press, January,2002), p.278.
14. The Knitting Circle: History, "Stonewall Rebellion" Found at http://myweb.lsbu.ac.uk/~stafflag/stonewall.html
15. Elizabeth Wright, "In the Name of "Civil Rights" Homosexuals Remake Society" (Issues and Views, New York, NY 10025, December 31, 2003). Taken from Spring 1996 issue Found at http://www.issues-views.com/index.php/sect/2004/article/2061
16. Found at Log Cabin Republicans website at www.lcr.org
17. Murray Healy, Gay Skins: *Class, Masculinity and Queer Appropriation*, Cassell, 1996. Found in Scott Lively and Kevin Abrams, *The Pink Swastika* (Veritas Aiterna Press, January, 2002), P.281.
18. R.D. Flavin, "Frank Collin: From new-Nazi to Hyper-Diffusionist and Witch" Found at http://www.flavinscorner.com/collin.htm A previous version appeared in The Greenwich Village Gazette (Feb.21, 1997) As "The Many Faces of Frank Collin."
19. "Gay nazi-A contradiction in terms?" Searchlight Magazine, September 1999. Found at http://www.searchlightmagazine.com/stories/GayNazi.htm
20. Scott Lively and Kevin Abrams, The Pink Swastika (Veritas Aiterna Press, January, 2002), p283.
21. Shelly Anderson, "Youth," The Advocate, January 26, 1993.

Found in *Pink Swastika*
22. Judith Reisman, "Content Analysis of The Advocate (a national homosexual Magazine) 1972,1991" 1992, p.57. Found in Tony Marco "Gay Rights" Strategies Involve Conscious Deception And Wholesome Manipulation of Public Opinion" Found at http://www.leaderu.com/marco/special/spc15.html
23. George Grant and Mark Horne, Legislating Immorality (Chicago, Moody Press1993), p104.
24. Scott Lively and Kevin Abrams, *The Pink Swastika* (Veritas Aeterna Press, January, 2002), p. 293.
25. Ibid., p.293-294

Notes-19
HOMOSEXUAL MANIFESTO

1. Greg Hoadley, "The Homosexual Agenda: It's No Longer about Tolerance," Reclaim America, The INSIDE TRACK, May 9, 2002. Found at http://www.reclaimamerica.org/PAGES/NEWS/newspage.asp?story=911&SC
2. Ibid.
3. Rev. Louis P. Sheldon, Traditional Values Special Report, "Homosexual Propaganda Campaign Based on Hitler's "Big Lie" Technique," (Traditional Values, Washington DC., Vol. 18, No.10) Found at www.traditionalvalues.org
4. Paul Rondeau, "Selling Homosexuality To America," p. 447. Found at http://www.regent.edu/acad/schlaw/lawreview/issues/v14n2.html
5. Ibid.
6. Ibid., p.447.
7. Rev. Louis P. Sheldon, TraditionalValues Special Report, "Homosexual Propaganda Campaign Based on Hitler's "Big Lie" Technique," (Traditional Values, Washington DC, Vol. 18, No. 10). Found at www.traditionalvalues.org

8. Paul Rondeau, "Selling Homosexuality To America," p.449. Found at http://www.regent.edu/acad/schlaw/lawreview/issues/v14n2.html

9. Rev. Louis P. Sheldon, TraditionalValues Special Report, "Homosexual Propaganda Campaign Based on Hitler's "Big Lie" Technique,"(Traditional Values, Washington DC, Vol.18, No.10). Found at www.traditionalvalues.org

10. Affidavit of the Jesse Dirkhissing murder. Found at http://www.americansfortruth.com/affidavit.html

11. Rev. Louis P. Sheldon, Traditional Values Coalition, "Some Victims Of Hate Murders Are More Equal Than Others," (Traditional Values, Washington DC2003)

12. Ibid.

13. L. Brent Bozell III, "Wrapping Up The Dirkhissing Story," (Bozell's Weekly Syndicated Column, March 29, 2001).

14. Dr. Joseph Nicolosi, "Is This Really Good for Kids?" Teachers in Focus (Website of Focus on the Family) Found at http://www.family.org/cforum/teachersmag/features/a0013018.cfm

15. Jamie Malernee (Education Writer), "S. Florida teen girls discovering 'bisexual chic' trend," South Florida *Sun-Sentinel*, (Fort Lauderdale, Fl., December 30, 2003). Found at http://www.sun-sentinel.com/news/local/southflorida/sfl-ccoolbidec30,0,5644616.story?coll=sfla-news-sfla Found through Mission America at www.missionamerica.com

16. Roy Waller and Linda A. Nicolosi, "Spitzer Study Just Published: evidence Found for Effectiveness of Reorientation Therapy," (NARTH, Oct. 2003) http://www.narth.com/docs/evidencefound.html

17. Ibid.

18. Homosexual Urban Legends The Series... "Born Gay" (Traditional Values Coalition, Washington DC). Found at http://traditionalvalues.org/urban/three.php Taken from National Association for Research and Therapy of Homosexuality Website

19. Ibid.

20. Ibid.

21. Ibid.
22. Dr. Joseph Nicolosi, "Is This Really Good for Kids?" Teachers in Focus (Website of Focus on the Family) Found at Http://www.family.org/cforum/teachersmag/features/a001301 8.cfm
23. Ibid.
24. Traditional Values Coalition, "Press Releases: New FBI Hate CrimeStatistics Expose Homosexual Lies," Found at http://www.traditionalvalues.org/modules.php?name=News&f ile=article&sid=66
25 St. Louis Region, "2002 FBI Hate Crime Statistics Act (HCSA)," October 29, 2003. Found at http://www.nccjstl.org/stories/storyReader$610
26 Traditional Values Coalition, "TVC Weekly News: Texas Decision Highlights Homosexual Violence," Vol. 6, Issue 26, July 3, 2003. Found at http://www.trditionalvalues.org/modules.php?name=News&fi le=article&sid=1036
27. Ibid.
28. Traditional Values Coalition, "Domestic Battering," (Traditional Values Coalition, Washington, DC). Found at http://www.traditionalvalues.org/pdf_files/DomesticBattering .pdf
29. Robert T. Michael, *Sex in America*, Little Brown Publishing Company, 1994.
30. Traditional Values Special Report, " Same-sex Marriages And Domestic Partnerships: Are They Good For Families And Society." (Traditional Values Coalition, Washington DC). Found at www.traditionavalues.org
31. Ibid.
32. Ibid.
33. Paul Rondeau, "Selling Homosexuality To America," p.449. Found at http://www.regent.edu/acad/schlaw/lawreview/issues/v14n2.h tml

34. Marshall Kirk and Hunter Madsen, *After the Ball: How America will Conquer is fear and hatred of Gays in the 90's*, Plume Books, (Penquin Group, New York, NY, 1990)

35. Ibid., p.179.

36. Jim Brown and Sherrie Black, "Lutherans Contend with Issues of Homosexuality, Same-Sex Unions," Christian News Service, (Agape Press) Found at http://headlines.agapepress.org/archive/5/272003a.asp

37. Scott lively and Kevin Abrams, *Pink Swastika* (Veritas Aeterna Press, January 2002), p.7.

38. Ibid., p.8

39. *The Bible*, Luke 17 verses 1-3

40. Henry Makow Ph.D., "Is this Gay Behavior Sick?," March 5, 2004. Found http://www.savethemales.ca/201101.html

41. Ibid.

42. Michael Swift, Boston Gay Community News, February 15-21, 1987

Notes-21

PEDAGOGY

1. National SEED Project on Inclusive Curriculum, "Research, Education, % Action" Found at http://www.wcwonline.org/seed/index.html

2. Girouz, H.A. and McLaren, P. (Eds). Between Borders: "Pedagogy and the Politics of Cultural Studies" (New York, Routledge, 1994). Found at http://newton.uor.edu/FacultyFolder/Mboya/ICRITPED.HTM-

3. Thomas S. Popkewitz and Philip Higgs, "Critical Thinking and Critical Pedagogy: Relations, Differences and Limits" (Butterworth's, 1997)Found at http://www.ed.uiuc.edu/facstaff/burbules/ncb/papers/critical.html

4. Education Week, "Assessment," (December 23, 2003). Found http://www.edweek.org/context/topics/issuespage.cfm?id=41

5. The Journal of Pedagogy Pluralism & Practice, "Table of Contents" Found at http://www.lesley.edu/journals/jppp/2/jppp_issue_2.toc.html
6. Moacir Gadotti and Carlos Alberto Torres, "Paulo Freire: An Homage," American Educational Research Association. Found at www.gseis.ucla.edu/cide/projects/Torres.pdf
7. Ibid.
8. Y. Robinson, Executive Director of Minnesota Inclusiveness Program. S.E.E.D Information found at website http://www.miprog.org/newsletterSPRING02.html

Notes-22
SYSTEMIC INQUIRY and TRANSFORMATION

1. Peggy McIntosh and Emily Style, *The National SEED Project on Inclusive Curriculum: Developing Teachers as Sources of Systemic Inquiry &Transformation* Found at http://www.lesley.edu/journals/jppp/2/mcintosh_style.html
2. Ibid.
3. Ibid.
4. Ibid.
5. Ibid.
6. Ibid.
7. NCREL North Central Regional Educational Laboratory, Professional Development Programs, Found at
8. http://www.ncrel.org/sdrs/areas/issues/educatrs/leadrshp/le4p ppd.htm
9. Peggy McIntosh and Emily Style, "The National SEED Project on Inclusive Curriculum: Developing Teachers as Sources of Systemic Inquiry & Transformation. Found at http://www.lesley.edu/journals/jppp/2/mcintosh_style.html
10. Ibid.
11. Ibid.
12. Ibid.
13. Ibid.

Notes-23
WHITE PRIVILEGE

1. "Examining White Skin Privilege," p. 2. Found at
   http://racerelations.about.com/library/weekly/aa060200b.html
2. Peggy McIntosh, "White Privilege: Unpacking the Invisible
   Napsack." Found at
   http://www.anarchistblackcross.org/org/wp/peggy.html
3. Ibid.
4. Ibid.
5. Ibid.
6. Gregory J. Krupey, "Black-On-White: The Invisible Hate
   Crimes" Found at
   http://onix.gtcomm.net/~cozenage/kiosk/black.html
7. Ibid.
8. Ibid.
9. Peggy McIntosh, "White Privilege: Unpacking the Invisible
   Napsack." Found at
   http://www.anarchistblackcross.org/org/wp/peggy.html
10. Ibid.
11. Thomas Sowell, *Civil Rights: Rhetoric or Reality?* (New
    York:William Morrow Co., 1994), pp. 80-81. Found in Jesse
    Petersens book *From Rage to Responsibility*
12. Richard Miniter, "Why Is America's Black Middle Class
    Strangely Fragile?" *The American Enterprise*,
    November/December 1998, p.32. Found in Jesse Petersens
    Book From *Rage to Responsibility*
13. Karl Zinsmeister, "When Black and White Turn Gray," *The
    American Enterprise,* November/December,1998, p.5. Found
    in Jesse Petersens book *From Rage to Responsibility*
14. Peggy McIntosh, "White Privilege: Unpacking the Invisible
    Napsack," Found at
    http://www.anarchistblackcross.org/org/wp/peggy.htm
15. Danny Ball, "The Night I met George Skelton" Found at
    www.donnyball.com
16. Peggy McIntosh, "White Privilege: Unpacking the Invisible
    Napsack" Found at
    http://www.anarchistblackcross.org/org/wp/peggy.htm
17. Ibid.

18. Ibid.
19. Ibid.

Notes-24
SEED MATERIAL
1. Melissa Suarez, "Rigoberta Menchu and The search for Truth," *Clarion* (Volume 3, No.9, May 1999). Found at http://www.popecenter.org/clarion/1999/May/0599cover.html
2. Ibid., p. p2
3. "An Interview with Bill Bigelow," Found at History Matters http://historymatters.gmu.edu/d/6433
4. *Education Reporter*, The Newspaper of Education Rights, Number215, December 2003.
5. Gregory Cajete, "Look to the Mountain An Ecology of Indigenous Education, Kivaki Press, 1994. Found at http://www.great-ideas.org/30-3.htm
6. Ibid.
7. Ibid.
8. Mark Belletini, "Liturgical Materials for Sunday the 16th of June, 2002" Material taken from "Sermon The Living Tradition" Found under "On Being a Man" http://www.firstuucolumbus.org/sermons/mb20020616.htm#p.5
9. Jean Baker Miller, speaks about her " Relational/Cultural Approach" at the Rational Practice: Illustrations from Union Alliance-Building May 4, 2000. Center for Gender in Organizations at Simmons Graduate School of Management. Found at http://www.simmons.edu/gsm/cgo/relational_practice.html, p.1 and at http://www.brc21.org/tenth/rel_psych.html
10. Ibid., p.2
11. Ibid., p.3
12. Ibid.
13. Forward by Susan J. Tchudi, Weaving In the Women: Transforming the High School English Curriculum, Heinemann: Weaving In the Women Found at http://www.heinemann.com/shared/products/0459.asp

14. Alix North, "Aphra Behn," Isle of Lesbos Website Found at http://www.sappho.com/poetry/a_behn.html
15. Zora Neale Hurston, "Biography of Zora Neale Hurston" Found at http://www.classicnote.com/ClassicNotes/Authors/about_zora_neale_hurston.html
16. "Zora Neale Hurston, Women's History. Found at http://womenshistory.abut.com/library/bio/blhurston.htm?once=true&
17. Richard Cornwall, "Education for the VT Queen," Out in the Mountains.
    Found at http://www.mountainpridemedia.org/oitm/issues/1990/01jan1990/queen.html.

Notes-25
DECEPTIVE SKITS
1. Michael Fowlin Biography, Found at http://www.michaelfowlin.com/biography.htm
2. Michael Fowlin, You Don't Know Me Until You Know Me, Found at http://www.michaelfowlin.com/booking.htm
3. Michael Fowlin, YES Education Programs. Found at http://www.michaelfowlin.com/Yes.htm

Notes-27
THE DIALECTIC and PRAXIS
1. Dean Gotcher, *The Dialectic and Praxis: Diaprax and the End of the Ages*, (Institute for Authority Research, Herndon, KS, 1996), Vol. No. 1, p.3.
2. Ibid., pp.4-5
3. Ibid.,p.5
4. Dean Gotcher, "What is Diaprax?" (The Institution for Authority Research ,Herndon, KS.), *Readings In The Dialectic*, Papers Presented at The Institute for Authority Research Diaprax Conferences, p.4.

5. L.J. Lebret, "Marxism as Humanism," Source: *The Last Revolution: The Destiny of Over-and-Underdeveloped Nations*, (Sheed & Ward, 1965). Found at http://www.nathanielturner.com/marxismashumanism.htm
6. Dean Gotcher, "The Dialectic and Praxis: Diaprax and the End of the Ages"(Institute for Authority Research, Herndon, KS, 1996), Vol. No. 1, p.2.
7. Dean Gotcher, "What is Diaprax" (The Institution for Authority Research, Herndon, KS.), *Readings In The Dialectic*, Papers Presented at The Institute for Authority Research Diaprax Conferences, p.3.
8. Dean Gotcher, "The Dialectic & Praxis: Diaprax And The End Of The Ages,"
   (The Institution for Authority Research, Herndon,KS.), pp24-25 in booklet.   Found at http://www.professionalserve.com/doublespeak/diaprax1.htm
9. Ibid.
10. Marc Tucker, "How We Plan to Do It," Proposal to the New American School Development Corporation: National Center for Education and the Economy, July 9, 1992.
11. Berit Kjos, "Mind Control How to resist three UNESCO strategies for training students to reject truth and conform to a pre-planned group consensus,"
    Found at http://www.crossroad.to/text/articles/mc9-24-98.html
12. Ibid.
13. Ibid.

Notes-28
PURPOSE DRIVEN INSTITUTIONAL CHANGE
1. Steven R. Goss, "Diaprax The Dialectic Process, TQM and Technology," *Readings In The Dialectic*, Papers Presented at the Institute for Authority Research Diaprax Conferences, (The Institute for Authority Research, Herndon, KS.), p.50.
2. Ibid., p51
3. Rick Warren, *The Purpose Driven Church* (Zondervan Publishing Hourse, 1995), p.190.

4. Robert Klenck, *Diaprax and the Church*, (Institution for Authority Research, Herndon, KS.), p. 9.
5. Ibid., p.9.
6. Ibid.
7. Ibid., pp. 11-13
8. Ibid., p.17
9. Ibid., p.16
10. Steven R. Goss, "Diaprox The Dialectic Process, TQM and Technology," *Readings In The Dialectic*, Papers Presented at the Institute for Authority Research Diaprax Conferenced, (The Institute for Authority Research, Herndon,KS), p.64.
11. Dean Gotcher, "What is Diaprax?" Readings In The Dialectic, Papers PresentedAt the Institute for Authority Research Diaprax Conferences, (The InstituteFor Authority Research, Herndon, KS), p.5.
12. Judy McLemore, *The Aspen Institue and Marxist Praxis* (Institution for Authority Research, Herndon, KS.), Vol. 1, Second Editon, pp. 5-6. Information for her research from Sidney Hyman, *The Lives of William Benton*, (University of Chicago Press, 1969).
13. Ibid., p.9. Information for her research from Sidney Hyman, *The Aspen Idea* (University of Oklahoma Press, 1975).
14. Ibid., p.13.
15. Ibid., p. 15
16. Ibid., p.17
17. Ibid., pp31-33
18. Ibid., p33
19. Ibid., p21
20. Ibid., p29
21. Ibid.
22. Ibid., p23
23. Ibid., p30
24. Ibid., p31
25. Ibid., p.16. Information for her research from Paul T. Hill and David Hornbeck, *The Business Roundtable Participation Guide: A Primer for Business on Educaiton*, Second Editon, 1991.

26. Allen Quist, *Fed Ed: The New Federal Curriculum and How It's Enforced* (Maple River Education Coalition, St. Paul, MN. 2002). pp16-17.
27. Center for Civic Education, *We The People: The Citizen And The Constitution* (Center for Civic Education, Calabasas, CA., 2003), p.1.
28. Ibid., p.207
29. Allen Quist, We The People: "The Citizen And The Constitution, How It Teaches The Federal Curriculum A Textbook Review" by Allen Quist, 2003.
30. Center for Civic Education, *We The People: The Citizen And The Constitution* (Center for Civic Education, Calabasas, CA., 2003), p.208.
31. David Barton, *America To Pray? or Not To Pray?* (Wallbuilders Press, Aledo, Texas), August, 2002.
32. Mark Matta information can be found at www.preserveliberty.com
33. Chuck Baldwin, "Bible Inspired America's Founding Documents," May 30, 2003. Found at http://www.truthusa.org/articles/misc/bible.htm
34. Tony Nassif, "Abortion, The Declaration of Independence and the Constitution"(Cedars Cultural and Educational Foundation), January 21, 2004. Via e-mail.
35. Allen Quist, "We The People: The Citizen And The Constitution, How It Teaches The Federal Curriculum A Textbook Review" by Allen Quist, 2003.
36. Center for Civic Education, *We The People: The Citizen And The Constitution* (Center for Civic Education, Calabasas, CA, 2003), p. X of Introduction.
37. Allen Quist, Fed Ed: *The New Federal Curriculum and How It's Enforced*(Maple River Education Coalition, St. Paul, MN. 2002)
38. Ann Wilson, Pavlov's Children: *A Study of Performance-Outcome-Based Education.* Found at Say No to Psychiatry! http://www.sntp.net/education/OBE_2.htm
39. Judy McLemore, The Aspen Institute and Marxist Praxis (Institution for Authority Research, Herndon, KS.), Vol. 1, Second Edition, p.40.

Notes-30
SEED SURPRISE
1. Clarence L. Barnhart, *The American Dictionary* (Random House, New York, 1949), p. 1049.
2. A curriculum from Social Justice Education . Org, " Tools For Building Justice" Found at http://www.socialjusticeeducation.org/tools.htm

Notes-32
MASSACHUSETTS SCANDAL
1. "Kids Get Graphic Instruction," The Massachusetts News, Found at Steve Kane Show at http://www.stevekaneshow.com/glsnmass.htm
2. Ibid.
3. Ibid.
4. Ibid.
5. The Massachusetts News, "The Fistgate Report." Found http://www.massnews.com/past_issues/2000/Schools/fist rep.htm
6. Dean Sullivan, "Teach Out" Exposed as Instructional Child Abuse, Found in Liberation Journal at http://www.libertocracy.com/Transfer/Articles/Education /queer/teachout.htm
7. The Massachusetts News, "Fistgate Comes Back to Haunt Governor Cellluci." Found at http://www.massnews.com/past_issues/2001/march%202 001/marfist.htm
8. Phyllis Schlafly, "The Education Reporter," June 2001. Found at http://www.eagleforum.org/educate/2001/june01/gay-teach-out.shtml
9. Ibid.
10. Ibid.
11. Ibid.
12. Ibid.
13. Phyllis Schlafly, "The Education Reporter," August 2003. Found at

http://www.eagleforum.org/educate/2003/aug03/lobbying.shtml
14. Phyllis Schlafly, "Education Reporter," June 2001. Found at http://www.eagleforum.org/educate/2001/june01/gay-teach-out.shtml
15. Agape Press, (July, 23,2003). Found in "The Education Reporter"(August 2003) Found at http://www.eagleforum.org/educate/2003/aug03/lobbying.shtml

Notes-33
HOMOSEXUAL FRIENDSHIP
1. Linda Harvey, "How Homosexual Friends Can Influence Our Kids," Found at Mission America .com at http://www.missionamerica.com/homosexual.php?articlenum=12
2. Ibid.
3. Ibid.
4. Ibid.
5. Ibid.

Notes-34
PEDOPHILIA
1. American Psychiatric Association, *Diagnostic and Statistical Manual of Mental Disorders IV* (Washington, D.C. 1994), p. 523. Found in Frank V. York and Robert H. Knight, "Homosexual Behavior & Pedophilia," Found at http://us2000.org/cfmc/Pedophilia.pdf , p.9.
2. Raymond D. Fowler, M.D., letter to Hon. Tom DeLay, Office of the Majority Whip, June9, 1999. Found at Ibid., p.10.
3. Steven M. Mirin, M.D., letter to Robert Knight, director of Cultural Studies, Family Research Council, May 27, 1999. Found at Ibid.
4. James Kincaid, Child-Loving: The Erotic Child and Victorian Culture, (New York, Routledge, 1992), cited at http://www.nambla.org and Found at

Ibid., p. 16
5. Ibid.
6. Robert Bauserman, "Objectivity and Ideology Criticism of Theo Sandfort's Research on Man-Boy. Found at http://www.ipce.info/ipceweb/Library/bauserman_objectivity.htm
7. Daniel Tsang, "The Age Taboo: Gay Male Sexuality, Power and Consent" A 2001 review by Rod Powell. Found at http://cellar.usc.edu:9673/review/iglr/review.html?rec_id=10
8. Daniel Tsang, "Slicing Silence:Asian Progressives Come Out" Found at http://www.kqed.org/w/snapshots/01transforming/09tsang_daniel.html
9. Pat Califia, *Public Sex*, (Cleis Press, 1994) Excerpt from this book
10. Frank V. York and Robert H. Knight, "Homosexual Behavior & Pedophilia," p.16 Found at http://us2000.org/cfmc/Pedophilia.pdf
11. Ibid., p.17
12. Ibid., p.16
13. Ibid., p.3-4
14. Bill O'Reilly, Fox News Channel, Interviews and footage on "Vagina Monologue" given in Amherst Massachusetts. February 16, 2004.
15. Julia Duin, "Gay priests cited in abuse of boys," The Washington *Times*, Washington, D.C., February 27, 2004.

Notes-35
GLSEN

1. Kevin Jennings speech at Human Rights Campaign, 1995. Quoted in Peter LaBarera "Head of Homosexual Teachers' Group Lays Out Victim Strategy," Spring,1996, p.3. Found at http://tdmea.tripod.com/homosexualtop10strategiesbyfrc.htm

2. Brian Clowes, Debating the "Gay Rights" Issue. Oregon Citizens Alliance, (Brooks Oregon), 1993. Found in Scott Lively and Kevin Abrams, *The Pink Swastika* (Veritas Aeterna Press, January, 2002), pp.332-333

3. Paul Russell, The Gay 100: A Ranking of the Most Influential Gay Men and Lesbians. Cited by Peter LaBarbera in "Top Ten Strategies Used ByHomosexual Activists In Schools" Found at http://tdmea.tripod.com/homosexualtop10strategiesbyfrc.htm

4. Peter LaBarbera, "L.A.Educator Asserts Lincoln Had Homosexual Affairs"*Lambda Report on Homosexuality*, April-June, 1995.

5. Paul Rondeau, "Selling Homosexuality To America," p.472 Found at http://www.regent.edu/acad/schlaw/lawreview/issues/v14n2.html

6. Ibid.

7. Ibid.,p.469

8. Ibid., p.470

9. "Help Expose 'Marriage Protection Week's A Gay Agenda," Found at http://www.glaad.org/action/alerts_detail.php?id=3498

10. Ibid.

11. Paul Rondeau, "Selling Homosexuality To America," p. 471. Found at http://www.regent.edu/acad/schlaw/lawreview/issues/v14n2.html

12. GLSEN book link site http://www.glsen.org.

13. Bennett Singer, *Growing Up Gay/Growing Up Lesbian* (New Press, 1994), p.100.
14. William J. Letts IV and James T. Sears, eds., *Queering Elementary Education*, (Rowman and Littlefield Publishers , 1999), pp. 71-81.
15. Alex Sanchez, *Rainbow Boys* (Simon and Schuster, 2001), pp. 51-51.
16. Ibid., p.148.
17. Mary L. Gray, *In Your Face: Stories From the Lives of Queer Youth* (Harrington Park Press, 1999), p.23.
18. Ibid., p111.
19. Ibid., pp86-87
20. Ibid., p.58
21. Traditional Values Coalition, "TVC Distributes James Hormel Sex Coloring Book To Freshmen Senators" January 25, 2001.Found at http://www.freerepublic.com/forum/a3a703e335240.htm

Notes-36
HEROES
1. American Humanist Association, "Humanist Manifestos I and II, Found at http://www.jcn.com/manifestos.html
2. "Is the religion of Secular Humanism being taught in public school classrooms?" Found at http://www.christiananswers.net/q-sum/sum-g002.html

Notes-38
THE LAST SAMURAI
1. Thomas R. Eddlem, The New American, June 19, 2000, Vol. 6 no 13. Found at http://www.thenewamerican.com/tna/2000/06-19-2000/vo16no13_education.htm

Notes-39
ADVOCACY PROGRAM

1. Jon Dougherty, "Planned Parenthood concealing crimes," (World Net Daily), May 21, 2002, Found at http://wnd.com/news/article.asp?ARTICLE_ID=27687&OVR AW=planned%20parenthood&OVKEY=parenthood%20plann ed&OVMTC=standard

2. Traditional Values Coalition, "Child Sex Abuse Cover Up At Planned Parenthood & National Abortion Federation," Found at http://traditionalvalues.org/1/pph/

3. "Myth Conceptions about School Choice," Found at http://www.schoolchoices.org/roo/myths.htm

4. Gilbert J. Botkin, *Life Skills Training* (Princeton Health Press, Inc.), Sixth Grade Teachers Guide, p. 6.

5. Questionnaires found at Toby Johnson Middle School, Advocacy Program, Elk Grove CA.

6. Ibid.

7. Ibid.

Notes-40
ONE LAST CHAPTER

1. The Pew Forum On Religion and Public Life, "Religious Beliefs Underpin Opposition to Homosexuality," Found at http://pewforum.org/docs/index.php?DocID=37?source=ggm

2. Michael Paulson, "Black clergy rejection stirs gay marriage backers," (The Boston Globe), February 10, 2004. Found at http://www.boston.com/news/local/articles/2004/02/10/black_ clergy_rejection_stirs_gay_marriage_backers?mode=PF

3. Ibid.

4. Ibid.

5. Ibid.

6. Ibid.

7. Steve Jordahl, "California Agency Rejects Gay Marriages" Found in Family News at Focus on Family website http://www.family.org/cforum/fnif/news/a0030885.cfm

8. Gene Edward Veith, "The Nordic Track," WORLD ON THE WEB, March 6, 2004, Found at

http://www.worldmag.com/world/issue/03-06-04/cover_2.asp

9. Pastor Matt Trewhella, "A Time for War," Found at http://www.covenantnews.com/trewhella040220.htm

10. "Taft's Statement Concerning Signing of HB 272," February 06, 2004, Found at Fair Marriage.org at http://www.fairmarriage.org/news/comments.php?id=27_0_1_0_C

11. Rev Lou Sheldon, "Defense of Marriage Act State Law Update," February 9, 2004 from Traditional Values Coalition.

12. Ibid.

13. Traditional Values Cooalition, "TVC Weekly News: Arlington Group And President Issues Statements On Same-Sex Marriage" Found at http://www.traditionalvalues.org/modules.php?name=News&file=article&sid=1407

14. Ibid.

15. Zell Miller, 'Miller Delivers Floor Speech on 'Deficit of Decency' in America," February 12, 2004, Found at http://miller.senate.gov/press/2004/02-12-04decency.html

16. Rick Schatz, "Stop MTV," (Cincinnati, Ohio), sent to me on February 11, 2004. National Coalition for the Protection of Children and Family Found at http://www.nationalcoalition.org

17. Arielle Grossman, "Some parents are too blind to realize the disturbance in their own kids," *Elk Grove Citizen*, February 18, 2004.

18. Larry Higgs, "Liberal agenda seen in diversity studies," Daily Record. Found at http://frontpage.montclair.edu/stuehlerd/engl105/Readings/seed.htm

19. American Humanist Association, "Humanist Manifestos I and II, Found at http://www.jcn.com/manifestos.html

20. Ibid.

21. Judge Roy Moores quotation and Found at http://www.fundyourcause.com/JudgeRoyMooreInterview.html

22. *LORD of THE RINGS-FELLOWSHIP of THE RING* Movie

GEORGIANA PRESKAR

Georgiana was born in Chicago, Illinois and raised in Downers Grove, Illinois. Following her Graduation from Michael Reese School of Nursing, she moved to San Francisco. She worked as a Registered Nurse in the Acute Neurosurgical Unit at San Francisco General Hospital, while finishing her BA in Sociology from San Francisco State University.

After her marriage to Michael, they moved to Denver where their first child Michael was born. Georgiana became a full time Homemaker. Upon completion of Michael's Education Program, they returned to California and eventually moved to Sacramento where their second child Michelle was born. They have lived in Elk Grove for 23 years.

Georgiana has pursued part time work in Real Estate and managed two home based businesses. She has been Prayer Coordinator for the South Sacramento Christian Women's Club and taught Sixth Grade Religion Education for ten years. Her plan was to Substitute School Teach when the children left for College, but she decided to direct Eagle Forum of Sacramento in June of 2002.